Newlywed's
Official Reception
Certificate

D0255393

This Wedding M.C. Reception Book and Official Record

Presented To

_____ & _____
(Bride's first name)   (Groom's first name)

on the occasion of their

marriage and wedding reception

on

_____
(date)

at

_____
(place)

Presented by your Wedding M.C.

_____
(signature)

Brian Lee's – The Wedding M.C.

Autograph Page

We want you to know who was here! *(circulate during meal time)*

Please return to: _____

From our Readers

Praise for - Brian Lee's The Wedding M.C.

"Not knowing the first thing about weddings, your book really made the day. Without it, the wedding would have cost us a fortune for a professional planner. Having your book made all the difference."
> *- Bob & Mary Anne Ward*

"It was the first time I was to be an MC and I wanted to do a good job. With your book "The Wedding MC", it went very well. So well that I got a standing ovation!

I would recommend "The Wedding MC" to anyone who will be MC'ing a wedding, especially if it is their first time. Congratulations on putting together such a helpful and easy to use book."
> *- Warren Pickard*

"Eliminates the "butterflies" of Mc'ing events."
> *- Bradley Dixon, MC*

"The Wedding Couple were astounded by my performance - as were others - I was even asked if I attended a Toastmasters public speaking course. Everyone loved it!"
> *- Paul J. Lemoine*

"There were 900 guests and a head table of 50 people. Thanks to the Wedding MC, I had every single detail in perfect order. All I had to do was fill in the blanks.

The big day finally came and needless to say, I was a bundle of nerves. But I had my Wedding MC in front of me with everything laid out and all I had to do was read it. At first, I tripped over my tongue, but as soon as I heard everyone laugh at my first joke, you couldn't drag me away from the podium!

All I can say is, "Thanks a Million, Brian."
> *- George Safaris*

Praise for - Brian Lee's The Wedding M.C. (Continued)

"I found The Wedding M.C. to be fantastic guide for anyone wanting to emcee a wedding, be it their first time or their tenth. I recommend this book to everyone, it is the very best guide anyone can use to be a successful wedding emcee."
  - Gordon Shrake, Member of the Alberta Legislature

"My brother used your notes, and was a superb MC. I will recommend your book to others."
  - Carmen Madden

"I now know that I could not have completed the task successfully without it. Your material is very concise, yet extremely thorough and comprehensive. The bottom line is you leave nothing to chance. I believe the best way I can show my appreciation to you Brian is to share the contents of the "Thank You" card I received from the grooms' parents."
  - W.G. (Bill) Yard

  "Bill: We would like to thank you for being such a great MC.
  Everybody talked about it and wondered if this is what you do for a living!
  You truly helped to make that evening such a success and a night to remember."
    - Klaus & Christel Duszywski

"I always find myself wondering if I have done the proper preparation, thus causing some anxiety. Your book has solved that problem completely. I found I had the confidence to be able to carry out a first class presentation. Most of the comments afterwards astounded me. Professional, smooth and polished, and after all, that is the way it should be."
  - Les Hartland, President, The Hartland Group

"I am, an experienced speaker with 27 years experience in both radio and television. Using "The Wedding MC" has made me a more confident speaker and was very helpful in laying out all the protocols and practices. I received raves from everyone at the wedding on my masterful and relaxed way of doing things. Everyone said it was the best MC job they had ever heard (including the minister.)"
  - Robert A. (Chuck) Howard, Canada Trust

Toll Free: 1-800-66-Speak
www.customlearning.com

Praise for - Brian Lee's The Wedding M.C. (Continued)

"Last fall I was asked to perform the duties of Master of Ceremonies at a large wedding for a close friend. At first I was apprehensive, but upon acquiring a copy of your book "The Wedding MC" I settled in to the program and used your book to the fullest and did the job.

Close to a dozen people approached me after the formalities and asked such questions as "you're obviously a professional, do you do a lot of weddings?"

My thanks to you Brian. Your book is brilliant and it appears to have opened up a new part-time career opportunity for me. I've been asked to perform four more weddings and I will promote your book at each and every one."

- Dave Clark, Manager, Limousine Division, The Checker Group

"Very valuable information to know well ahead of time of the event."
- Agathe Fournier, Mother of the Bride

"I purchased your "Wedding MC" book for my brother to use at our wedding and everything went fantastic. I highly recommend it and it made him a lot more comfortable. We had a lot of positive comments. Thank you.
- Dianne Or, Bride

"The wedding reception was a great success as a result of The Wedding M.C. I found the book helpful for organizing the wedding as well as fulfilling the requirements of an emcee. I would, and have recommended, your book to any person planning to emcee a wedding in the future."
- Kevin J. Phillips

"How interesting and yet how fun it really can be . . ."
- Tim & Cindy Haverlock, Bride & Groom

Praise for - Brian Lee's The Wedding M.C. (Continued)

"Your Wedding MC is a timely and practical guide for the on-the-job MC who wants to avoid being on-the-spot, woefully lacking preparation and advice. Congratulations are in order for sharing your obvious expertise in this often neglected area.
  - James A. Patchell

"The format, method of presentation and outline of information and helpful hints were of great assistance to both the professional and novice Public Speaker."
  - James M. Maxim, Government of Canada

"Recently I was asked to be an MC for a wedding. Fortunately for me, I have a friend who was already in possession of your book, which he in turn lent me. Frankly, it saved me from a disaster. Now that the celebrations are behind me, I realize that being a Master of Ceremonies is not an unpleasant task, not if you are PREPARED.

A special thanks to the author for time and effort put into a very valuable book."
  - Colleen Randal

Toll Free: 1-800-66-Speak
www.customlearning.com
copyright © 1988

The Wedding M.C.

How To M.C. and Speak at Weddings:

A Step by Step How-to Guide to M.C. and speak at Weddings
The definitive organizers handbook.

Brian C. Lee, CSP

ISBN 0-921328-05-2

Published by: Mastery Publishing
#201, 1505 - 17 Avenue SW
Calgary, Alberta   T2T 0E2
Phone: 403-245-2428
Fax: 403-228-6776
Toll Free: 1-800-66 SPEAK
Email: brian@customlearning.com
Website: www.customlearning.com

Mastery Publishing is a Division of Custom Learning Systems Group Ltd.

First Edition 1986 by Brian Lee, CSP

Revised Edition 1988 by Brian Lee Reprinted 1991,1992,1993,1994, 1995, 1996, 1997

Revised Edition 1998 by Brian Lee

Mastery Publishing Co.

#201, 1505 - 17 Avenue SW

Calgary; Alberta   T2T 0E2

Phone: (403) 245-2428

Fax: (403) 228-6776

Toll Free: 1-800-66-SPEAK

Email: brian@customlearning.com

Website: www.customlearning.com

Canadian Cataloguing with Publication Data

Lee, CSP, Brian

ISBN 0-921328-O5-2

1. Masters of ceremonies.   2. Wedding etiquette.   I. Title.

BJ2065.M37L43 1998   395'.22   C98-910635-7

Printed and bound in Canada

Copyright 1988

Brian Lee CSP
Profile of an Author and World Class Professional Speaker

Active as a public speaker from the age of 15 when he completed a Junior Achievement course, Brian Lee CSP has applied his exceptional communications skills in a host of ways.

Becoming successful in business as the Vice-President of a major retail firm by the age of 25, he then entered politics 2 years later and was elected Calgary's youngest-ever Alderman. Nine productive years in public life on City Council and as a Provincial MLA provided Brian with public speaking opportunities on a daily basis.

Authored by Brian Lee, CSP
"Mr. Customer Satisfaction"
"Canada's "Mr. Enthusiasm"

Brian Lee's Career Highlights

❏ With twenty-one years (and some 60 weddings) M.C.'ing experience behind him, Brian Lee is also a past president of the Canadian Association of Professional Speakers (Alberta Chapter) and past Assistant Area Governor, Toastmasters International as well as past president of the University of Calgary Oxford Debating Society.

❏ Brian Lee, CSP is one of North America's leading experts in the field of World Class Customer Satisfaction and Change Leadership and is author of 4 books including "Satisfaction Guaranteed . . . How to Master the 6 Secrets of Lifetime Customer Loyalty."

❏ For two consecutive years, Brian has been evaluated by the International Customer Service Association Conference as the number one rated Customer Service Speaker in the World.

❏ Mr. "Customer Satisfaction" travels over 200,000 miles a year, delivering over 200 keynotes and seminars, and has spoken in 54 states and provinces and 12 countries worldwide.

❏ As both a speaker and implementation consultant to over 100 Fortune 500 corporations and Health Care Organizations, Brian is sought after as an advisor/ coach to senior management, specializing in long term strategic solutions.

❏ He has been awarded the National Speakers Association Professional Designation CSP (Certified Speaking Professional), becoming one of only nine in Canada, and 270 in the world.

❏ Brian and his wife, Valerie Cade Lee, reside in Calgary, Alberta.

Put Brian Lee to work for your next conference or meeting.

1-800-66-SPEAK (667-7325)

Keynotes * Seminars * Consulting * Coaching
(for further information, see Customer Service Section)

Acknowledgments

My Very Special Thanks To:

- Charly Pazdor and Elizabeth Magnifico *for being the first to invite me to M.C. a Wedding (theirs!)*

- My Mother Margo *for encouraging me to be the best I could be.*

- Sharyn Krause *for getting the first edition to print.*

- Ray McLeod *for making the second edition possible.*

- Leo Peters *for his creative ideas and graphics.*

- Nomi Whalen *for her enlightened editorial review.*

- Allan John *for his spectacular cover design and creative input.*

- Candis McLean *for getting the book to the people*

- So many Wedding M.C.'s *for taking the time to share with me their best ideas.*

- 60 Couples *for allowing me to experiment with and share their family and friends as their Master of Ceremonies.*

- Neil Gow and Gary Robertson D.J. Services *for their valuable assistance with the Dance Program Chapter.*

- Elcheshen's Photography, Winnipeg, Manitoba *for the fabulous cover photo.*

- Our Custom Learning Systems Group Ltd. 1998 Editing Team *for their terrific ideas and insights:*

  - Valerie Cade Lee
  - Pat Goodberry-Dyck
  - Bruce Lee
  - Nicole Hofferd

Meet the Editor

The story of the success of the second edition of The Wedding M.C. would be incomplete without special acknowledgment of our editor, Ray McLeod.

The fine attention to detail, organizational structure, understandable plain English and easy flow are due in large part to Ray's personal experience and remarkable career as an educator, businessman, speaker, travel consultant and journalist.

Ray resides in Calgary, Alberta with his wife, Maureen, and their two children.

Toll Free: 1-800-66-Speak
www.customlearning.com
copyright © 1988

*This book is dedicated to my mother,
Margo, with love, respect and
enthusiasm.*

Table of Contents

A   Introduction

Chapter I   Get Yourself Organized   **17**

    Our Mission. . . A Perfect Reception   19

    What IS a Wedding?   21

    Who to Select as Your M.C.   22

    Types of Wedding Receptions   23

    6 Easy Steps to M.C. Success   24

    The M.C.'s Master Checklist   25

    Author Feedback - Request   32

    Author Feedback - Report   33

Chapter II   What Every Speaker Needs To Know   **35**

    How to be a Great Wedding M.C.   37

    The 13 Strengths of a Great Wedding M.C.   40

    How to Beat Nervousness and Relax   41

Chapter III   The Wedding Couple Interview -
**   Designing the Reception**   **43**

    Wedding Couple Interview - Checklist   45

    Wedding Day Schedule   46

    Reception Program Planner   47

    Pre-Meal Announcements   50

    Dance Program Planner   51

    Who to Contact   52

    Reception Set up Floor Plan   57

    P.S. To the Bride and Groom   58

Toll Free: 1-800-66-Speak
www.customlearning.com
copyright © 1988

Table of Contents (continued)

Chapter IV Assembling Personal Information   **59**

How To Use This Chapter   61

The Makings of a Great Story/Anecdote   62

Personal Summary Forms   63

(Head Table and Family, Program Presenters,
Out-of-Town Guests, Special Guests,
Acknowledgments)

Chapter V Multicultural Programs   **89**

Cultural Diversity   91

Example - Chinese Cultural   92

Multicultural Toasting   93

To Translate or Not to Translate   94

Chapter VI Planning The Receiving Line   **95**

Why Bother With a Receiving Line?   97

Receiving Line - Plan Sheet   98

How to Handle a Receiving Line   99

Suggestions For Hosting At A Reception   100

Chapter VII Planning The Head Table   **101**

Head Table - Seating Suggestions   103

Head Table - Seating Diagrams   104

Head Table - Planner   105

Sub-Head Table - Rectangle   106

Sub-Head Table -Round   107

Table of Contents (continued)

Chapter VIII Starting The Program   **109**

Opening the Reception - Checklist   111

Head Table - Entrance Announcement   112

The Invocation (How To, Introduction, Example)   113

M.C.'s Welcome (Outline, Example, Notes)   115

Food Service (Suggestions, Announcement)   120

Pre-Meal Announcements   122

Chapter IX Introducing The Head Table   **123**

How To Use This Chapter   125

Head Table Guest Introductions   126

    (The Notion, The Forms, An Example)

M.C.'s Program Opening Comments   129

    (The Notion, An Outline, Examples of Humour)

Head Table Introductions Opening   133

Introduction Forms   135

Chapter X Conducting The Main Program   **157**

How To Use This Chapter   159

Speaker Introductions   160

Telegrams   163

The "Key" Ceremony   170

This Is Your Life Slide Show   174

Out-of-Town Guests   178

Entertainment   197

Special Program Opportunities   201

Toast To The Bride   205

Toll Free: 1-800-66-Speak
www.customlearning.com
copyright © 1988

Table of Contents (continued)

Chapter X   **(Continued)**

Groom's Reply To The Toast To The Bride	212
Groom's Interview	219
Bride's Reply To The Toast	221
Special Guest Introductions	228
Toast To The Maid of Honour & Bridesmaids	240
Reply to the Toast to the Maid of Honour & Bridesmaids	247
Reply to the Toast to the Groomsmen	254
Roving "Donahue"	257
Father Of The Bride/Mother of the Bride - Address	261
Father of the Groom/Mother of the Groom - Address	269
Optional Toasts	277
"Open" Toast	283
Acknowledgments	286
Ceremonial Cake Cutting	303
Closing Announcements	305
Final Advice	308

Chapter XI   **Organizing The Dance Program**   **311**

How To Use This Chapter	313
Dance Program Planner	314
Dance Program Event Options	315
M.C.'s Dance Program - Notes	322
Wedding Dance Music Selection	323

Toll Free: 1-800-66-Speak
www.customlearning.com
copyright © 1988

Table of Contents (continued)

Chapter XII Treasury Of Wit and Wisdom   **325**

    Alphabetical Listings (by category) of Jokes,

    Quotations and Poems   325

    How To Use This Chapter   327

    How To Tell A Really Funny Joke Every Time   328

    Nine (9) Humour Techniques and Resources   332

Addendum   **419**

**Speech Master - A Short Course on
Public Speaking**   **421**

- Speech Writing   422
- Physical Delivery   424
- Vocal Delivery   426
- Speech Types   427
- Graceful Speeches (and how to respond to them)   429
- Professional Insights   431
- One Minute Name Memory   435
- The L.I.S.T.E.N. Name Memory Formula   438
- Dress for Speaking Success   439

Customer Service   **445**

  6 Reasons to put Brian Lee to work for you   447

  Topic List   448

  Brian Lee Quotations   449

  Reader Satisfaction Survey   450

  World Class Presentation Skills Training Tools   453

  World Class Customer Satisfaction
  and Service Empowerment Leadership Training Tools   454

  World Class Sales and Marketing Training Tools   455

  World Class Professional Development Training Tools   456

  Brian Lee Book Library   457

  Product Order Form   459

Toll Free: 1-800-66-Speak
www.customlearning.com
copyright © 1988

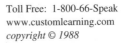

CHAPTER 1

Get Yourself Organized

Our Mission . . . A Perfect Reception   19

What Is A Wedding?   21

Who To Select As Your M.C.   22

Types of Wedding Receptions   23

Six Easy Steps to M.C. Success   24

The M.C.'s Master Checklist   25

Author Feedback - Request   32

Author Feedback - Report   33

Toll Free: 1-800-66-Speak
www.customlearning.com
copyright © 1988

From the Author

Our Mission. . . A Perfect Reception!

The purpose of this book. . . it's mission. . . is that every wedding reception be the best it can be. Why shouldn't it be?

After all, there are too few times when family and friends really get together - funerals, weddings, Christmas . . . therefore, we owe it to ourselves to make the best of every opportunity.

We look at this book as a kind of Insurance Policy - one that removes the risk of having an average, adequate or even a poor experience.

Now, we know for certain that a minister or other wedding officiant will conduct an excellent marriage ceremony and generally the price is minimal. The reception, however, costs an average of $10,000.00. So why risk the investment on a program that isn't thought out or on an M.C. who is unaware of the basic ingredients for success?

Many years ago, since I M.C.'d my first wedding I have seen and heard about many horror stories including:

- an M.C. who brought a bride to tears by attempting to force her to speak;
- a groom who left the reception and went home to watch TV rather than kiss his bride in public;
- guests frequently being offended by bad jokes or comments made in poor taste;
- a wedding annulled as a result of the groom's inopportune comments;
- guests simply bored to daydreaming.

Such disasters need never occur. In fact, many of the users of this book are frequently asked if they are professional speakers.

So how did this book come about? Like others, I panicked the first time I was asked to M.C. a wedding. I visited the library only to find an aging collection of not very relevant articles and decaying joke books. I asked friends and relatives. The assistance was small. Finally, I drew upon my speaking experience and delivered an enjoyable and entertaining program. As a result, I was asked to repeat it many times. (As you will be).

Eventually, getting tired of reinventing the wedding wheel, I decided to produce a system for my own use. It most have worked well as friends and fellow Toast-masters began asking to borrow these notes. So, I revised my method again. Eventually a story appeared in the Alberta press and as a result of the many requests for copies, I really couldn't afford to photocopy the embryo of this book any longer.

Therefore I teamed up with a wedding consultant, Sharyn Krause, to produce the first edition. It sold out at the bookstores and wedding boutiques immediately; hence this

Our Mission. . . A Perfect Reception! (continued)

new and greatly revised edition, for which I wish to acknowledge invaluable input from Ray McLeod.

I don't know why you've purchased this book - you may be a parent who wants to assist your son/daughter or a friend giving a gift to the couple. Perhaps you are the person who finally gave in and agreed to M.C. the event (an average two out of three decline) or maybe it is you who must give the Toast to the Bride. Whatever the reason, we wish you the very best for there is no greater honour than to M.C. or speak at a Wedding Reception.

The key to using this book is to see it as a menu and select the ideas you like. For the Golden Rule of Wedding Receptions is. . . there are no rules. There may be traditions and appropriate protocol and etiquette, which we've attempted to identify systematically throughout, but the bottom line is whatever works for you. . . is OK, provided of course, it's done in good taste.

And remember, with 3% of the population getting married every year. . . there is no right way to organize an event: whether it's a young couple getting married for the first time or seniors getting remarried the 2nd or 3rd time; whether the event is held in a restaurant, community hall or hotel; whether you're Catholic, Protestant, Muslim or Buddhist; or whether you're Irish, Chinese or Hindu. We know you'll find the answers and ideas you're looking for within these covers. (And if you don't, we'd like to hear from you).

The essential ingredient to success is preparation, so I urge you to follow the six (6) key steps. And make note, Mr./Madam Master of Ceremonies, your special challenge is a great honour. So:

- Take charge of the reception and co-ordinate the participation of all concerned. You are the 'producer.' This will allow the bride and groom the opportunity to enjoy;
- Don't show off, but rather train the spotlight on the bride and groom and the wedding party.

To you, all the best. When you're done, let me know how it went. . . with a phone call and/or by mail and please complete the Author Feedback Report

And if you need any advice, give me a call in Calgary at (403)245-2428. And above all, have fun! Best wishes for a terrific Wedding Reception!!

Brian Lee, CSP
Author , The Wedding M.C.

Toll Free: 1-800-66-Speak
www.customlearning.com
copyright © 1988

What Is a Wedding?

* The word originates from the Anglo-Saxon word "wed."

* The "wed" was the price paid by the male for the female or

* It was the "security deposit" paid by the groom's family to the bride's family when they were betrothed by both families.

* The "wedding" was the ceremony of pledging the troth of the bride to the groom and the posting of the "wed."

* Today's wedding and reception is a time for the families (or clans) to gather.

* The reception is the celebration of the marriage.

* We trust "The Wedding M.C." will assist you to have a wonderful and memorable experience.

Brian Lee, CSP

Who To Select As Your M.C.

Use the blank spaces on this page to make a list of all the people you might ask to be the M.C. at your Wedding reception.

• A good friend or relative of either family - preferably someone not in the bridal party

_____

• Someone who loves, likes or enjoys speaking.

_____

• A member of Toastmasters International or someone with experience in training or communication.

_____

• Someone who is willing to spend time properly preparing (8 -24 hours).

_____

• Any speaker you've heard whose style you admire.

_____

• A professional person, eg. lawyer, teacher - someone who speaks as part of their daily duties.

_____

• A duo (male, female) eg, husband and wife, brother and sister, etc.

_____

• A person who has self confidence and a clean sense of humour.

_____

Toll Free: 1-800-66-Speak
www.customlearning.com
copyright © 1988

Types Of Wedding Receptions

Morning Wedding Reception (Wedding Breakfast)

- follows a morning wedding
- usually a noon event (or later)
- can involve light lunch or buffet
- service format is optional
- bar format - punch, wine, beer

Afternoon Wedding Reception

- generally a stand-up event
- food is hors d'oeuvres, sandwiches
- bar format - punch, wine, beer

Early Evening Wedding Reception (Standard)

- most common
- generally drinks prior to (6-7:00 PM)
- full meal service or buffet optional
- full bar

Evening Wedding Reception

- later reception (eg. 8-9:00 p.m.)
- usually simple meal served buffet style

Any wedding reception may take place in a home/public hall/hotel/restaurant.

Notes About A "Standing" Reception

- Some couples today are hosting a "standing" or shorter reception.
- Regardless of format, if program is longer than ten (10) minutes, be sure to provide seating for everyone.
- Even if program is shorter than ten (10) minutes, provide seating for handicapped and elderly.

6 Easy Steps to M.C. Success

Quickly Review the book

- Invest 10 - 15 minutes to familarize yourself with the Chapter Guides and Key forms/checklists.

2

Interview the couple

- Meet with the couple's (family(ies)) as soon as possible.

- Use the Wedding Couple Interview Checklist to plan/organize for the reception. (Chapt III)

Fill in the Blanks

- After you have completed all the pertinent information (Chpts. III - VII) complete the Speaker's Notes forms (as required).

Post-it note your chosen program pages

Copy Key pages for other Presenters (i.e. Toast to the Bride)

- Then review your notes 3 times before the reception

Stand, deliver and M.C. **6**

- Have Fun!

- Don't forget to complete and mail c "Author Feedback Report"

Toll Free: 1-800-66-Speak
www.customlearning.com
copyright © 1988

The M.C.'s Master Checklist

The details in this section represent a complete catalogue of all the things a successful M.C. will do to prepare for and deliver a great Wedding Reception.

When this checklist has been completed, your job will be done.

1. ❏   Reviewing the Book

2. ❏   Meeting With The Wedding Couple (the first time)

3. ❏   Meeting With the Wedding Couple (the second time)

4. ❏   Preparing the M.C.'s Notes

5. ❏   Attending the Rehearsal/Stag/Shower

6. ❏   Preparing the Day Before

7. ❏   Getting Ready on the Wedding Day

8. ❏   Checking the Reception Facility/Set Up

9. ❏   Conducting Yourself as Guests Arrive

10. ❏   Leaving the Reception

The M.C.'s Master Checklist (continued)

1. Reviewing The Book

When: 2-4 weeks in advance

❏ Become familiar with how the book should be used. (See 6 Easy Steps To M.C. Success page 20)
❏ Read enough to become comfortable with your role.
❏ Arrange your first meeting with the Wedding Couple.

2. Meeting With The Wedding Couple (the first time)

When: 14-21 days in advance

❏ Help the couple decide on the details of the reception.
❏ Complete as many of the items on the Wedding Couple Interview Checklist (page 41) as possible.

3. Meeting With The Wedding Couple (the second time)

(Include the best man and maid of honour)
When: 3-7 days in advance

❏ Complete all the items on the Wedding Couple Interview Checklist (page 41).
❏ If the couple plan to print a reception program, review the final content.

4. Preparing The M.C.'s Notes

When: 2-3 days in advance

❏ Check every detail on the program and be sure you have a note to cover each one.

5. Attending The Rehearsal/Stag/Shower

When: As they are scheduled. Make sure your attendance at any of these is approved beforehand.

❏ Meet as many people as possible since you will be introducing many of them at the reception. Here you can obtain feedback on the story/anecdote you have been given about them. This is also a great source of added material about everyone else.
❏ Take a list of questions for which you need answers/clarification or additional direction.

Toll Free: 1-800-66-Speak
www.customlearning.com
copyright © 1988

The M.C.'s Master Checklist (continued)

6. Preparing The Day Before

- ❏ Confirm the time the physical set up of the reception hall will be complete. (This should be no later than 2 hours before the guests will arrive.)
- ❏ Confirm that the decoration of the hall will be completed at least 3 hours before guests arrive.
- ❏ Confirm the name of the person in charge of the facility with whom you will be working at the reception.
- ❏ Check your clothes:
  - • suit/dress cleaned?
  - • no loose buttons?
  - • shoes shined?
- ❏ Check yourself
  - • hair, make-up, etc.

7. Getting Ready On The Wedding Day

- ❏ Check with the couple regarding any changes of people to be introduced. (Especially out-of town guests, and the pronunciation.)
- ❏ Change your notes where required.
- ❏ Review your notes three (3) times before you leave home. This will give you a complete grasp of the materials. There will be no need to worry or review them again.
- ❏ Check your personal appearance:
  - • shoes shined?
  - • personal hygiene?
  - • brush teeth, gargle?
- ❏ Speak with minister/officiant before the ceremony. Give him/her an announcement of the details of the reception's exact time and place guests are expected to arrive.

8. Checking The Reception Facility - Set Up

When: 1¹/₂ - 2 hours before guests arrive.

Immediately upon your arrival, check the following:

- ❏ Notice is posted in lobby
- ❏ Direction signs are posted (if necessary)
- ❏ Doors are unlocked
- ❏ Manager/key volunteer is available
- ❏ Name of room matches name on the invitation
- ❏ If buffet style, note table #'s - you may want to announce tables by draw.

The M.C.'s Master Checklist (continued)

Then meet with the facility coordinator and check the location of the following:

- ❏ Lighting controls
- ❏ Heating controls
- ❏ Air conditioning controls
- ❏ Sound system controls
- ❏ Emergency exits
- ❏ Loading area - doors, dollies
- ❏ Kitchen
- ❏ Table/chair storage
- ❏ Coat room
- ❏ Bathrooms
- ❏ Telephones
- ❏ Other

❏ Find out how to page the key contact if there is a problem.

❏ Determine what events are taking place in adjoining rooms and if the noise from them would adversely impact your program, and vice-versa (eg. music, P.A. system, speeches.)

Furniture

With the key contact, check the physical set up of the furniture for the following:

- ❏ The correct number of banquet tables & chairs
- ❏ Table near entrance for guest book with two chairs
- ❏ Head table - correct number of places
- ❏ Sub-head table(s) - correct number of places
- ❏ Floor length podium/table top lectern
- ❏ Storage table behind podium for M.C. materials
- ❏ Table for audio recording (if required)
- ❏ Risers for head table (if large reception)
- ❏ Table(s) for D.J.
- ❏ Riser(s) for band
- ❏ Tables for buffet service
- ❏ Table for slide show (extension cord), if required (optional)
- ❏ Table for cake display/cutting
- ❏ Coat rack and gift table(s)
- ❏ Smoking/non-smoking area, ashtrays (smoking should be outside)

Toll Free: 1-800-66-Speak
www.customlearning.com
copyright © 1988

The M.C.'s Master Checklist (continued)

Also check on the following equipment:

- ❑ The microphone/sound system - personally check how it works, and make adjustments now
- ❑ Audio recording set up and tested
- ❑ Video recording set up - will it get best view? Obstructions?
- ❑ D.J. or Band set up

Food Service

With the key person responsible for food service, review the following:

- ❑ Estimated program start time _____
- ❑ Estimated food service start time _____
- ❑ Timing of wine service _____
- ❑ Timing of wine service - for toasts _____
- ❑ Timing of coffee service _____
- ❑ Timing of table clearance _____
- ❑ Timing of cake service _____
- ❑ Timing of evening snack service _____
- ❑ Timing of bar service _____

Pre-meal _____

Post-meal _____

Last call _____

Close _____

- ❑ Timing of facility cleaning _____
- ❑ Arrangements/timing for management, cooks, servers, and/or volunteers to be acknowledged by audience.
- ❑ The requirements re: unnecessary kitchen noise. Double check that head table and sub-head table seating place cards have been set out in the exact same order as your notes for the introductions.
- ❑ If guest seating is pre-arranged, check that place cards or table #'s have been assigned.

The M.C.'s Master Checklist (continued)

Key Organizers

Meet with key organizers to confirm the following details with the D.J. or Band that:

- ❏ the set-up is complete before guests arrive
- ❏ background music (pre-meal) is ready
- ❏ background music (during meal) is ready
- ❏ all special music requirements for program are understood
- ❏ background music (pre-dance) is ready
- ❏ they have a copy of the dance program
- ❏ timing for the last dance is understood

With the Photographer that:

- ❏ he/she understands details of the program eg. cake-cutting ceremony

With the video recordist that:

- ❏ he/she understands details of the program
- ❏ Check that decorations are completed.
- ❏ Check with the host/hostess to confirm they are ready
- ❏ Check that coat check facility is prepared.

Receiving Line

(See Chapter VI - Planning the Receiving Line for logistics)

- ❏ 20 minutes before guests are scheduled to arrive (they always come early) organize the receiving line.
- ❏ Brief the head table guests re: how and when the program will begin.
- ❏ Don't forget to take a break before guests arrive to check your personal appearance.
- ❏ Last minute questions (for bride and groom, etc.)

List Below

_____

_____

_____

_____

Toll Free: 1-800-66-Speak
www.customlearning.com
copyright © 1988

The M.C.'s Master Checklist (continued)

9. Conducting Yourself As Guests Arrive

When: as guests arrive

Be sure to personally greet every person scheduled to participate in or be introduced during the program to confirm that:

- ❏ they are present
- ❏ they are prepared and know their timing
- ❏ they are aware of their place on the program
- ❏ you know how to pronounce their name
- ❏ you understand their special requirements (such as slow walking, hard of hearing, etc.)

❏ Check to be sure all participants are present. If there is a "no-show," arrange a replacement but be prepared yourself to fill in.

❏ If you have extra time, visit with friends. This can help reduce nervousness.

❏ Be sure to attend to your spouse's/guests'/family's needs. Advise the bar service person 15 minutes before you are to begin. The bar may be closing then.

❏ Announce (on P.A. system) that the program begins in 15 minutes and the bar will close/remain open at that time. Also good time for one last bathroom break. Announce 5 minutes to beginning.

❏ Assist the head table guests in lining up in correct order according to seating assignment (not necessarily the same as the receiving line).

❏ Confirm that the piper, DJ or other musician is ready. Confirm the route for the procession and agree on the starting cue with the person at the head of the line.

❏ Announcement: "Ladies and Gentlemen, please take your seats"

10. Leaving the Reception

- ❏ Check the podium/head table for valuables that may have been left behind.
- ❏ Turn over telegrams, letters etc. to the bride and groom.
- ❏ Pat yourself on the back for a job well done!

Author Feedback - Request

Dear Fellow Wedding M.C.,

This book came about as the result of years of experience combined with suggestions and ideas from hundreds of sources.

If feedback is truly the genius of continued growth, then your experience, ideas and suggestions would contribute to making this book better for future users.

Accordingly, I would appreciate it if you would share with me your observations by completing the attached Author Feedback Report.

With thanks in advance,

Brian C. Lee, CSP
Author
The Wedding M.C.™

Toll Free: 1-800-66-Speak
www.customlearning.com
copyright © 1988

Author Feedback Report

(Brian, now that the wedding is complete, I'd like you to know . . .)

To: **Brian Lee, CSP**
The Wedding M.C.
Custom Learning Systems Group Ltd.
#201, 1505 - 17 Avenue SW
Calgary, Alberta Canada T2T 0E2

From: Name: _____

             Address: _____

             City: _____

             Province/State: _____ P C./Zip _____

             Bus. Phone: (   ) _____ Fax: (   ) _____

             Email: _____

Re: Comments/Observations - The Wedding M.C.

1.   Most useful feature/idea of this book:

_____

_____

_____

2.   Comments, feedback received from Wedding Couples and others in attendance:

_____

_____

_____

3.   Suggestions for improving existing ideas, format:

_____

_____

_____

4.   Suggested "Best Idea" that could be added:

_____

_____

_____

Author Feedback Report - continued

5. I became aware of the book by/through:

_____

_____

_____

6. For the Archives: _____

    Wedding Date: _____

    City/Location: _____

    Bride's Name: _____

    Groom's Name: _____

    Size of Reception: _____

General Reception Features: •eg. meal? dance?)

_____

_____

_____

_____

_____

_____

_____

_____

_____

_____

_____

7. Please find attached a photo(s)/wedding invitation/of the couple/event:

Toll Free: 1-800-66-Speak
www.customlearning.com
copyright © 1988

CHAPTER II

What Every Speaker Needs To Know

How to Be a Great Wedding M.C.   37

The 13 Strengths of a Great Wedding M.C.   40

How to Beat Nervousness and Relax   41

How To Be A Great Wedding M.C.

The Master of Ceremonies - Defined

An M.C. is:
- a coordinator
- a stage setter
- an umpire
- a humourist

- a speaker
- a translator
- an emergency technician
- a housekeeping/facilitator

An M.C. is "The frame around the picture, but YOU AIN'T THE STAR!"

The M.C.'s Mission: To plan and deliver the best wedding reception the bride, groom, family and guests will ever experience.

Six Key Personal Qualities of The Great M.C.

The Great M.C. is a person who:

1. is positive, good-natured and diplomatic; BE A FRIENDLY FRIEND
2. takes his/her job seriously - but not himself/herself too seriously
3. expects the unexpected
4. lets other people look good - and by so doing, looks good himself/herself. eg. doesn't try to tell a joke after a humourist - doesn't try to add a motivational point after a motivator, etc.
5. knows there is no substitute for preparation and practice
6. always assumes personal responsibility for the success of the event.

The M.C. Must Plan, Coordinate and Take Charge

"Take Charge" of the event. You're not only the "coach," but the producer as well. Systematically review all physical and technical set-up details well in advance of guests arriving. (This book contains a checklist just for this purpose.) Contact every organizer, manager, staff person and volunteer in advance to coordinate their efforts and ensure a smooth program. (See the same checklist.)

The M.C. Must Prepare All Speakers and Prepare For Them

Meet every person on the program beforehand in order to get to know them, their "hot buttons" and their feelings for the occasion. Learn the correct spelling and pronunciation of every name on your program. This applies to people's titles, too.

If in doubt as to the appropriateness of a particular introduction, check with the person involved and ask them.

Determine each speakers' special requirements, eg. remote microphone, music, props, etc. Diplomatically ensure that all speakers are aware of their specific time objectives. Inform them as to the sequence of their appearance (who they follow) and the approximate timing.

Double check and verify the attendance of individuals who may not be speaking but are to be recognized by way of an introduction.

The M.C. Must Use Only Suitable Material

In consultation with others, develop a special "theme" that is consistent with most program events and appropriate to the audience. This will give continuity to the program.

Determine the most effective method of gaining the audience's attention at the beginning of the program. Organize a head table "march in" (led by a piper or musician?), make a strong "call to order" or use a musical build up.

Your material must always be in good taste and never overly embarrass anyone. Approach politics and religion with care and don't "pick on" anyone unless you are certain they can take a little ribbing. Avoid "filling" time between program events with lengthy stories, jokes, etc. unless absolutely necessary.

Avoid using "trite" phrases. eg. "Unaccustomed as I am. . .", "It is a rare privilege. . ." etc.

The M.C. Must Be a Coordinator

Always lead the audience in applause. Stay at the lectern and shake hands with every speaker as they arrive and depart. Always create "bridges" or transitions from one program event to the next.

Toll Free: 1-800-66-Speak
www.customlearning.com
copyright © 1988

The M.C. Must Be Very Aware Of Time

Create a schedule for the program which includes a specific starting time, a time estimate for each event and a specific concluding time. Be as brief as possible in everything and maintain a sense of momentum - almost an urgency to keep going.

As much as possible, let guests enjoy their meal with a minimum of interruption.

Note: Take a battery operated clock to put on the lectern to ensure all speakers are aware of the time - avoid looking at your watch.

The M.C. Must Recognize That Things Could Go Wrong

If a speaker doesn't show, relax. Find a replacement or do the job yourself - without complaining. If the reception is delayed, keep your audience informed about the rearrangements.

Don't lose your temper or let little incidents upset you. Always be prepared to make decisions.

For Your M.C. File

Pre-Plan "Fill" Material

Keep a list of material with time codes (ie. the ideas and how much time it takes) on the lectern.

This can provide you with ready "fill" material that is appropriate and takes the right amount of time. (To be used only when absolutely necessary.)

Keep Records

Record material you have used by day, date and group spoken to. This is valuable when speaking to the same group for a second or third time.

Also works for speakers.

The 13 Strengths of a Great Wedding M.C.

A Great M.C.:

1. Has a positive attitude;

2. Plans the program carefully in close consultation with the families and participants. This includes the receiving line, head table sequence and introductions, the program sequencing and the dance;

3. Coordinates the involvement of organizers and volunteers;

4. Is an effective speaker committed to developing his/her personal speaking abilities through control of his/her content, delivery and audience;

5. Takes pride in his/her appearance and dresses for speaking success;

6. Does personal research for facts by getting to know the families and speakers in a personal way;

7. Creates a great physical environment by overseeing the physical and technical set-up - leaving nothing to chance;

8. Coordinates the creation of an appropriate receiving line;

9. Performs the head table introductions efficiently and humourously;

10. Shows sensitivity towards the program's speakers and the audience; he/she is particularly aware of timing;

11. Acknowledges all participants with enthusiasm;

12. May coordinate a dance program that is lively and entertaining;

13. Always has FUN and projects a good sense of humour.

Toll Free: 1-800-66-Speak
www.customlearning.com
copyright © 1988

How to Beat Nervousness and Relax

The following suggestions should help you to relax and use your nervous energy to your advantage:

- Be aware that nervousness causes the adrenaline to flow, which puts you on your toes and brings out your best;

- Review your notes with someone else and explain exactly how you are going to handle the program from beginning to end;

- Review your notes privately three times;

- Get to the event early, so that you have a sense of control;

- Informally visit with as many of the audience as possible;

- Take 6 -10 deep breaths;

- Mentally "see" the audience as receptive and friendly. Remember - **they** want the reception and you to succeed!

- Avoid drinking alcohol;

- Try hugging!!!

CHAPTER III

The Wedding Couple Interview - Designing the Reception
"Doing Your Homework"

This section contains a set of forms which, when completed, will provide the M.C. with all the information needed to masterfully take charge of the reception.

Wedding Couple Interview - Checklist   45

Wedding Day Schedule.   46

Reception Program Planner   47

Pre-Meal Annoucements   50

Dance Program Planner   51

Who to Contact   52

Reception Set-Up Floor Plan   57

P.S. to the Bride and Groom   58

Wedding Couple Interview - Checklist

Meet with the bride and groom and/or parents as early as possible. Allow at least 2 hours for the first meeting.

How to use this checklist:

1. Use this page as a guide.

2. Obtain the information required to complete each form.

3. Check off each form as you complete it.

Remember, you will need ALL of this information to do the job well.

Tentative	Confirmed	Form	Page #
❏	❏	1. Wedding Day Schedule	46
❏	❏	2. Reception Program Planner/Timetable	47
❏	❏	3. Pre-Meal Announcements	50
❏	❏	4. Dance Program Planner	51
❏	❏	5. Key Locations	52
❏	❏	6. Key Phone Numbers	
		Family	53
		Bridal Party	54
		Organizers	56
❏	❏	7. Reception Set-Up Floor Plan	57
❏	❏	8. Receiving Line Plan Sheet	98
❏	❏	9. Head Table Plan Sheet	105
❏	❏	Sub Head Table "A"	106
❏	❏	Sub Head Table "B"	106
❏	❏	10. Head Table Introductions. (See Pages 63-70)	
❏	❏	11. Program Presenter Introductions	
		(See Pages 71-75)	
❏	❏	12. Out-of-Town Guest Introductions	
		(See Pages 76-82)	
❏	❏	13. Special Guest Introductions	
		(See Pages 83-84)	
❏	❏	14. Acknowledgments	
		(See Pages 85-88)	

 Toll Free: 1-800-66-Speak
www.customlearning.com
copyright © 1988

45

Wedding Day Schedule

Determine which of the following events will take place and estimate times:

	From	To
Wedding Ceremony		
Wedding Party Photos		
First Guests Arrive for Reception (Bar Opens)		
Receiving Line Begins		
Bar Closes		
Guests to be Seated		
"Head Table" Enters		
Meal Served/Buffet		
Introduce "Head Table"		
Reception Program		
Adjourn Program		
Bar Re-opens		
1st Dance Begins		
Evening Snack Served		
Bouquet Toss		
Bar Closes		
Music Ends		
Out of Hall		

Toll Free: 1-800-66-Speak
www.customlearning.com
copyright © 1988

Reception Program Planner

This page is to be used to assist in determining which events will be part of the reception program. Simply check the ones you wish to use and fill in the blanks as to the participant and the time required. The reference page numbers are a guide to information about each event.

Ref. pg.#	Program Event	Speaker/ Key Person	Time
98 ❏	*Receiving Line	_____	_____
112 ❏	*Procession	_____	_____
113 ❏	*Invocation	_____	_____
116 ❏	Welcome (M.C.)	_____	_____
120 ❏	*Meal	_____	_____
125 ❏	Introductions -Head Table	_____	_____
163 ❏	*Telegrams (fictitious)	_____	_____
168 ❏	Telegrams (genuine)	_____	_____
170 ❏	*The Key Ceremony (Bride)	_____	_____
170 ❏	*The Key Ceremony (Groom)	_____	_____
174 ❏	*"This is Your Life" Slide Show	_____	_____
178 ❏	Introductions - Out-of-Town Guests	_____	_____
197 ❏	*Entertainment	_____	_____
205 ❏	Toast to the Bride	_____	_____
213 ❏	Reply - Groom	_____	_____
219 ❏	* - Groom Interview	_____	_____
221 ❏	* Bride's Reply	_____	_____

*This event is considered optional. All others are mandatory.

Reception Program Planner

Ref. pg.#	Program Event	Speaker/ Key Person	Time
228 ❑	Introductions - Parents/Family	_____	_____
228 ❑	* - Special Guests	_____	_____
240 ❑	*Toast to the Maid of Honour/Bridesmaids	_____	_____
247 ❑	*Maid's Reply	_____	_____
257 ❑	*Roving "Donahue"	_____	_____
261 ❑	*Address - Father of the Bride/ Mother of the Bride	_____	_____
269 ❑	*Address - Father of the Groom/ Mother of the Groom	_____	_____
277 ❑	Optional Toasts	_____	_____
283 ❑	*"Open Toast" opportunity	_____	_____
286 ❑	Acknowledgments	_____	_____
❑	- Flower Girl	_____	_____
❑	- Ring Bearer	_____	_____
❑	- Usher	_____	_____
❑	- Photographer	_____	_____
❑	- Caterers/Volunteers / Staff	_____	_____

*This event is considered optional. All others are mandatory.

Toll Free: 1-800-66-Speak
www.customlearning.com
copyright © 1988

Reception Program Planner

Ref. pg.#	Program Event	Speaker/ Key Person	Time
303 ❑	Cake Cutting Ceremony	_____	_____
305 ❑	Announcement - Remaining Program	_____	_____
308 ❑	Closing Remarks (M.C.)	_____	_____

Number of guests expected: _____

Special Program Opportunities:

_____

_____

_____

Multicultural Traditions (see Chapter V - Multicultural Programs)

_____

_____

_____

"Ringing" of Glasses (see pg. 50)

_____

_____

_____

Pre-Meal Announcements

- **Bar Opens/Closes**

- **Wine service** (re: potential toasts

- **Meal service arrangements**

- **"Ringing of glasses IDEA!"** (optional)
  Instead of "ringing" glasses to inspire bride and groom to kiss, why not announce that the wedding couple will only respond to a "spontaneous" poem, joke, anecdote or song that extols their virtues (with the word LOVE in it).

- **"Open" Toast-Notice** (optional) (see page 278) Remind anyone who feels so inclined, who has not been previously scheduled on the program that they may propose a short toast at the conclusion of, the program.

- **Other:**

- On with the meal. ENJOY!!

Toll Free: 1-800-66-Speak
www.customlearning.com
copyright © 1988

Dance Program Planner

❏ copy for M.C. ❏ copy for D.J./Band ❏ Other_____

Event Option		**Time Est.**

❏ 1.   Post program break _____

❏ 2.   Bar Details: Open _____   Close: _____

❏ 3.   Band/D.J. Begins Playing_____ Concludes _____
         Breaks/Details _____

❏ 4.   Wedding Cake Delivery _____

❏ 5.   Ceremonial First Dance(s) _____

                 Dancers   Music (see list, page 323)
        ❏ #1 _____   _____
        ❏ #2 _____   _____
        ❏ #3 _____   _____

❏ 6.   Bingo Dance (optional) : Starts with _____

❏ 7.   Bouquet Toss _____

❏ 8.   Garter Toss _____

❏ 9.   Dance Options   Notes: _____

        ❏ bunny hop   ❏ bump _____
        ❏ cha-cha   ❏ butterfly _____
        ❏ chicken   ❏ schottische _____
        ❏ hokey-pokey   ❏ fox-trot _____
        ❏ polka   ❏ jive (contest) _____
        ❏ waltz _____

❏ 10.   Entertainment _____
        Act #1 _____ Act #2 _____

❏ 11.   Bride & Groom Change Clothes _____

❏ 12.   Spot Dance _____
        Prize(s) _____
        Spotter _____

❏ 13.   Evening Snack _____

❏ 14.   Ladies' Choice _____

❏ 15.   Train Trap _____

❏ 16.   For They Are Jolly Good Fellows _____

❏ 17.   Last Call for the Bar _____

❏ 18.   Last Dance & Music _____

❏ 19.   Auld Lang Syne _____

❏ 20.   Drink Up _____

❏ 21.   Hall Cleared and Closed by Volunteer _____

Who to Contact

Key Locations

Wedding Day _____ Date _____

Bride's Name _____

Address _____

Groom's Name _____

Address _____

Church/Wedding Location

Name _____

Address _____

Phone #'s _____

Reception Location

Name _____

Address _____

Phone #'s _____

Photographs Location

Name _____

Studio/Other Location _____

Name/Contact _____

Address _____

Phone #'s _____

Toll Free: 1-800-66-Speak
www.customlearning.com
copyright © 1988

Who to Contact

Key Phone Numbers - Family

Bride _____

Home Phone _____ Bus. Phone _____

Cell Phone: _____ Email: _____

Fax: _____

Groom _____

Home Phone _____ Bus. Phone _____

Cell Phone: _____ Email: _____

Fax: _____

Bride's Father _____

Home Phone _____ Bus. Phone _____

Cell Phone: _____ Email: _____

Fax: _____

Bride's Mother _____

Home Phone _____ Bus. Phone _____

Cell Phone: _____ Email: _____

Fax: _____

Groom's Father _____

Home Phone _____ Bus. Phone _____

Cell Phone: _____ Email: _____

Fax: _____

Groom's Mother _____

Home Phone _____ Bus. Phone _____

Cell Phone: _____ Email: _____

Fax: _____

Minister/Priest/Officiant _____

Home Phone _____ Bus. Phone _____

Cell Phone: _____ Email: _____

Fax: _____ Minister's Spouse

M.C. _____

Home Phone _____ Bus. Phone _____

Cell Phone: _____ Email: _____

Fax: _____ M.C.'s Guest:

Who to Contact

Key Phone Numbers - Bridal Party

Best Man _____

Home Phone _____ Bus. Phone _____

Cell Phone: _____ Email: _____

Fax: _____

Maid of Honour _____

Home Phone _____ Bus. Phone _____

Cell Phone: _____ Email: _____

Fax: _____

Groomsman #1 _____

Home Phone _____ Bus. Phone _____

Cell Phone: _____ Email: _____

Fax: _____

Maid #1 _____

Home Phone _____ Bus. Phone _____

Cell Phone: _____ Email: _____

Fax: _____

Groomsman #2 _____

Home Phone _____ Bus. Phone _____

Cell Phone: _____ Email: _____

Fax: _____

Maid #2 _____

Home Phone _____ Bus. Phone _____

Cell Phone: _____ Email: _____

Fax: _____

Groomsman #3 _____

Home Phone _____ Bus. Phone _____

Cell Phone: _____ Email: _____

Fax: _____

Maid #3 _____

Home Phone _____ Bus. Phone _____

Cell Phone: _____ Email: _____

Fax: _____

Toll Free: 1-800-66-Speak
www.customlearning.com
copyright © 1988

Who to Contact

Key Phone Numbers - Bridal Party

Ringbearer _____
Home Phone _____ Bus. Phone _____

Flower Girl _____
Home Phone _____ Bus. Phone _____

Usher #1 _____
Home Phone _____ Bus. Phone _____
Cell Phone: _____ Email: _____
Fax: _____

Usher #2 _____
Home Phone _____ Bus. Phone _____
Cell Phone: _____ Email: _____
Fax: _____

Usher #3 _____
Home Phone _____ Bus. Phone _____
Cell Phone: _____ Email: _____
Fax: _____

Other _____
Home Phone _____ Bus. Phone _____
Cell Phone: _____ Email: _____
Fax: _____

Other _____
Home Phone _____ Bus. Phone _____
Cell Phone: _____ Email: _____
Fax: _____

Other _____
Home Phone _____ Bus. Phone _____
Cell Phone: _____ Email: _____
Fax: _____

Who to Contact

Key Phone Numbers - Organizers

Catering Service _____
Home Phone _____ Bus. Phone _____
Cell Phone: _____ Fax: _____

Music Service _____
Home Phone _____ Bus. Phone _____
Cell Phone: _____ Fax: _____

Bar Service _____
Home Phone _____ Bus. Phone _____
Cell Phone: _____ Fax: _____

Guest Book _____
Home Phone _____ Bus. Phone _____
Cell Phone: _____ Fax: _____

Hall/Facility _____
Home Phone _____ Bus. Phone _____
Cell Phone: _____ Fax: _____

Photographer _____
Home Phone _____ Bus. Phone _____
Cell Phone: _____ Fax: _____

Other _____
Home Phone _____ Bus. Phone _____
Cell Phone: _____ Fax: _____

Other _____
Home Phone _____ Bus. Phone _____
Cell Phone: _____ Fax: _____

Other _____
Home Phone _____ Bus. Phone _____
Cell Phone: _____ Fax: _____

Toll Free: 1-800-66-Speak
www.customlearning.com
copyright © 1988

Reception Set-up Floor Plan   *Use this page to design layout.*

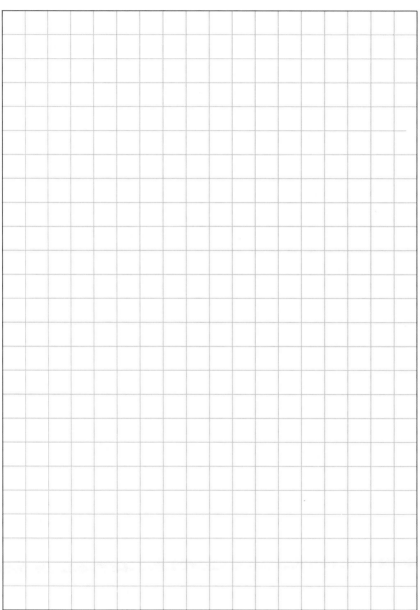

P.S. To The Bride and Groom

- Call or fax your parents the next day to Thank them for everything.

- It is appropriate to present the M.C. with a nice gift for his/her efforts.

- Be certain to say goodbye to parents prior to leaving reception.

- It's not necessary for a couple to have to leave a reception early. Stay and visit all night if you wish.

- It is no longer necessary for the bride to have to change out of her wedding dress part way through the evening. Keep it on if you choose, after all it's not very often that one gets the chance to use it.

Toll Free: 1-800-66-Speak
www.customlearning.com
copyright © 1988

CHAPTER IV

Assembling Personal Information

How to Use This Chapter 61

The Makings of a Great Story/Anecdote 62

Personal Summary Forms

Head Table Introductions 63

Program Presenter Introductions 71

Out-of-town Guest Introductions 76

Special Guest Introductions 83

Acknowledgements 85

How To Use This Chapter

- Review "The Makings of a Great Story/Anecdote" to gain an insight into how to ask questions to obtain this information.

- Review the "Personal Summary Forms" with Bride and Groom and cross off parts of pages not needed.

- Complete personal summary forms during discussion with Bride and Groom.

- If couple have difficulty providing colorful stories, have them complete and forward to you later.

- Set time for next meeting.

- Review couple's notes to achieve clarity and understanding.

- Next, transfer notes from personal summary pages onto actual introduction forms (page numbers are cross referenced.)

The Makings Of A Great Story/Anecdote

- Fact is stranger than fiction, so why tell someone else's joke when a true story can be:
    - funny;
    - of very personal interest to the audience;
    - more memorable;
    - given without memorization.

- Besides, a bad joke can bore, offend or do both.

- The hard part may be extracting a good anecdote from the participants. It's difficult to be "objective" about people you see every day.

- So we've provided a few sample questions that will help you find those great stories.

Sample Questions

1. What are their unusual habits?

2. For what funny things are they well known to friends and relatives?

3. What did they always fight over?

4. Is there a special nick name?

5. What is unique about your relationship with them?

6. What do they consider funny? Do they have unique hobbies?

To Summarize

If your helpers can't think of anything, then be patient. . . they will eventually. When in doubt as to the appropriateness of a story. . . ask!

The Objective

To have fun, but not overly embarrass.

Now use the remaining pages in this chapter to make your notes on all of the information you will need about the participants.

Toll Free: 1-800-66-Speak
www.customlearning.com
copyright © 1988

Head Table Introductions

Personal Summary Forms

Bride and Groom

Groom's Story:

_____

_____

_____

_____

_____

(transfer to pages #135 to 154)

Bride's Story

_____

_____

_____

_____

_____

(transfer to pages #135 to 154)

How did the Bride and Groom meet? What was their initial impression?

_____

_____

_____

_____

_____

_____

(transfer to pages #135 to 154)

Head Table Introductions

Best True Story/Anecdote-Summary

Bride's Family

Bride's Mother _____

Story:_____

_____

_____

_____

(transfer to pages #135 to 154)

Bride's Father _____

Story:_____

_____

_____

_____

(transfer to pages #135 to 154)

Bride's Grandmother _____

Story:_____

_____

_____

_____

(transfer to pages #135 to 154)

Bride's Grandfather _____

Story:_____

_____

_____

_____

(transfer to pages #135 to 154)

Toll Free: 1-800-66-Speak
www.customlearning.com
copyright © 1988

Head Table Introductions

Groom's Family

Groom's Mother _____

Story:_____

_____

_____

_____

(transfer to pages #135 to 154)

Groom's Father _____

Story:_____

_____

_____

_____

(transfer to pages #135 to 154)

Groom's Grandmother _____

Story:_____

_____

_____

_____

(transfer to pages #135 to 154)

Groom's Grandfather _____

Story:_____

_____

_____

_____

(transfer to pages #135 to 154)

Head Table Introductions

Bridal Party

Maid of Honour _____

Story:_____

_____

_____

_____

(transfer to pages #135 to 154)

Bridesmaid #1 _____

Story:_____

_____

_____

_____

(transfer to pages #135 to 154)

Bridesmaid #2 _____

Story:_____

_____

_____

_____

(transfer to pages #135 to 154)

Bridesmaid #3 _____

Story:_____

_____

_____

_____

(transfer to pages #135 to 154)

Toll Free: 1-800-66-Speak
www.customlearning.com
copyright © 1988

Head Table Introductions

Bridal Party

Best Man _____

Story:_____

_____

_____

_____

(transfer to pages #135 to 154)

Groomsman #1 _____

Story:_____

_____

_____

_____

(transfer to pages #135 to 154)

Groomsman #2 _____

Story:_____

_____

_____

_____

(transfer to pages #135 to 154)

Groomsman #3 _____

Story:_____

_____

_____

_____

(transfer to pages #135 to 154)

Head Table Introductions

Bride's Family

Bride's Brother/Sister _____

Story:_____

_____

_____

_____

(transfer to pages #135 to 154)

Bride's Brother/Sister _____

Story:_____

_____

_____

_____

(transfer to pages #135 to 154)

Bride's Brother/Sister _____

Story:_____

_____

_____

_____

(transfer to pages #135 to 154)

Bride's Brother/Sister _____

Story:_____

_____

_____

_____

(transfer to pages #135 to 154)

Toll Free: 1-800-66-Speak
www.customlearning.com
copyright © 1988

Head Table Introductions

Groom's Family

Groom's Brother/Sister _____

Story:_____

_____

_____

_____

(transfer to pages #135 to 154)

Groom's Brother/Sister _____

Story:_____

_____

_____

_____

(transfer to pages #135 to 154)

Groom's Brother/Sister _____

Story:_____

_____

_____

_____

(transfer to pages #135 to 154)

Groom's Brother/Sister _____

Story:_____

_____

_____

_____

(transfer to pages #135 to 154)

 Toll Free: 1-800-66-Speak
www.customlearning.com
copyright © 1988

Head Table Introductions

Minister/Priest/Officiant

Story:_____

_____

_____

_____

_____

(transfer to pages #135 to 154)

Officiant's Spouse/Guest _____

Story:_____

_____

_____

_____

_____

(transfer to pages #135 to 154)

Others _____

Story:_____

_____

_____

_____

_____

_____

(transfer to pages #135 to 154)

Toll Free: 1-800-66-Speak
www.customlearning.com
copyright © 1988

Program Presenter Introductions

Best True Story/Anecdote-Summary

Program Event: **Invocation** (optional - to tell a story)

Name(s): _____

Relationship: _____

Story:_____

_____

_____

_____

(transfer to page 115)

Program Event: **"This is Your Life" Slide Show**

Name(s): _____

Relationship: _____

Story:_____

_____

_____

_____

(transfer to page 176)

Program Event: **Entertainment #1**

Name(s): _____

Relationship: _____

Story:_____

_____

_____

_____

(transfer to page 199)

Program Presenter Introductions

Best True Story/Anecdote-Summary

Program Event: **Entertainment #2**

Name(s): _____

Relationship: _____

Story:_____

_____

_____

_____

(transfer to page 199)

Program Event: **Special Program #1**

Name(s): _____

Relationship: _____

Story:_____

_____

_____

_____

(transfer to page203)

Program Event: **Special Program #2**

Name(s): _____

Relationship: _____

Story:_____

_____

_____

_____

(transfer to page 203)

Toll Free: 1-800-66-Speak
www.customlearning.com
copyright © 1988

Program Presenter Introductions

Best True Story/Anecdote Summary

Program Event: **Toast to the Bride**

Name(s): _____

Relationship: _____

Story:_____

_____

_____

_____

(transfer to page 210)

Program Event: **Groom's Reply**

Name(s): _____

Relationship: _____

Story:_____

_____

_____

_____

(transfer to page 213)

Program Event: **Bride's Reply**

Name(s): _____

Relationship: _____

Story:_____

_____

_____

_____

(transfer to page 222)

 Toll Free: 1-800-66-Speak
www.customlearning.com
copyright © 1988

Program Presenter Introductions

Best True Story/Anecdote - Summary

Program Event: **Toast to the Bridesmaids** (optional)

Name(s): _____

Relationship: _____

Story:_____

_____

_____

(transfer to page 245)

Program Event: **Maid's Reply** (optional)

Name(s): _____

Relationship: _____

Story:_____

_____

_____

(transfer to page 252)

Program Event: **Father of the Bride/Mother of the Bride**

Name(s): _____

Relationship: _____

Story:_____

_____

_____

(transfer to page 267)

Toll Free: 1-800-66-Speak
www.customlearning.com
copyright © 1988

Program Presenter Introductions

Best True Story/Anecdote-Summary

Program Event: **Father of the Groom/Mother of the Groom**

Name(s): _____

Relationship: _____

Story:_____

_____

_____

(transfer to page 275)

Program Event:_____

Name(s): _____

Relationship: _____

Story:_____

_____

_____

Out of Town Guest Introductions

(Note: to save time, stories are optional)

Best True Story/Anecdote-Summary

Name(s): _____

Relationship: _____

Story:_____

_____

_____

(transfer to pages #182 - 195)

Name(s): _____

Relationship: _____

Story:_____

_____

_____

(transfer to pages #182 - 195)

Name(s): _____

Relationship: _____

Story:_____

_____

(transfer to pages #182 - 195)

Name(s): _____

Relationship: _____

Story:_____

_____

(transfer to pages #182 - 195)

Toll Free: 1-800-66-Speak
www.customlearning.com
copyright © 1988

Out of Town Guest Introductions

Best True Story/Anecdote-Summary

Name(s): _____

Relationship: _____

Story:_____

_____

_____

(transfer to pages #182 - 195)

Name(s): _____

Relationship: _____

Story:_____

_____

_____

(transfer to pages #182 - 195)

Name(s): _____

Relationship: _____

Story:_____

_____

(transfer to pages #182 - 195)

Name(s): _____

Relationship: _____

Story:_____

_____

_____

(transfer to pages #182 - 195)

Out of Town Guest Introductions

Best True Story/Anecdote-Summary

Name(s): _____

Relationship: _____

Story:_____

_____

_____

(transfer to pages #182 - 195)

Name(s): _____

Relationship: _____

Story:_____

_____

_____

(transfer to pages #182 - 195)

Name(s): _____

Relationship: _____

Story:_____

_____

_____

(transfer to pages #182 - 195)

Name(s): _____

Relationship: _____

Story:_____

_____

_____

(transfer to pages #182 - 195)

Toll Free: 1-800-66-Speak
www.customlearning.com
copyright © 1988

Out of Town Guest Introductions

Best True Story/Anecdote-Summary

Name(s): _____

Relationship: _____

Story:_____

_____

_____

(transfer to pages #182 - 195)

Name(s): _____

Relationship: _____

Story:_____

_____

_____

_____

(transfer to pages #182 - 195)

Name(s): _____

Relationship: _____

Story:_____

_____

_____

(transfer to pages #182 - 195)

Name(s): _____

Relationship: _____

Story:_____

_____

_____

(transfer to pages #182 - 195)

Out of Town Guest Introductions

Best True Story/Anecdote-Summary

Name(s): _____

Relationship: _____

Story:_____

_____

_____

(transfer to pages #182 - 195)

Name(s): _____

Relationship: _____

Story:_____

_____

_____

(transfer to pages #182 - 195)

Name(s): _____

Relationship: _____

Story:_____

_____

_____

(transfer to pages #182 - 195)

Name(s): _____

Relationship: _____

Story:_____

_____

_____

(transfer to pages #182 - 195)

Toll Free: 1-800-66-Speak
www.customlearning.com
copyright © 1988

Out of Town Guest Introductions

Best True Story/Anecdote-Summary

Name(s): _____

Relationship: _____

Story:_____

_____

_____

(transfer to pages #182 - 195)

Name(s): _____

Relationship: _____

Story:_____

_____

_____

_____

(transfer to pages #182 - 195)

Name(s): _____

Relationship: _____

Story:_____

_____

_____

(transfer to pages #182 - 195)

Name(s): _____

Relationship: _____

Story:_____

_____

_____

(transfer to pages #182 - 195)

Out of Town Guest Introductions

Best True Story/Anecdote-Summary

Name(s): _____

Relationship: _____

Story:_____

_____

_____

(transfer to pages #182 - 195)

Name(s): _____

Relationship: _____

Story:_____

_____

_____

(transfer to pages #182 - 195)

Name(s): _____

Relationship: _____

Story:_____

_____

_____

(transfer to pages #182 - 195)

Name(s): _____

Relationship: _____

Story:_____

_____

_____

(transfer to pages #182 - 195)

Toll Free: 1-800-66-Speak
www.customlearning.com
copyright © 1988

Special Guest Introductions
(Note: to save time, stories are optional)

Best True Story/Anecdote-Summary

Name(s): _____

Relationship: _____

Story:_____

_____

_____

(transfer to pages #232 - 239)

Name(s): _____

Relationship: _____

Story:_____

_____

_____

_____

(transfer to pages #232 - 239)

Name(s): _____

Relationship: _____

Story:_____

_____

_____

(transfer to pages #232 - 239)

Name(s): _____

Relationship: _____

Story:_____

_____

_____

(transfer to pages #232 - 239)

Special Guest Introductions

Best True Story/Anecdote-Summary

Name(s): _____

Relationship: _____

Story:_____

_____

_____

(transfer to pages #232 - 239)

Name(s): _____

Relationship: _____

Story:_____

_____

_____

(transfer to pages #232 - 239)

Name(s): _____

Relationship: _____

Story:_____

_____

_____

(transfer to pages #232 - 239)

Name(s): _____

Relationship: _____

Story:_____

_____

_____

(transfer to pages #232 - 239)

Toll Free: 1-800-66-Speak
www.customlearning.com
copyright © 1988

Acknowledgements

Best True Story/Anecdote-Summary

Activity: **Flower Girl**

Name(s): _____

Relationship: _____

Story:_____

_____

(transfer to pages #288 - 301)

Activity: **Ring Bearer**

Name(s): _____

Relationship: _____

Story:_____

_____

(transfer to pages #288 - 301)

Activity: **Guest Book Hosting**

Name(s): _____

Relationship: _____

Story:_____

_____

(transfer to pages #288 - 301)

Activity: **Guest Book Hosting**

Name(s): _____

Relationship: _____

Story:_____

_____

(transfer to pages #288 - 301)

Toll Free: 1-800-66-Speak
www.customlearning.com
copyright © 1988

Acknowledgements

Best True Story/Anecdote-Summary

Activity: **Usher #1**

Name(s): _____

Relationship: _____

Story: _____

_____

(transfer to pages #288 - 301)

Activity: **Usher #2**

Name(s): _____

Relationship: _____

Story: _____

_____

(transfer to pages #288 - 301)

Activity: **Usher #3**

Name(s): _____

Relationship: _____

Story: _____

_____

(transfer to pages #288 - 301)

Activity: **Usher #4**

Name(s): _____

Relationship: _____

Story: _____

_____

(transfer to pages #288 - 301)

Toll Free: 1-800-66-Speak
www.customlearning.com
copyright © 1988

Acknowledgements

Best True Story/Anecdote-Summary

Activity:　　**Photographer**

Name(s): _____

Relationship: _____

Story:_____

_____

(transfer to pages #288 - 301)

Activity:　　**Video**

Name(s): _____

Relationship: _____

Story:_____

_____

(transfer to pages #288 - 301)

Activity:　　**Maitre D', Manager, Cook and Serving Staff and/or Volunteers and/or Caterer**

Name(s): _____

Relationship: _____

Story:_____

_____

(transfer to pages #288 - 301)

Activity:　　**Bartender**

Name(s): _____

Relationship: _____

Story:_____

_____

(transfer to pages #288 - 301)

Acknowledgements

Best True Story/Anecdote-Summary

Activity: **Entertainment #1**

Name(s): _____

Relationship: _____

Story:_____

_____

(transfer to pages #288 - 301)

Activity: _____

Name(s): _____

Relationship: _____

Story:_____

_____

(transfer to pages #288 - 301)

Activity: _____

Name(s): _____

Relationship: _____

Story:_____

_____

(transfer to pages #288 - 301)

Activity: _____

Name(s): _____

Relationship: _____

Story:_____

_____

(transfer to pages #288 - 301)

Toll Free: 1-800-66-Speak
www.customlearning.com
copyright © 1988

Chapter V

Multicultural Programs

Cultural Diversity - Our Way of Life   91

Example - Chinese Cultural   92

Multicultural Toasting   93

To Translate or Not to Translate   94

Toll Free: 1-800-66-Speak
www.customlearning.com
copyright © 1988

Cultural Diversity - Our Way of Life

- We have observed a fascinating variety of multicultural, ethnic and regional practices and rituals at weddings and wedding receptions.

- We have attempted to present this "how-to" book with content and structure that is flexible enough to accommodate almost any cultural context.

- To build on this format, and to add to it, we take this opportunity to invite readers to write us and let us know about their own cultural traditions that may be added for inclusion in our next edition.

- We have attached an example of Chinese tradition on the next page and look forward to hearing about your special cultural practices.

Forward Ideas To: THE WEDDING M.C.
Suite #201, 1505 - 17 Avenue SW
Calgary, Alberta   T2T 0E2
Phone: 403-245-2428
Fax: 403-228-6776
Email: brian@customlearning.com

Example - Chinese Cultural

Wedding Reception Practices & Traditions

• Language	Toast	Yum-Boy
	Welcome	Fon-Gin
	Ladies	Nui (Noi)
	Please	M-Koi
	Gentlemen	Nam
	Thank You	Doe-Jeh

Note: Gentlemen always first, before Ladies.

• **Program Format**

Most of the formalities, ie: introduction of the head table, etc. are conducted BEFORE the meal is served.

• **Introductions**

Introductions of all family members takes precedence over introducing out-of-town guests.

• **Vegetable "BOB"**

During the meal, M.C. calls bride and groom forward and dangles fruit or vegetable (cherry, carrot stick, radish etc.) on a string. Bride and Groom are to jointly consume the "delicacy." This can go on for quite some time.

• **Clothing Change**

The bride leaves to change her clothes about halfway through the meal. At the same time the M.C. interviews the Groom (see Groom's Intterview, page 219).

• **Family Toasting**

Towards the end of the meal, the Bride and Groom and immediate family tour each table and toast their guests.

Toll Free: 1-800-66-Speak
www.customlearning.com
copyright © 1988

Multicultural Toasting

Our communities have become so diverse with citizens from all over the world. Proposing a toast in more than English is fun and often appreciated by others. So why not try giving one of the nicest greetings of all . . . best wishes for health, in the Wedding Family's original tongue?

Language/Nationality	Phonetic Pronunciation
Chinese	Gan-bay
Croatian	Jee-vel-see
Danish	Skoll
Dutch	Prost
French	en Bonne Sante
German	Prost
Goan	Viva
Greek	Ee-see-he-yin
Hungarian	Agay-shay-ga-dra
Ismaili	Man-nee-du-say-oh
Sikh	Chak-koe, Chak-koe
Italian	Salud
Japanese	Kamp-eye
Jewish	Mmuzzle-toff
Lebanese	Kah-sack
Polish	Nos-trove-ya
Spanish	Salud
Ukranian	Nos-trove-ya
Yugoslavia	Jee-vel-eee
P.S. Canadian	Chee-moe

P.P.S.   If we've missed your language, please send us a note with the toast and its phonetic spelling!

To Translate or not to Translate?

Background

- Today's society is remarkably diverse, made up of citizens from all over North America and the world.

- Often times when either the bride, groom or both come from a particular cultural heritage the audience is made up of a large number of guests who may or may not speak English.

- The decision to translate a reception simultaneously into a second language is not an easy one and we offer the following tips and suggestions:

Tips and Suggestions

- Translate into a second language if 10% or more of the audience do not speak, or have difficulty with English.

- The translator MUST be articulate in both languages.

- Both M.C.'s need to meet and carefully review notes in advance and decide:

  - which events really need to be translated;

  - which items begin in English and which begin in the 2nd language.

- The first speaker should speak in relatively short sentences to allow the translator to catch up.

- Remember translating takes time, so budget an extra 30-60 minutes for the length of the program.

- Be sure to have 2 microphones.

- Have fun! You'll love it, and so will your audience!

Toll Free: 1-800-66-Speak
www.customlearning.com
copyright © 1988

CHAPTER VI

Planning the Receiving Line

Why Bother With a Receiving Line?   97

Receiving Line Plan Sheet   98

How to Handle a Receiving Line   99

Suggestions For Hosting At A Reception   100

Why Bother With A Receiving Line?

- All guests want to visit with the couple, to congratulate them and make them aware of their attendance.

- A Receiving Line saves time by reducing the amount of socializing during the reception.

- Many who attend the reception may not have been at the wedding ceremony and will not yet have greeted the couple.

- This is a "structured" opportunity for guests and relatives to meet the bridal party.

- It is a simple, yet valuable, way for guests who are quiet or shy to say "hello."

- IT'S FUN TOO!

Receiving Line - Plan Sheet

✓	**Suggested Line-Up**	**Actual Line-Up (Print Name)**

Begin

❑ Father of Bride _____

❑ Mother of Bride _____

❑ Father of Groom _____

❑ Mother of Groom _____

❑ Best Man _____

❑ Maid of Honour _____

❑ Groom _____

❑ Bride _____

❑ Groomsman #1 _____

❑ Maid #1 _____

❑ Groomsman #2 _____

❑ Maid #2 _____

❑ Groomsman #3 _____

❑ Maid #3 _____

❑ _____

❑ _____

❑ _____

End

Toll Free: 1-800-66-Speak
www.customlearning.com
copyright © 1988

How To Handle A Receiving Line

Physical Set Up

- Set up a **gift table**, prior to the receiving line, so that guests need not carry gifts with them.

- The receiving line **should be ready 15-20 minutes** before the expected guest arrival time, as guests tend to come early.

- For receiving line order, see recommended line up on page 98.

- **Coat rack** and **guest book** should be set up in advance of receiving line.

Greeting Suggestions

- Couples should **stand together**.

- It is not uncommon for each person in the receiving line to introduce the next person beside him.

- It is **NOT** appropriate to hold a **drink,** as both hands are required for greeting (ie. hugging.)

- Use your **right hand** to shake with unless the guest has a disability with his/hers.

- Handicapped or individuals in ill health may take their place in line in a wheel chair or on a stool.

- If you don't recognize the guest, then **offer your name** (if they hesitate or do not offer theirs.)

- **Avoid lengthy** conversations (for obvious reasons.) "We'll have to chat later."

- If either parent is not living, then it is OK to substitute a close relative.

Suggestions For Hosting At A Reception

Objective: To assist guests as they arrive at the reception.

Volunteers: Depending on the size of the reception, one (1) to four (4) volunteers can do the job nicely.

Duties:

Set Up:

- Set up door or hallway directional signs as required.

- See that tables are set up for:

    - signing the guest book

    - displaying gifts

- Decorate tables and entranceway.

Hosting:

- Welcome guests to the reception.

- Invite guests to sign the guest register with name, city and fun comment for the bride and groom. (Be sure to catch anyone who arrived before set-up.)

- Accept gifts and place upon gift table prior to guests going through the receiving line, or have presentation (usually money in some instances) placed in a basket or mailbox.

- Give directions to coat room, bathrooms, etc.

- Time permitting, take coat for guest.

- Provide name tags. (Optional)

- In the event of pre-assigned seating by table:

    - ask guests for their name

    - check alphabetical guest list to identify table number

    - give direction to the table

*   Later on, towards the end of the evening, take responsibility for moving the gifts to the location they are to be opened (to avoid double handling) or to a safe storage location, in case gifts are opened the next day.

Toll Free: 1-800-66-Speak
www.customlearning.com
copyright © 1988

CHAPTER VII

Planning the Head Table

Head Table - Seating Suggestions   103

Head Table - Seating Diagrams   104

Head Table Planner   105

Sub-Head Table - Planner - Rectangle   106

Sub-Head Table - Planner - Round   107

Toll Free: 1-800-66-Speak
www.customlearning.com
copyright © 1988

Toll Free: 1-800-66-Speak
www.customlearning.com
copyright © 1988

Head Table Seating - Suggestions:

- M.C. should be at the far right or far left, or at a separate table (convenient to the lectern.)

- Possibly alternate male, female.

- Males should be seated at the ends of a table.

- Any arrangement you feel good about is OK, although the following principles could be considered:
    - bride and groom in the middle;
    - bridal party closest to the couple;
    - parents or family representatives anchored at the table end.

- We suggest parents of bride and groom be mixed, ie. father of the bride, mother of the groom, etc. (optional.)

- If parents are divorced, you may want to consider seating them at separate sub-head tables so they may visit with their respective escorts.

- If Head Table is too large for the room, or your liking, then consider setting a Sub-Head Table (or two.)

Head Table Seating Diagram
(Suggested)

Introduction Order

A.   Outside to Inside

B.   Outside to Inside (Groom, then Bride last)

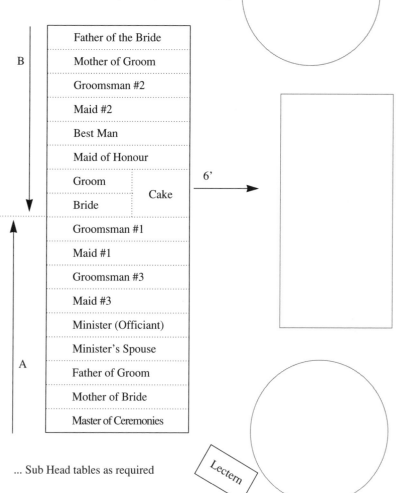

... Sub Head tables as required

Toll Free: 1-800-66-Speak
www.customlearning.com
copyright © 1988

Head Table - Planner

✓   Suggested   Actual Line-Up (Print Name)

Beginning

❏   Father of the Bride   _____

❏   Mother of Groom   _____

❏   Groomsman #2   _____

❏   Maid #2   _____

❏   Best Man   _____

❏   Maid of Honour   _____

❏   Groom   _____

❏   Bride   _____

❏   Groomsman #1   _____

❏   Maid #1   _____

❏   Groomsman #3   _____

❏   Maid #3   _____

❏   Minister (Officiant)   _____

❏   Minister's Spouse   _____

❏   Father of Groom   _____

❏   Mother of Bride   _____

❏   Master of Ceremonies   _____

End

Sub Head Table

- Planner - Rectangle

Do you wish the people at this table to be introduced as part of (before) the main head table or later as Special Guests?

Toll Free: 1-800-66-Speak
www.customlearning.com
copyright © 1988

Sub Head Table

- Planner - Round

1. _____

2. _____

3. _____

4. _____

5. _____

6. _____

7. _____

8. _____

9. _____

10. _____

Typical 8 places

Crowded 10 places

Do you wish the people at this table to be introduced as part of the head table (before main head table) or later as special guests?

_____

_____

Toll Free: 1-800-66-Speak
www.customlearning.com
copyright © 1988

CHAPTER VIII

Starting the Program

Opening the Reception - Checklist   111

Head Table - Entrance Annoucements   112

How to Give the Invocation   113

Invocation - Introduction   115

M.C.'s Welcome - Outline   116

Opening Poem - Example   117

M.C.'s Welcome - Notes   119

Food Service - Suggestions   120

Food Service - Annoucements   121

Pre-Meal Annoucements   122

Toll Free: 1-800-66-Speak
www.customlearning.com
copyright © 1988

Opening The Reception - Checklist

The opening of the reception is critical. A confident, successful start to the program will set the tone for what is to come.

This chapter is organized to reflect the order of events as they should take place for the proper opening of the reception.

M.C. Final Pre-Program Checklist ✓

❏ 1. **Bathroom Break Notice**

Give audience 5-10 minutes advance notice that program is about to begin, so that they have time for a bathroom break.

❏ 2. **When To Start**

It is OK to begin the program just as soon as the dessert is served. If possible have tables cleared and coffee served first.

❏ 3. **Check With Food Service**

Double check with food service that:

❏ wine has been served for toasting purposes (OK with person paying);

❏ tables will not be cleared during the speaking;

❏ cooks and servers will be available to be recognized at a specific time;

❏ the kitchen will be as quiet as possible during the program.

❏ 4. **Speakers Present**

Do a final check that all speakers and individuals to be introduced are, in fact, present.

❏ 5. **Cake Ready**

The cake is ready for ceremonial cutting.

Head Table - Entrance Announcement

Why have a procession?

- It's a good focal point to start the program.
- It gets everyone's attention.
- It's fun!

You might want to try marching in to the music of a piper or other musician. Be sure to lead the applause.

Announcement

Made by   _____

"Ladies and Gentlemen

Will you please stand and join me in welcoming

Mr. and Mrs.   _____

(Groom's first name)

and   _____

(Bride's first name)

_____

(Couple's last name)

and their head table/bridal party."

*Note: If the Bride has retained her maiden name or is using a hyphenated last name, double check with the Bride and Groom for specific instructions on how they prefer to be introduced.

(Photocopy and give to announcer)

Toll Free: 1-800-66-Speak
www.customlearning.com
copyright © 1988

How To Give The Invocation

(Photocopy this page for the person giving Invocation)

- If there is a microphone being used, then move up to the microphone.

- If no microphone, stand up behind your chair.

- If audience is seated, ask them to "please stand."

- Instruct guests: "Please bow your heads."

- Keep it short.

- Adjourn with "Amen."

Invocation Notes: (sample invocation on next page)

_____

_____

_____

_____

_____

_____

_____

_____

Invocation - Examples

ALL GOOD GIFTS

God and Father of us all,
you are the giver of all good gifts.
We praise and thank you today
for the love you have placed in the hearts
of _____ and _____,
and allowing us to share in that love.

THE JOY WE FEEL

We thank you for the joy we feel when we gather with friends.
We thank you for the food we are about to share.
Let this banquet be for us a sign of your constant care.

SING YOUR PRAISE

Bless us, Father, and the food we eat.
Give us grateful hearts to sing your praise.
In God's name, Amen.

Toll Free: 1-800-66-Speak
www.customlearning.com
copyright © 1988

Invocation Introduction

Invocation

"Would you all please (stand)/remain standing as I call upon

_____

of the _____

to lead us in the blessing."

"Thank You _____

Please Be Seated."

M.C.'s - Welcome Outline

- The next few pages contain the basic ingredients for the M.C.'s welcome.

- Feel free to use ours, or create your own.
    - The purpose of the welcome is to:
    - make guests feel welcome;
    - set a theme or tone of humour and fun;
    - create a mood of positive anticipation by the audience towards the program;
    - make the necessary announcements prior to supper, in order to prevent meal interruptions and/or confusion.

- Don't forget:
    - the welcome should be as short as possible.
    - the Head Table introductions should follow the meal, in order to give guests a chance to visit.

Toll Free: 1-800-66-Speak
www.customlearning.com
copyright © 1988

Opening Poem - Example

(Optional)

The Marriage Bond Divine

> What is there in the
> vale of life
> Half so delightful
> as a wife,
> When friendship, love and place combine
> To stamp the
> marriage bond divine.
> > William Cowper

The use of an appropriate poem may add a touch of class and provide the ideal opening for the M.C.

Use our example or choose one of your own.

M.C.'s - Welcome (Example)

- *"On behalf of Mr. & Mrs.* _____

  and _____

  I take great pleasure in welcoming you all." _____

  _____

  _____

  _____

- *"It has been said: 'Man is not complete until he's married . . . and then he's finished. But, boy, what a finish!' "*

- *"We are all delighted to join with* _____
  and _____ *on this special occasion, but I know you're all dying to find out how it happened:*

  Well, at great danger to myself, I obtained a transcript of how _____
  popped the question."

  " _____ *said, 'You know , I'm thinking of asking some girl/guy to marry me. What do you think of the idea?'*
  To which _____ *replied, 'It's a great idea, if you ask me!'*
  and _____ *did, and that's why we're all here."*

- *"We have an (choose which of these are appropriate)*
  - interesting, exciting, fun, entertaining humorous, romantic program planned for you."

  _____

  _____

  _____

  _____

  _____

  _____

Toll Free: 1-800-66-Speak
www.customlearning.com
copyright © 1988

M.C.'s Welcome - Notes

_____

_____

_____

_____

_____

_____

_____

_____

_____

_____

_____

_____

_____

_____

_____

_____

_____

_____

_____

_____

_____

_____

_____

_____

_____

Food Service Suggestions

Table Service

- Wish guests an enjoyable meal.

Buffet Service

- There is NO easy way to announce the order of tables that makes everyone happy, but you must give direction in order to avoid confusion and needless, lengthy lineups.

- Suggest tables be pre-numbered.

- Be sure Head Table is FIRST! (Even with buffet, bridal party could receive table service.)

Optional Methods

1. Ask each table to wait and watch until preceding table is standing, or

2. Draw table numbers from a hat and announce, or

3. Assign the task to the caterer or someone who owes you money!

YOUR JOB IS TO MAKE SURE THIS
PROCEDURE IS SMOOTH AND EFFICIENT!

Toll Free: 1-800-66-Speak
www.customlearning.com
copyright © 1988

Food Service Annoucement

(Note actual method of food service below and any other annoucements before meal begins)

_____

_____

_____

_____

_____

_____

_____

_____

_____

_____

_____

_____

_____

_____

_____

_____

_____

_____

_____

_____

_____

_____

Pre-Meal Announcements

- **Bar Opens/Closes**

  _____

  _____

- **Wine service** (re: potential toasts)

  _____

  _____

- **Meal service arrangements**

  _____

  _____

  _____

- **"Ringing" of glasses IDEA!** (optional)
  Instead of "ringing" glasses to inspire bride and groom to kiss, why not announce
  that the wedding couple will only respond to a "spontaneous" poem, joke,
  anecdote or song that extols their virtues. (with the word LOVE in it)

  _____

  _____

- **"Open" Toast-Notice** (optional) (see page 283)
  Remind anyone who feels so inclined, who has not been previously scheduled on
  the program that they may propose a short toast at the conclusion of the program.

  _____

  _____

  _____

- Other:

  _____

  _____

- On with the meal. ENJOY! !

Toll Free: 1-800-66-Speak
www.customlearning.com
copyright © 1988

CHAPTER IX

Introducing the Head Table

How to Use This Chapter 125

Head Table Guest Introductions
    The Notion 126
    How to Use the Forms 127
    Example 128

M.C.'s Program Opening Comments
    The Notion 129
    An Outline 130
    Head Table Introductions - Opening 133
    Introduction Humour - Example 134
    Introduction Forms 135
    (20 copies)
    Head Table Introductions- Closing 155

Introducing The Head Table

How To Use This Chapter

- Refer to your Head Table Plan Sheets.

- Confirm seating order.

- Assign one page for every introduction.

- Photocopy and sort pages into exact order of actual introductions. (See next page for details)

- Review each introduction with wedding couple for:
  - correct spelling and pronunciation
  - appropriate story/anecdote

- If Wedding Couple is unable to help, SEEK OUT others who are more knowledgeable.

- When in doubt as to appropriateness of remark, ask someone else or possibly even person to be introduced, eg: *"Would you be comfortable if I said. . .?"*

_____

_____

The Notion of: **The Head Table Guest Introductions**

Presented by: The M.C.

Purpose: To introduce Head Table Guests to the audience in an informative, humourous and enjoyable way in order to set everyone at ease.

Suggested Content:

- Preface your remarks by asking each Head Table guest to STAND and PLEASE REMAIN STANDING (table by table.)

   (This is by far the least awkward procedure, especially for those who are shy.)

- Avoid attempting to stifle applause with *"Please withhold applause until everyone is introduced"* because it never works, and usually ends up embarrassing all concerned.

- In fact we suggest the opposite. . .
   "and don't you dare withhold your applause."

- Introduction Sequence:

   A.   Outside to inside right

   B.   Outside to inside left

   (Groom, then Bride last)

   - Sub-Head Tables first

   - Head Table Last

   - Yourself the very last.

Toll Free: 1-800-66-Speak
www.customlearning.com
copyright © 1988

How To Use Head Table Form(s)
(see example on next page)

- **Seated** - describe where person is seated relative to previous introduction, i.e. on "John's left" or "next on your right."

  IS guest's first and/or last name.

- (**Position in Wedding Party**) - i.e. role they play in the proceeding e.g. . . . . "Father of the Bride", or "Best Man", or "Sister of the Groom."

- **Brief (humourous) true story or anecdote** - see page 62, "The makings of a great story/anecdote." Remember it should be funny, but never overly embarrass.

- If you are unable to obtain an appropriate anecdote or story, then try a joke or quotation from the Treasury of Wit and Wisdom chapter and insert here.

- **Sincere, Positive Comment** to "balance" the previous story. Conclude with a sincere, positive comment, i.e. their nicest quality, personal achievement, etc.

- **Please help me welcome** - pronounce name correctly and lead the applause. If you're not absolutely certain then spell it out phonetically in the space provided.

Don't Forget To:

- Meet each Head Table guest beforehand in order to:
  - see that they are actually present;
  - get to know them and their feelings about being introduced;
  - learn the correct spelling and pronunciation of both their names;
  - obtain their approval as to the appropriateness of the introduction you have prepared (if you're not certain it's true or in good taste, or might overly embarrass);
  - let them know when they will be introduced;
  - lead the audience in applause before and after.

Suggested Length:

- As quickly as possible – no longer than 60 seconds.

Head Table Guest Introductions – Example

(Maximum 60 seconds)

- Seated   *to the Groom's left* is   *Cindy*
       (describe location - e.g. next to)

- (Position in wedding party) *The Maid of Honour*
       and the *Bride's older sister*
       (personal relationship, eg. friend of, cousin to)

- Brief (humorous) true anecdote or story. (notes)
       "Cindy was always sedate
       she always came home rather late
       But then she met Tim
       and we all know about him
       So now they are setting a date."

  (if using prepared joke/quotation, copy or clip from HUMOUR section and insert above)

- Sincere, positive comment (notes)

     "Kind person who is always there for you."

- Please help me welcome (pronounce names correctly and lead the applause).

       Cindy   *O'Callahan*
       First Name   Last Name

(Phonetic spelling - if required for correct pronunciation)

The Notion of: **M.C.'s Program Opening Comments**

Presented by: The M.C.

Purpose: To share with the audience a brief outline of the events to follow
and set the stage for a terrific program.

**Suggested
Content:**   See outline, on the following page.

**Suggested
Length:**   1$^1/_2$ - 2 minutes.

M.C.'s Program Opening Comments
An Outline

- *"Welcome (back)!"*

  _____

  _____

  _____

- *"I trust you had a good meal and enjoyed the company of your table companions."*

  _____

  _____

  _____

- (Possibly acknowledge cooks, servers, meal time entertainers.)

  _____

  _____

  _____

- (If table centerpieces are for guests to keep, explain method of choosing who should keep them, i.e. tape under plate or chair – or let the table decide)

  _____

  _____

  _____

- (Share a brief, humourous, true anecdote, story, joke or quotation.)

  _____

  _____

  _____

  _____

  _____

Toll Free: 1-800-66-Speak
www.customlearning.com
copyright © 1988

M.C. Program Opening Comments

* (Provide brief outline of highlights of the program).

  _____

  _____

  _____

  _____

  _____

* (Welcome any late arrivals that should be acknowledged or recognized.)

  _____

  _____

  _____

  _____

* Remind audience about two (2) optional program features:

❑ **Ringing of glasses**
Instead of "ringing" glasses to inspire Bride and Groom to kiss, why not announce that the wedding couple will only respond to a "spontaneous" poem, joke, anecdote or song that extols their virtues (with the word LOVE in it!) To be presented by either:

    ❑   Individual(s)   ❑   All the guests at a table

_____

_____

❑ **"Open" Toast Notice** (see page 283)
Remind anyone who feels so inclined, who has not been previously scheduled on the program, that they may propose a short toast at the conclusion of the program, so be thinking about it!

_____

_____

_____

M.C. Program Opening Comments

• (Announcements about wine service for toasts).

_____

_____

_____

_____

_____

• Other

_____

_____

_____

_____

_____

_____

• (Now ON with the program!!)

_____

_____

_____

_____

_____

_____

_____

_____

Toll Free: 1-800-66-Speak
www.customlearning.com
copyright © 1988

Head Table Introductions – Opening

(Don't begin until after dessert is served.)

- *"I will ask our Head Table guests to stand and please remain standing until you are all introduced."*

- *"And don't you dare withhold your applause."*

- Notes:

_____

_____

_____

_____

_____

_____

_____

_____

_____

_____

_____

_____

_____

_____

_____

_____

_____

_____

Example - Introduction Humour

Suggestions

Groom:

> *"The bridal veil was fragile net,*
>> *The bridal gown was lace,*
> *The bride wore slippers on her feet,*
>> *A smile upon her face.*
> *The bride wore gloves of softest silk,*
>> *And garlands in her hair,*
> *The bride's bouquet was white*
>> *P.S. The groom was also there."*

Bride:

> *"The Lady, who turned* _____
> *from a night hawk - into a homing pigeon."*

> *"Who may very well have been the inspiration for Charley Rich when he wrote the words, 'Hey, did you happen to see the most beautiful girl in the world.' "*

Best Man:

> *"The trouble with being the Best Man at a wedding - is that you get no chance to prove it!"*

Toll Free: 1-800-66-Speak
www.customlearning.com
copyright © 1988

Head Table Guest Introductions

(Maximum 60 seconds)

- Seated _____ is _____
  (describe location - e.g. next to)   (name)

- **(Position in wedding party)** _____

  _____
                    (personal relationship e.g. friend of, cousin to)

- **Brief (humourous) true story or anecdote.** (notes)

  _____

  _____

  _____

  _____

  (if using prepared joke/quotation, copy or clip from HUMOUR section and insert above)

- **Sincere, positive comment.** (notes)

  _____

  _____

  _____

  _____

- ***"Please help me welcome"*** (pronounce name correctly and lead the applause)

  _____   _____
              (First Name)   (Last Name)

  _____
              (Phonetic spelling - if required for correct pronunciation)

Head Table Guest Introductions

(Maximum 60 seconds)

- Seated _____ is _____
          (describe location - e.g. next to)   (name)

- **(Position in wedding party)** _____

  _____
         (personal relationship e.g. friend of, cousin to)

- **Brief (humourous) true story or anecdote.** (notes)

  _____

  _____

  _____

  _____

  (if using prepared joke/quotation, copy or clip from HUMOUR section and insert above)

- **Sincere, positive comment.** (notes)

  _____

  _____

  _____

  _____

- *"Please help me welcome"* (pronounce name correctly and lead the applause)

  _____ _____
        (First Name)   (Last Name)

  _____
  (Phonetic spelling - if required for correct pronunciation)

Toll Free: 1-800-66-Speak
www.customlearning.com
copyright © 1988

Head Table Guest Introductions

(Maximum 60 seconds)

- Seated _____ is _____
             (describe location - e.g. next to)   (name)

- **(Position in wedding party)** _____

  _____
               (personal relationship e.g. friend of, cousin to)

- **Brief (humourous) true story or anecdote**. (notes)

  _____

  _____

  _____

  _____

  (if using prepared joke/quotation, copy or clip from HUMOUR section and insert above)

- **Sincere, positive comment.** (notes)

  _____

  _____

  _____

  _____

- *"Please help me welcome"* (pronounce name correctly and lead the applause)

  _____   _____
           (First Name)   (Last Name)

  _____
       (Phonetic spelling - if required for correct pronunciation)

Head Table Guest Introductions

(Maximum 60 seconds)

- Seated _____ is _____
  (describe location - e.g. next to)   (name)

- **(Position in wedding party)** _____

  _____
  (personal relationship e.g. friend of, cousin to)

- **Brief (humourous) true story or anecdote**. (notes)

  _____

  _____

  _____

  _____

  _____
  (if using prepared joke/quotation, copy or clip from HUMOUR section and insert above)

- **Sincere, positive comment.** (notes)

  _____

  _____

  _____

  _____

- *"Please help me welcome"* (pronounce name correctly and lead the applause)

  _____   _____
  (First Name)   (Last Name)

  _____
  (Phonetic spelling - if required for correct pronunciation)

Toll Free: 1-800-66-Speak
www.customlearning.com
copyright © 1988

Head Table Guest Introductions

(Maximum 60 seconds)

- Seated _____ is _____
  (describe location - e.g. next to)   (name)

- **(Position in wedding party)** _____

  _____
              (personal relationship e.g. friend of, cousin to)

- **Brief (humourous) true story or anecdote.** (notes)

  _____

  _____

  _____

  _____

  (if using prepared joke/quotation, copy or clip from HUMOUR section and insert above)

- **Sincere, positive comment.** (notes)

  _____

  _____

  _____

  _____

- ***"Please help me welcome"*** (pronounce name correctly and lead the applause)

  _____ _____
            (First Name)   (Last Name)

  _____
            (Phonetic spelling - if required for correct pronunciation)

Head Table Guest Introductions

(Maximum 60 seconds)

- Seated _____ is _____
        (describe location - e.g. next to)   (name)

- **(Position in wedding party)** _____

  _____
        (personal relationship e.g. friend of, cousin to)

- **Brief (humourous) true story or anecdote.** (notes)

  _____

  _____

  _____

  _____

  _____

  (if using prepared joke/quotation, copy or clip from HUMOUR section and insert above)

- **Sincere, positive comment.** (notes)

  _____

  _____

  _____

  _____

- ***"Please help me welcome"*** (pronounce name correctly and lead the applause)

  _____   _____
        (First Name)   (Last Name)

  _____

  (Phonetic spelling - if required for correct pronunciation)

Toll Free: 1-800-66-Speak
www.customlearning.com
copyright © 1988

Head Table Guest Introductions

(Maximum 60 seconds)

- Seated _____ is _____
          (describe location - e.g. next to)   (name)

- **(Position in wedding party)** _____

    _____
          (personal relationship e.g. friend of, cousin to)

- **Brief (humourous) true story or anecdote.** (notes)

    _____

    _____

    _____

    _____

    (if using prepared joke/quotation, copy or clip from HUMOUR section and insert above)

- **Sincere, positive comment.** (notes)

    _____

    _____

    _____

    _____

- ***"Please help me welcome"*** (pronounce name correctly and lead the applause)

    _____   _____
          (First Name)   (Last Name)

    _____
    (Phonetic spelling - if required for correct pronunciation)

Head Table Guest Introductions

(Maximum 60 seconds)

- Seated _____ is _____
  (describe location - e.g. next to)   (name)

- **(Position in wedding party)** _____

  _____
  (personal relationship e.g. friend of, cousin to)

- **Brief (humourous) true story or anecdote.** (notes)

  _____

  _____

  _____

  _____

  (if using prepared joke/quotation, copy or clip from HUMOUR section and insert above)

- **Sincere, positive comment.** (notes)

  _____

  _____

  _____

  _____

- ***"Please help me welcome"*** (pronounce name correctly and lead the applause)

  _____ _____
  (First Name)   (Last Name)

  _____
  (Phonetic spelling - if required for correct pronunciation)

Toll Free: 1-800-66-Speak
www.customlearning.com
copyright © 1988

Head Table Guest Introductions

(Maximum 60 seconds)

- Seated _____ is _____
         (describe location - e.g. next to)   (name)

- **(Position in wedding party)** _____

_____

(personal relationship e.g. friend of, cousin to)

- **Brief (humourous) true story or anecdote**. (notes)

_____

_____

_____

_____

_____

(if using prepared joke/quotation, copy or clip from HUMOUR section and insert above)

- **Sincere, positive comment**. (notes)

_____

_____

_____

_____

- ***"Please help me welcome"*** (pronounce name correctly and lead the applause)

_____   _____
         (First Name)   (Last Name)

_____

(Phonetic spelling - if required for correct pronunciation)

Head Table Guest Introductions

(Maximum 60 seconds)

- Seated _____ is _____
        (describe location - e.g. next to)   (name)

- **(Position in wedding party)** _____

  _____
       (personal relationship e.g. friend of, cousin to)

- **Brief (humourous) true story or anecdote.** (notes)

  _____

  _____

  _____

  _____

  (if using prepared joke/quotation, copy or clip from HUMOUR section and insert above)

- **Sincere, positive comment.** (notes)

  _____

  _____

  _____

  _____

- ***"Please help me welcome"*** (pronounce name correctly and lead the applause)

  _____   _____
       (First Name)   (Last Name)

  _____
  (Phonetic spelling - if required for correct pronunciation)

Toll Free: 1-800-66-Speak
www.customlearning.com
copyright © 1988

Head Table Guest Introductions

(Maximum 60 seconds)

- Seated _____ is _____
       (describe location - e.g. next to)   (name)

- **(Position in wedding party)** _____

  _____

       (personal relationship e.g. friend of, cousin to)

- **Brief (humourous) true story or anecdote.** (notes)

  _____

  _____

  _____

  _____

  (if using prepared joke/quotation, copy or clip from HUMOUR section and insert above)

- **Sincere, positive comment.** (notes)

  _____

  _____

  _____

  _____

- *"Please help me welcome"* (pronounce name correctly and lead the applause)

  _____   _____
       (First Name)   (Last Name)

  _____

  (Phonetic spelling - if required for correct pronunciation)

Head Table Guest Introductions

(Maximum 60 seconds)

- Seated _____ is _____
  (describe location - e.g. next to)   (name)

- **(Position in wedding party)** _____

  _____
  (personal relationship e.g. friend of, cousin to)

- **Brief (humourous) true story or anecdote.** (notes)

  _____

  _____

  _____

  _____

  (if using prepared joke/quotation, copy or clip from HUMOUR section and insert above)

- **Sincere, positive comment.** (notes)

  _____

  _____

  _____

  _____

- ***"Please help me welcome"*** (pronounce name correctly and lead the applause)

  _____   _____
  (First Name)   (Last Name)

  _____
  (Phonetic spelling - if required for correct pronunciation)

Toll Free: 1-800-66-Speak
www.customlearning.com
copyright © 1988

Head Table Guest Introductions

(Maximum 60 seconds)

- Seated _____ is _____
  (describe location - e.g. next to)   (name)

- **(Position in wedding party)** _____

  _____
                    (personal relationship e.g. friend of, cousin to)

- **Brief (humourous) true story or anecdote.** (notes)

  _____

  _____

  _____

  _____

  _____
  (if using prepared joke/quotation, copy or clip from HUMOUR section and insert above)

- **Sincere, positive comment.** (notes)

  _____

  _____

  _____

  _____

- *"Please help me welcome"* (pronounce name correctly and lead the applause)

  _____   _____
          (First Name)   (Last Name)

  _____
        (Phonetic spelling - if required for correct pronunciation)

Head Table Guest Introductions

(Maximum 60 seconds)

- Seated _____ is _____
  (describe location - e.g. next to)   (name)

- **(Position in wedding party)** _____

  _____
  (personal relationship e.g. friend of, cousin to)

- **Brief (humourous) true story or anecdote.** (notes)

  _____

  _____

  _____

  _____

  (if using prepared joke/quotation, copy or clip from HUMOUR section and insert above)

- **Sincere, positive comment.** (notes)

  _____

  _____

  _____

  _____

- *"Please help me welcome"* (pronounce name correctly and lead the applause)

  _____   _____
  (First Name)   (Last Name)

  _____
  (Phonetic spelling - if required for correct pronunciation)

Toll Free: 1-800-66-Speak
www.customlearning.com
copyright © 1988

Head Table Guest Introductions

(Maximum 60 seconds)

* Seated _____ is _____
    (describe location - e.g. next to)   (name)

* **(Position in wedding party)** _____

    _____
                (personal relationship e.g. friend of, cousin to)

* **Brief (humourous) true story or anecdote.** (notes)

    _____

    _____

    _____

    _____

    (if using prepared joke/quotation, copy or clip from HUMOUR section and insert above)

* **Sincere, positive comment.** (notes)

    _____

    _____

    _____

    _____

* ***"Please help me welcome"*** (pronounce name correctly and lead the applause)

    _____   _____
            (First Name)   (Last Name)

    _____
        (Phonetic spelling - if required for correct pronunciation)

Head Table Guest Introductions

(Maximum 60 seconds)

- Seated _____ is _____
           (describe location - e.g. next to)   (name)

- **(Position in wedding party)** _____

  _____
           (personal relationship e.g. friend of, cousin to)

- **Brief (humourous) true story or anecdote**. (notes)

  _____

  _____

  _____

  _____

  (if using prepared joke/quotation, copy or clip from HUMOUR section and insert above)

- **Sincere, positive comment.** (notes)

  _____

  _____

  _____

  _____

- *"Please help me welcome"* (pronounce name correctly and lead the applause)

  _____   _____
         (First Name)   (Last Name)

  _____

  (Phonetic spelling - if required for correct pronunciation)

Toll Free: 1-800-66-Speak
www.customlearning.com
copyright © 1988

Head Table Guest Introductions

(Maximum 60 seconds)

• Seated _____ is _____
          (describe location - e.g. next to)   (name)

• **(Position in wedding party)** _____

_____
      (personal relationship e.g. friend of, cousin to)

• **Brief (humourous) true story or anecdote**. (notes)

_____

_____

_____

_____

(if using prepared joke/quotation, copy or clip from HUMOUR section and insert above)

• **Sincere, positive comment.** (notes)

_____

_____

_____

_____

• *"Please help me welcome"* (pronounce name correctly and lead the applause)

_____   _____
      (First Name)   (Last Name)

_____

(Phonetic spelling - if required for correct pronunciation)

 Toll Free: 1-800-66-Speak
www.customlearning.com
copyright © 1988

151

Head Table Guest Introductions

(Maximum 60 seconds)

- Seated _____ is _____

          (describe location - e.g. next to)   (name)

- **(Position in wedding party)** _____

      _____

         (personal relationship e.g. friend of, cousin to)

- **Brief (humourous) true story or anecdote.** (notes)

  _____

  _____

  _____

  _____

  (if using prepared joke/quotation, copy or clip from HUMOUR section and insert above)

- **Sincere, positive comment.** (notes)

  _____

  _____

  _____

  _____

- ***"Please help me welcome"*** (pronounce name correctly and lead the applause)

  _____ _____

      (First Name)   (Last Name)

  _____

  (Phonetic spelling - if required for correct pronunciation)

Toll Free: 1-800-66-Speak
www.customlearning.com
copyright © 1988

Head Table Guest Introductions

(Maximum 60 seconds)

* Seated _____ is _____
         (describe location - e.g. next to)   (name)

* **(Position in wedding party)** _____

  _____
             (personal relationship e.g. friend of, cousin to)

* **Brief (humourous) true story or anecdote.** (notes)

  _____

  _____

  _____

  _____

  (if using prepared joke/quotation, copy or clip from HUMOUR section and insert above)

* **Sincere, positive comment.** (notes)

  _____

  _____

  _____

  _____

* **_"Please help me welcome"_** (pronounce name correctly and lead the applause)

  _____   _____
        (First Name)   (Last Name)

  _____
  (Phonetic spelling - if required for correct pronunciation)

Head Table Guest Introductions

(Maximum 60 seconds)

- Seated _____ is _____
  (describe location - e.g. next to)   (name)

- **(Position in wedding party)** _____

  _____
  (personal relationship e.g. friend of, cousin to)

- **Brief (humourous) true story or anecdote.** (notes)

  _____

  _____

  _____

  _____

  (if using prepared joke/quotation, copy or clip from HUMOUR section and insert above)

- **Sincere, positive comment.** (notes)

  _____

  _____

  _____

  _____

- *"Please help me welcome"* (pronounce name correctly and lead the applause)

  _____   _____
  (First Name)   (Last Name)

  _____
  (Phonetic spelling - if required for correct pronunciation)

Toll Free: 1-800-66-Speak
www.customlearning.com
copyright © 1988

Head Table Introductions - Closing

•   *"And this, Ladies and Gentlemen, is your Head Table!"*
    (Audience may automatically applaud - be sure to lead the applause).
    (if guests don't sit down, then say, "Please be seated.")

•   *"Finally, Ladies and Gentlemen, my name is:"*

    _____   _____
    (First Name)   (Last Name)

    (Comment about yourself)

    _____

    _____

    _____

    _____

    _____

    _____

    _____

    _____

    _____

    _____

    _____

    _____

    _____

    _____

•   *"And I'm your Master of Ceremonies!"*

 Toll Free: 1-800-66-Speak
www.customlearning.com
copyright © 1988

155

CHAPTER X

Conducting the Main Program

How to Use This Chapter 159

Program Speaker Introductions 160

Telegrams 163

The "Key Ceremony" 170

The "This is Your Life" Slide Show 174

Out-of-Town Guest Introductions 178

Entertainment 197

Special Program Opportunities 201

Toast to the Bride 205

Groom's Reply to the Toast to the Bride 212

Bride's Reply to the Toast 221

Special Guest Introductions 228

Toast to the Maid of Honour & Bridesmaids 240

Reply to the Toast to the Maid of Honour & Bridesmaids ... 247

Reply to the Toast to the Groomsmen 254

Roving "Donahue" 257

The Father of the Bride/Mother of the Bride - Address ... 261

The Father of the Groom/Mother of the Groom - Address ... 269

Optional Toasts 277

"Open" Toast Opportunity 283

Acknowledgements 286

Ceremonial Cake Cutting 303

Closing Announcements 305

M.C.'s Final Advice 308

How To Use This Chapter

- There is no "perfect" or "right" program.

- Whatever works or is the wish of the family is OK!

- Any of the Program Events should be considered optional.

- The format for most items in this chapter is as follows:

The Notion	this explains the concept and ideas for each program event.
M.C. Opening Comments	the M.C.'s form for planning and writing notes to introduce the program item.
Introduction Forms	a form for speaker and other guest introductions.
Presenter Outline	suggested outline for speakers to assist in developing their presentation.
M.C. Closing Comments	is M.C.'s form for planning and writing notes to conclude the program event.

- Review each item with the Couple to determine their specific preferences (see program planner, page 47)

- It is suggested the order in which the program events are presented in this chapter be followed at the reception. Contact every speaker regarding the need for:

  - brevity
  - clean humour
  - special requirements
  - their introduction

- When you are done, paper clip or "post-it-note".

The Notion of: **Program Speaker Introductions**

Presented by: The M.C.

Purpose: To inform the audience as to the purpose and objective of the presenter(s) in an informative, friendly and entertaining way, and to introduce the speaker and make him/her feel welcome.

Suggested Content:

Follow the outline on the speaker introduction forms that are provided with each of the program events.

Note: A program speaker is anyone who will be addressing the entire audience and therefore requires a proper introduction.

Toll Free: 1-800-66-Speak
www.customlearning.com
copyright © 1988

How To Use Introduction Form(s)

- **Our Next Presentation is** - in your own words, inform audience as to the next program event, i.e. toast to the bride, maid's reply, etc.

- **Brief (humorous) true story or anecdote** - see page 62,"The Makings of a Great Story (Anecdote.)" Remember it should be funny, but never overly embarrass.

- If you are unable to obtain an appropriate anecdote or story, then try a joke or quotation from the Treasury of Wit and Wisdom chapter and insert here.

- **Reason speaker was asked to perform task and/or relationship to Bride and Groom and Family** should be an accurate, sincere, positive comment describing the program speaker's nicer attributes and/or their involvement with the family.

- **Restate Speaking Assignment**, (i..e. "And now to propose a toast to The Maid of Honour.")

- **Please help me welcome** - pronounce name correctly and lead the applause. If you're not absolutely certain, then spell it out phonetically in the space provided.

Don't Forget To:
- Meet each speaker/presenter beforehand in order to:
  - ensure that they are **actually** present;
  - get to know them and their feelings about being introduced;
  - learn the **correct spelling** and **appropriateness** of the introduction you have prepared (if you're not certain it's true or in good taste, or might overly embarrass);
  - let them know **when** they will be introduced;
  - **diplomatically** make them aware of time objective.

- **Lead** the audience in applause before and after.

- **Shake hands** with each presenter as they arrive and depart.

Suggested Length:

- As quickly as possible - No longer than 60 seconds

Program Speaker Introduction - Example

- "Our next presentation is" (name of program event ie. Telegrams, etc.)

  "The Toast To The Bride"

  _____

  _____

- (Brief, humorous, true anecdote or story about speaker. Should not overly embarrass guest or audience).

  "He is the bride's closest friend. In fact, rumour has it he proposed to her when he was nine (9) years old. She said 'no'. He was absolutely dejected and didn't talk to her for three (3) days!"

  _____

  _____

  _____

- (Reason speaker was asked to perform task and/or relationship to Bride & Groom & Family)

  *"What better person to propose the **Toast to the Bride** than her lifelong best friend!"*

  _____

  _____

- (Restate speaking assignment)

  *"To propose the **Toast To The Bride**"*

  _____

- *"Please help me welcome"* (pronounce name correctly)

  _____   _____
  (First Name)   (Last Name)

  _____
  (Phonetic spelling)

Toll Free: 1-800-66-Speak
www.customlearning.com
copyright © 1988

Telegrams

M.C. Opening Comments

(Transition comment from previous event.)

_____

_____

_____

_____

_____

(Brief, humorous anecdote or true story relevant to this topic or next speaker. Do not overly embarrass.)

_____

_____

_____

_____

_____

OR (Prepared joke, poem, quotation that is relevant. See Chapter XII Treasury of Wit and Wisdom).

_____

_____

_____

_____

_____

Now introduce next speaker or conduct next event.

The Notion Of: **Telegrams**

Presented by: The M.C., or any volunteer.

Purpose: 1.   To communicate best wishes from friends and relatives unable to be present.

2.   To have a little fun with fictitious messages.

Suggested Content:

- collect telegrams, letters and phone messages from both families

- edit and/or highlight lengthy messages for key passages

- "customize" fictitious telegrams you feel are appropriate and/or create your own (in good taste)

- read real messages first

- don't forget to return messages to the bridal couple when you're done

Suggested Length: 1¹/₂ - 3 minutes.

Toll Free: 1-800-66-Speak
www.customlearning.com
copyright © 1988

Telegram #1 (Hotel Room Rent-Out)

_____   _____
            (City)   (Province)

Dear Mr. _____

    So you are really getting married this time.

    Congratulations!

    Does this mean we can rent Room 123 to somebody else on Friday nights?

                               Manager

_____
                                   Name

_____
                                   Hotel

Telegram #2 (Don't Forget)

_____   _____
            (City)   (Province)

Dear _____

    You are so lucky to get a wife already. Don't
forget to visit me and the other girls once in a
while. . . and it will be just like old times.

    Love Mitzy

Telegram #3 (Broken Heart)

_____   _____
           (City)   (Province)

Dear_____
                                    (nickname)

Best wishes for a long and happy marriage . . . even though you're breaking our hearts.

Joe, Jim, Dale, Gerald, etc. (and the rest of _____.)
                                                        (sports team)

Telegram #4 (Overtime)

_____   _____
           (City)   (Province)

Dear Mr. _____

My personal congratulations and best wishes for the future to you and
_____ (bride's name).

We expect great things from you and our firm, and hope you enjoy working overtime every evening for the next three months.

President

_____
                                    Name

_____
                                  Company

Toll Free: 1-800-66-Speak
www.customlearning.com
copyright © 1988

Telegram #5 (Two Singles)

From: _____ Hotel

_____   _____
            (City)   (Province)

Dear Mr. _____

We are unable to confirm your request for the honeymoon room.

Instead, we have reserved 2 singles . . .

-     one on the 4th floor

-     and the other on the 22nd floor

Please advise if this arrangement is suitable.

The Management

Telegram #6 (The Queen)

_____   _____
            (City)   (Province)

Dear _____

Congratulations on your great achievement. Although I am unable to attend this function due to other commitments, I am happy to declare this tractor factory officially open.

Queen Elizabeth

"Real" Telegrams

• Paper clip or attach real telegrams, letters and/or special telephone call messages.

Toll Free: 1-800-66-Speak
www.customlearning.com
copyright © 1988

Telegrams

M.C. Closing Comments

(Acknowledge presenter(s) speaker(s)

_____

_____

_____

_____

_____

(Prepared joke, poem, quotation that is relevant)
(See Chapter XII, Treasury of Wit and Wisdom)

_____

_____

_____

_____

_____

OR (Brief, humorous anecdote or true story relevant to this topic or previous speaker.
Do not overly embarrass.)

_____

_____

_____

_____

_____

The Notion of: **The Key Ceremony (optional)**

Presented by: The M.C. or any volunteer(s)

Purpose: To entertain

Suggested Content:

- This is an optional event

- If in doubt as to appropriateness, DO NOT USE! ! !

- Speaker announces that the Bride was very popular as a single person.

- She was courted by a select group of most eligible bachelors.

- However, very close to her Mother, who lived so close, that she had a key to her apartment/house.

- It would be helpful if Mother and any other "relatives" who did have a key, would now turn them in to the Groom.

- Speaker tees up 5-20 young men to come forward and turn in a key.

- Project assigned to: _____

- Special Note: This event may also be "played out" for the groom as well!

- We suggest using old useless keys that don't need to be returned.

Suggested Length: 1-2 minutes.

Toll Free: 1-800-66-Speak
www.customlearning.com
copyright © 1988

The "Key" Ceremony

M.C. Opening Comments

(Transition comment from previous event.)

_____

_____

_____

_____

_____

(Brief, humorous anecdote or true story relevant to this topic or next speaker. Do not overly embarrass.)

_____

_____

_____

_____

_____

OR (Prepared joke, poem, quotation that is relevant. See Chapter XII Treasury of Wit and Wisdom).

_____

_____

_____

_____

_____

Now introduce next speaker or conduct next event.

Program Speaker Introduction

- *"Our next presentation is"* (name of program event ie. The Key Ceremony, etc.)

  _____

  _____

  _____

- (Brief, humorous, true anecdote or story about speaker. Should not overly embarrass guest or audience).

  _____

  _____

  _____

  _____

  _____

  _____

- (Reason speaker was asked to perform task and/or relationship to Bride & Groom & Family)

  _____

  _____

  _____

  _____

  _____

- (Restate speaking assignment)

  _____

- *"Please help me welcome"* (pronounce name correctly)

  _____   _____
  (First Name)   (Last Name)

  _____
                    (Phonetic spelling)

Toll Free: 1-800-66-Speak
www.customlearning.com
copyright © 1988

The "Key" Ceremony

M.C. Closing Comments

(Acknowledge presenter(s) speaker(s)

_____

_____

_____

_____

_____

(Prepared joke, poem, quotation that is relevant)
(See Chapter XII, Treasury of Wit and Wisdom)

_____

_____

_____

_____

_____

OR (Brief, humorous anecdote or true story relevant to this topic or previous speaker. Do not overly embarrass.)

_____

_____

_____

_____

_____

The Notion of: **"This Is Your Life"**

Presented by: A close friend(s) of the Bride and/or Groom

Purpose: To affectionately share pictures and stories about the Wedding Couple's lives before and after meeting.

Suggested Content:

- A new, but growing, idea for wedding receptions.
- Friend/relative compiles photographs of the bride and groom.
- Usually intermingle "phony" slides, i.e. zoo photos, fun shots
- Documents couple's lives apart (and together).
- Should be light-hearted, and never rude.
- Suggest male/female co-M.C. this event.
- Light background music during presentation.
- Conclusion could be romantic.
- Photo album of slides is presented to couple at conclusion of presentation.
- Should be clean enough to show it in a church.

Suggested Length: 3-7 minutes.

If presented as a slide show, ensure large screen everyone can see it, good music, good control of light switches. Some receptions have even had pictures taken in the morning or afternoon of the wedding, rushed for development, and added to the slide show that evening.

This could also be a well thought out video.

Toll Free: 1-800-66-Speak
www.customlearning.com
copyright © 1988

The "This is Your Life" Slide Show

M.C. Opening Comments

(Transition comment from previous event.)

_____

_____

_____

_____

_____

(Brief, humorous anecdote or true story relevant to this topic or next speaker. Do not overly embarrass.)

_____

_____

_____

_____

_____

OR (Prepared joke, poem, quotation that is relevant. See Chapter XII Treasury of Wit and Wisdom).

_____

_____

_____

_____

_____

Now introduce next speaker or conduct next event.

Program Speaker Introduction

- *"Our next presentation is"* (name of program event ie. This is Your Life, etc.)

  _____

  _____

  _____

- (Brief, humorous, true anecdote or story about speaker. Should not overly embarrass guest or audience).

  _____

  _____

  _____

  _____

  _____

- (Reason speaker was asked to perform task and/or relationship to Bride & Groom & Family)

  _____

  _____

  _____

  _____

  _____

- (Restate speaking assignment)

  _____

- *"Please help me welcome"* (pronounce name correctly)

  _____   _____
  (First Name)   (Last Name)

  _____
  (Phonetic spelling)

Toll Free: 1-800-66-Speak
www.customlearning.com
copyright © 1988

The "This is Your Life" Slide/Video Show

M.C. Closing Comments

(Acknowledge presenter(s) speaker(s)

_____

_____

_____

_____

_____

(Prepared joke, poem, quotation that is relevant)

(See Chapter XII, Treasury of Wit and Wisdom)

_____

_____

_____

_____

OR (Brief, humorous anecdote or true story relevant to this topic or previous speaker. Do not overly embarrass.)

_____

_____

_____

_____

_____

The Notion Of   **Out Of Town Guest Introductions**

Presented by: The M.C.

Purpose: To recognize and acknowledge out of town guests for taking the time to travel a distance to attend the wedding.

Suggested Content:

- It is recommended that every out of town guest be recognized.

- Prepare an introduction form for each family present (see example on page 180.)

- Take the time to get the first name of spouse(s) and/or children, and/or other relatives or guests present with the family.

Toll Free: 1-800-66-Speak
www.customlearning.com
copyright © 1988

How To Use Out-of-Town Form(s)

- **From** - provide name of city, town, province or state.

- **Relationship** - describe the relationship of the guest(s) being introduced to the bride and/or groom, or family, eg. cousin of the bride, groom's best friend, etc.

- **Brief (humorous) anecdote or true story** - see page 62, "The Makings of a Great Story/Anecdote." Remember it should be funny, but never overly embarrass. If you are unable to obtain an appropriate anecdote or true story, then try a joke or quotation from the Treasury of Wit and Wisdom chapter and insert here.

- **Please help me welcome:**

  Accompanied by - First state name(s) of children, other guests who may have traveled with this individual/family.

  Guest's First Name - state his/her first name.

  Spouse's First Name - state his/her first name.

  Last Name - if couple have same last name, pronounce name(s) correctly and lead the applause, OR if couple have different last names, then provide escort's first and last name. If you're not absolutely certain of the pronunciation, spell it out phonetically in the space provided.

Don't Forget To:

- Meet each Out-of-Town guest beforehand in order to:

  - ensure that they are **actually** present;

  - get to know them and their feelings about being introduced;

  - learn the **correct spelling** and **pronunciation** of **both** their names;

  - obtain names of others who may be traveling with them;

  - obtain their **approval** as to the **appropriateness** of the introduction you have prepared (if you're not certain it's true or in good taste, or might overly embarrass.);

  - let them know when they will be introduced.

- **Lead** the audience in applause.

Suggested Length:

- As quickly as possible – No longer than 30 seconds.

Out-of-Town Guest Introduction - Example

- From   ***Los Angeles***
                         (City, Province, State)

- Relationship   ***Wife of the Best Man - Henry***
                         (to member of the bridal party/family)

- (Anecdote/story - humorous but should not overly embarrass guest or audience.)

  "Used to live in Long Beach, California. Were out late one night skinny-dipping in the ocean and the beach patrol came along and took all their clothes. They had to sneak home down dark alleys and parked cars. Now they really know the meaning of "Long" Beach."

  _____

  _____

  _____

  _____

  Accompanied by (children) _____

  _____

  _____

- "Please (help me) welcome"   ***Irene***

                                (Guest first name)

  & _____   ***Johnson***
     (Spouse's first name)   (Last name)

  & _____
              (Escort's first and last name)

  _____

              (Phonetic spelling(s) - if required)

Toll Free: 1-800-66-Speak
www.customlearning.com
copyright © 1988

Out-of-town Guest Introductions

M.C. Opening Comments

(Transition comment from previous event.)

_____

_____

_____

_____

_____

(Brief, humorous anecdote or true story relevant to this topic or next speaker. Do not overly embarrass.)

_____

_____

_____

_____

_____

OR (Prepared joke, poem, quotation that is relevant. See Chapter XII Treasury of Wit and Wisdom).

_____

_____

_____

_____

_____

Now introduce next speaker or conduct next event.

Out-of-Town Guest Introduction

- From _____
    (City, Province, State)

- Relationship _____
    (to member of the bridal party/family)

- (Anecdote/story - humorous but should not overly embarrass guest or audience.)
    _____
    _____

    Accompanied by (children) _____
    _____

- "Please (help me) welcome" _____
    (Guest first name)

    & _____ _____
        (Spouse's first name)   (Last name)

    & _____
        (Escort's first and last name)

    _____
    (Phonetic spelling(s) - if required)

Out-of-Town Guest Introduction

- From _____
    (City, Province, State)

- Relationship _____
    (to member of the bridal party/family)

- (Anecdote/story - humorous but should not overly embarrass guest or audience.)
    _____
    _____

    Accompanied by (children) _____
    _____

- "Please (help me) welcome" _____
    (Guest first name)

    & _____ _____
        (Spouse's first name)   (Last name)

    & _____
        (Escort's first and last name)

    _____
    (Phonetic spelling(s) - if required)

Toll Free: 1-800-66-Speak
www.customlearning.com
copyright © 1988

Out-of-Town Guest Introduction

- From _____
  (City, Province, State)

- Relationship _____
  (to member of the bridal party/family)

- (Anecdote/story - humorous but should not overly embarrass guest or audience.)

  _____

  _____

  Accompanied by (children) _____

  _____

- "Please (help me) welcome" _____
  (Guest first name)

  & _____   _____
     (Spouse's first name)   (Last name)

  & _____
     (Escort's first and last name)

  _____
  (Phonetic spelling(s) - if required)

Out-of-Town Guest Introduction

- From _____
  (City, Province, State)

- Relationship _____
  (to member of the bridal party/family)

- (Anecdote/story - humorous but should not overly embarrass guest or audience.)

  _____

  _____

  Accompanied by (children) _____

  _____

- "Please (help me) welcome" _____
  (Guest first name)

  & _____   _____
     (Spouse's first name)   (Last name)

  & _____
     (Escort's first and last name)

  _____
  (Phonetic spelling(s) - if required)

Out-of-Town Guest Introduction

- From _____
  (City, Province, State)
- Relationship _____
  (to member of the bridal party/family)
- (Anecdote/story - humorous but should not overly embarrass guest or audience.)

  _____

  _____

  Accompanied by (children) _____

  _____

- "Please (help me) welcome" _____
  (Guest first name)

  & _____   _____
  (Spouse's first name)   (Last name)

  & _____
  (Escort's first and last name)

  _____
  (Phonetic spelling(s) - if required)

Out-of-Town Guest Introduction

- From _____
  (City, Province, State)
- Relationship _____
  (to member of the bridal party/family)
- (Anecdote/story - humorous but should not overly embarrass guest or audience.)

  _____

  _____

  Accompanied by (children) _____

  _____

- "Please (help me) welcome" _____
  (Guest first name)

  & _____   _____
  (Spouse's first name)   (Last name)

  & _____
  (Escort's first and last name)

  _____
  (Phonetic spelling(s) - if required)

Toll Free: 1-800-66-Speak
www.customlearning.com
copyright © 1988

Out-of-Town Guest Introduction

- From _____

  (City, Province, State)

- Relationship _____

  (to member of the bridal party/family)

- (Anecdote/story - humorous but should not overly embarrass guest or audience.)

  _____

  _____

  Accompanied by (children) _____

  _____

- "Please (help me) welcome" _____

  (Guest first name)

  & _____ _____

  (Spouse's first name)   (Last name)

  & _____

  (Escort's first and last name)

  _____

  (Phonetic spelling(s) - if required)

Out-of-Town Guest Introduction

- From _____

  (City, Province, State)

- Relationship _____

  (to member of the bridal party/family)

- (Anecdote/story - humorous but should not overly embarrass guest or audience.)

  _____

  _____

  Accompanied by (children) _____

  _____

- "Please (help me) welcome" _____

  (Guest first name)

  & _____ _____

  (Spouse's first name)   (Last name)

  & _____

  (Escort's first and last name)

  _____

  (Phonetic spelling(s) - if required)

Out-of-Town Guest Introduction

- From _____
  (City, Province, State)

- Relationship _____
  (to member of the bridal party/family)

- (Anecdote/story - humorous but should not overly embarrass guest or audience.)
  _____
  _____

  Accompanied by (children) _____
  _____

- "Please (help me) welcome"_____
  (Guest first name)

  & _____   _____
  (Spouse's first name)   (Last name)

  & _____
  (Escort's first and last name)

  _____
  (Phonetic spelling(s) - if required)

Out-of-Town Guest Introduction

- From _____
  (City, Province, State)

- Relationship _____
  (to member of the bridal party/family)

- (Anecdote/story - humorous but should not overly embarrass guest or audience.)
  _____
  _____

  Accompanied by (children) _____
  _____

- "Please (help me) welcome"_____
  (Guest first name)

  & _____   _____
  (Spouse's first name)   (Last name)

  & _____
  (Escort's first and last name)

  _____
  (Phonetic spelling(s) - if required)

Out-of-Town Guest Introduction

- From _____
  (City, Province, State)

- Relationship _____
  (to member of the bridal party/family)

- (Anecdote/story - humorous but should not overly embarrass guest or audience.)

  _____

  _____

  Accompanied by (children) _____

  _____

- "Please (help me) welcome" _____
  (Guest first name)

  & _____ _____
  (Spouse's first name)   (Last name)

  & _____
  (Escort's first and last name)

  _____
  (Phonetic spelling(s) - if required)

Out-of-Town Guest Introduction

- From _____
  (City, Province, State)

- Relationship _____
  (to member of the bridal party/family)

- (Anecdote/story - humorous but should not overly embarrass guest or audience.)

  _____

  _____

  Accompanied by (children) _____

  _____

- "Please (help me) welcome" _____
  (Guest first name)

  & _____ _____
  (Spouse's first name)   (Last name)

  & _____
  (Escort's first and last name)

  _____
  (Phonetic spelling(s) - if required)

Out-of-Town Guest Introduction

*   From _____
                          (City, Province, State)

*   Relationship _____
                          (to member of the bridal party/family)

*   (Anecdote/story - humorous but should not overly embarrass guest or audience.)

    _____

    _____

    Accompanied by (children) _____

    _____

*   "Please (help me) welcome" _____
                          (Guest first name)

    & _____   _____
          (Spouse's first name)   (Last name)

    & _____
                          (Escort's first and last name)

    _____
                          (Phonetic spelling(s) - if required)

Out-of-Town Guest Introduction

*   From _____
                          (City, Province, State)

*   Relationship _____
                          (to member of the bridal party/family)

*   (Anecdote/story - humorous but should not overly embarrass guest or audience.)

    _____

    _____

    Accompanied by (children) _____

    _____

*   "Please (help me) welcome" _____
                          (Guest first name)

    & _____   _____
          (Spouse's first name)   (Last name)

    & _____
                          (Escort's first and last name)

    _____
                          (Phonetic spelling(s) - if required)

Toll Free: 1-800-66-Speak
www.customlearning.com
copyright © 1988

Out-of-Town Guest Introduction

- From _____

    (City, Province, State)

- Relationship _____

    (to member of the bridal party/family)

- (Anecdote/story - humorous but should not overly embarrass guest or audience.)

    _____

    _____

    Accompanied by (children) _____

    _____

- "Please (help me) welcome" _____

    (Guest first name)

    & _____   _____

    (Spouse's first name)   (Last name)

    & _____

    (Escort's first and last name)

    _____

    (Phonetic spelling(s) - if required)

Out-of-Town Guest Introduction

- From _____

    (City, Province, State)

- Relationship _____

    (to member of the bridal party/family)

- (Anecdote/story - humorous but should not overly embarrass guest or audience.)

    _____

    _____

    Accompanied by (children) _____

    _____

- "Please (help me) welcome" _____

    (Guest first name)

    & _____   _____

    (Spouse's first name)   (Last name)

    & _____

    (Escort's first and last name)

    _____

    (Phonetic spelling(s) - if required)

Out-of-Town Guest Introduction

*   From _____

    (City, Province, State)

*   Relationship _____

    (to member of the bridal party/family)

*   (Anecdote/story - humorous but should not overly embarrass guest or audience.)

    _____

    _____

    Accompanied by (children) _____

    _____

*   "Please (help me) welcome" _____

    (Guest first name)

    & _____   _____

    (Spouse's first name)   (Last name)

    & _____

    (Escort's first and last name)

    _____

    (Phonetic spelling(s) - if required)

Out-of-Town Guest Introduction

*   From _____

    (City, Province, State)

*   Relationship _____

    (to member of the bridal party/family)

*   (Anecdote/story - humorous but should not overly embarrass guest or audience.)

    _____

    _____

    Accompanied by (children) _____

    _____

*   "Please (help me) welcome" _____

    (Guest first name)

    & _____   _____

    (Spouse's first name)   (Last name)

    & _____

    (Escort's first and last name)

    _____

    (Phonetic spelling(s) - if required)

Toll Free: 1-800-66-Speak
www.customlearning.com
copyright © 1988

Out-of-Town Guest Introduction

- From _____

  (City, Province, State)

- Relationship _____

  (to member of the bridal party/family)

- (Anecdote/story - humorous but should not overly embarrass guest or audience.)

  _____

  _____

  Accompanied by (children) _____

  _____

- "Please (help me) welcome" _____

  (Guest first name)

  & _____ _____

  (Spouse's first name)   (Last name)

  & _____

  (Escort's first and last name)

  _____

  (Phonetic spelling(s) - if required)

Out-of-Town Guest Introduction

- From _____

  (City, Province, State)

- Relationship _____

  (to member of the bridal party/family)

- (Anecdote/story - humorous but should not overly embarrass guest or audience.)

  _____

  _____

  Accompanied by (children) _____

  _____

- "Please (help me) welcome" _____

  (Guest first name)

  & _____ _____

  (Spouse's first name)   (Last name)

  & _____

  (Escort's first and last name)

  _____

  (Phonetic spelling(s) - if required)

Out-of-Town Guest Introduction

- From _____

  (City, Province, State)

- Relationship _____

  (to member of the bridal party/family)

- (Anecdote/story - humorous but should not overly embarrass guest or audience.)

  _____

  _____

  Accompanied by (children) _____

  _____

- "Please (help me) welcome" _____

  (Guest first name)

  & _____   _____

  (Spouse's first name)   (Last name)

  & _____

  (Escort's first and last name)

  _____

  (Phonetic spelling(s) - if required)

Out-of-Town Guest Introduction

- From _____

  (City, Province, State)

- Relationship _____

  (to member of the bridal party/family)

- (Anecdote/story - humorous but should not overly embarrass guest or audience.)

  _____

  _____

  Accompanied by (children) _____

  _____

- "Please (help me) welcome" _____

  (Guest first name)

  & _____   _____

  (Spouse's first name)   (Last name)

  & _____

  (Escort's first and last name)

  _____

  (Phonetic spelling(s) - if required)

Toll Free: 1-800-66-Speak
www.customlearning.com
copyright © 1988

Out-of-Town Guest Introduction

• From _____

(City, Province, State)

• Relationship _____

(to member of the bridal party/family)

• (Anecdote/story - humorous but should not overly embarrass guest or audience.)

_____

_____

Accompanied by (children) _____

_____

• "Please (help me) welcome"_____

(Guest first name)

& _____   _____

(Spouse's first name)   (Last name)

& _____

(Escort's first and last name)

_____

(Phonetic spelling(s) - if required)

Out-of-Town Guest Introduction

• From _____

(City, Province, State)

• Relationship _____

(to member of the bridal party/family)

• (Anecdote/story - humorous but should not overly embarrass guest or audience.)

_____

_____

Accompanied by (children) _____

_____

• "Please (help me) welcome"_____

(Guest first name)

& _____   _____

(Spouse's first name)   (Last name)

& _____

(Escort's first and last name)

_____

(Phonetic spelling(s) - if required)

Out-of-Town Guest Introduction

- From _____
  (City, Province, State)

- Relationship _____
  (to member of the bridal party/family)

- (Anecdote/story - humorous but should not overly embarrass guest or audience.)

  _____

  _____

  Accompanied by (children) _____

  _____

- "Please (help me) welcome" _____
  (Guest first name)

  & _____   _____
  (Spouse's first name)   (Last name)

  & _____
  (Escort's first and last name)

  _____
  (Phonetic spelling(s) - if required)

Out-of-Town Guest Introduction

- From _____
  (City, Province, State)

- Relationship _____
  (to member of the bridal party/family)

- (Anecdote/story - humorous but should not overly embarrass guest or audience.)

  _____

  _____

  Accompanied by (children) _____

  _____

- "Please (help me) welcome" _____
  (Guest first name)

  & _____   _____
  (Spouse's first name)   (Last name)

  & _____
  (Escort's first and last name)

  _____
  (Phonetic spelling(s) - if required)

Toll Free: 1-800-66-Speak
www.customlearning.com
copyright © 1988

Out-of-Town Guest Introduction

- From _____
  (City, Province, State)
- Relationship _____
  (to member of the bridal party/family)
- (Anecdote/story - humorous but should not overly embarrass guest or audience.)
  _____
  _____

  Accompanied by (children) _____
  _____

- "Please (help me) welcome" _____
  (Guest first name)
  & _____   _____
  (Spouse's first name)   (Last name)
  & _____
  (Escort's first and last name)

  _____
  (Phonetic spelling(s) - if required)

Out-of-Town Guest Introduction

- From _____
  (City, Province, State)
- Relationship _____
  (to member of the bridal party/family)
- (Anecdote/story - humorous but should not overly embarrass guest or audience.)
  _____
  _____

  Accompanied by (children) _____
  _____

- "Please (help me) welcome" _____
  (Guest first name)
  & _____   _____
  (Spouse's first name)   (Last name)
  & _____
  (Escort's first and last name)

  _____
  (Phonetic spelling(s) - if required)

Out-of-Town Guest Introductions

M.C. Closing Comments

(Acknowledge presenter(s) speaker(s))

_____

_____

_____

_____

_____

(Prepared joke, poem, quotation that is relevant)

(See Chapter XII, Treasury of Wit and Wisdom)

_____

_____

_____

_____

_____

OR (Brief, humorous anecdote or true story relevant to this topic or previous speaker. Do not overly embarrass.)

_____

_____

_____

_____

_____

Toll Free: 1-800-66-Speak
www.customlearning.com
copyright © 1988

The Notion of: **Entertainment**

Presented by: Volunteer friends and/or relatives.

Purpose: To entertain guests by calling upon talented friends or relatives to perform.

Suggested Content:

- This is an opportunity for friends and/or relatives to share their special talents with everyone there.
- It is a kind of special "gift" to the wedding couple.
- The entertainment could be presented as either:
  - background prior to program beginning
  - background or a feature during the meal
  - a feature during the main program
  - a feature during the dance program
- The type of entertainment need only be limited by the number and creativity of the guests, such as

solo or duet	solo musician
family band	lip-sync
dancing	magic
skit	poetry recitation

- Do take the time to prepare a good introduction (forms provided), as well as encouraging audience to acknowledge them

Suggested Length: 1 - 5 minutes per act

maximum three (3) acts

Entertainment

M.C. Opening Comments

(Transition comment from previous event.)

_____

_____

_____

_____

_____

(Brief, humorous anecdote or true story relevant to this topic or next speaker. Do not overly embarrass.)

_____

_____

_____

_____

_____

OR (Prepared joke, poem, quotation that is relevant. See Chapter XII Treasury of Wit and Wisdom).

_____

_____

_____

_____

_____

Now introduce next speaker or conduct next event.

Toll Free: 1-800-66-Speak
www.customlearning.com
copyright © 1988

Program Speaker Introduction

*   *"Our next presentation is"* (name of program event ie. Entertainment, etc.)

    _____

    _____

    _____

*   (Brief, humorous, true anecdote or story about speaker. Should not overly
    embarrass guest or audience).

    _____

    _____

    _____

    _____

    _____

    _____

*   (Reason speaker was asked to perform task and/or relationship to Bride & Groom
    & Family)

    _____

    _____

    _____

    _____

    _____

*   (Restate speaking assignment)

    _____

*   *"Please help me welcome"* (pronounce name correctly)

    _____   _____
    (First Name)   (Last Name)

    _____
    (Phonetic spelling)

Entertainment

M.C. Closing Comments

(Acknowledge presenter(s) speaker(s)

_____

_____

_____

_____

_____

(Prepared joke, poem, quotation that is relevant)

(See Chapter XII, Treasury of Wit and Wisdom)

_____

_____

_____

_____

_____

OR (Brief, humorous anecdote or true story relevant to this topic or previous speaker. Do not overly embarrass.)

_____

_____

_____

_____

_____

Toll Free: 1-800-66-Speak
www.customlearning.com
copyright © 1988

The Notion Of: **Special Program Opportunities**

Presented by: Anyone

Purpose: To capitalize on and use spontaneous ideas or unique program suggestions that might not normally occur.

Suggested Content:

A Few Ideas:

- presentation of a "unique" gift
- a special presentation from the bride and/or groom's favourite club or society
- a "put-on" story
- a video or slides from groom's stag, bride's shower or rehearsal (in good taste)
- welcome from the bride or groom's children (from an earlier marriage)
- a specially-prepared skit
- father presents a funny "dowry"
- couple opens a gag honeymoon gift
- pause for a moment of silence
- practice of a unique cultural tradition
- REMEMBER, event must be in good taste
- be sure to prepare a good introduction

Suggested Length: Two minutes per event.

Special Program Opportunities

M.C. Opening Comments

(Transition comment from previous event.)

_____

_____

_____

_____

_____

(Brief, humorous anecdote or true story relevant to this topic or next speaker. Do not overly embarrass.)

_____

_____

_____

_____

_____

OR (Prepared joke, poem, quotation that is relevant. See Chapter XII Treasury of Wit and Wisdom).

_____

_____

_____

_____

_____

Now introduce next speaker or conduct next event.

Toll Free: 1-800-66-Speak
www.customlearning.com
copyright © 1988

Program Speaker Introduction

- *"Our next presentation is"* (name of program event ie. Special Program Opportunities, etc.)

  _____

  _____

  _____

- (Brief, humorous, true anecdote or story about speaker. Should not overly embarrass guest or audience).

  _____

  _____

  _____

  _____

  _____

  _____

- (Reason speaker was asked to perform task and/or relationship to Bride & Groom & Family)

  _____

  _____

  _____

  _____

  _____

- (Restate speaking assignment)

  _____

- *"Please help me welcome"* (pronounce name correctly)

  _____   _____

  (First Name)   (Last Name)

  _____

  (Phonetic spelling)

Special Program Opportunities

M.C. Closing Comments

(Acknowledge presenter(s) speaker(s))

_____

_____

_____

_____

_____

(Prepared joke, poem, quotation that is relevant)

(See Chapter XII, Treasury of Wit and Wisdom)

_____

_____

_____

_____

_____

OR (Brief, humorous anecdote or true story relevant to this topic or previous speaker. Do not overly embarrass.)

_____

_____

_____

_____

_____

Toll Free: 1-800-66-Speak
www.customlearning.com
copyright © 1988

The Notion Of: **The Toast to the Bride**

Presented by: A relative or close family friend who knew the bride as she grew up.

Purpose: To acknowledge the bride, share insights into her life with the audience and with her as well.

Suggested Content:

See Toast to the Bride Presenter Outline, on next page.

Suggested Length: 2 - 4 minutes.

Note: The Toast to the bride may be replaced by a toast to the **Couple.** Or you may have a Toast to the Bride and a Toast to the Groom.

Presenter Outline

Toast To The Bride

Presented by: _____

Please Note: The following is an outline of a few ideas you may wish to cover in your remarks. Feel free to add or delete anything you wish as long as it is in good taste and does not exceed 2 - 4 minutes.

"Mr./Madame Master of Ceremonies, Head Table Guests, Ladies and Gentlemen, and especially"

_____

(Bride's first name)

(Explain relationship between you and the Bride):

_____

_____

_____

_____

(Share 2 or 3 personal humorous anecdotes involving the Bride growing up, dating, working, etc. Don't overly embarrass).

_____

_____

_____

_____

_____

(Photocopy page and give to Presenter/Speaker)

Toll Free: 1-800-66-Speak
www.customlearning.com
copyright © 1988

Presenter Outline

_____

_____

_____

_____

_____

_____

_____

(Point out a few of the Bride's achievements, better qualities. Flatter her.)

_____

_____

_____

_____

_____

(Perhaps offer a few words of advice to the Groom on how to get along with the Bride.)

_____

_____

_____

_____

_____

(Photocopy page and give to Presenter/Speaker)

Presenter Outline

(Wish her (and groom) success and happiness)

_____

_____

_____

_____

_____

_____

_____

(any other appropriate comments)

_____

_____

_____

Note: It is OK to bring props or whatever you may need to make your toast interesting. Ideas for Toasts:
- A "top 10 list" of why the bride and/or groom is so wonderful
- A few short stories that lead to a point

(Properly lead guest through toast)

"Ladies and Gentlemen

Would you please stand (pause till they do)

*a**nd raise your glasses***

in a toast to

THE BRIDE"

(audience will repeat *"to the Bride"*)

(no need to say thank you . . . return to your seat)

(Photocopy page and give to Presenter/Speaker)

Toll Free: 1-800-66-Speak
www.customlearning.com
copyright © 1988

Toast To The Bride

M.C. Opening Comments

(Transition comment from previous event.)

_____

_____

_____

_____

_____

(Brief, humorous anecdote or true story relevant to this topic or next speaker. Do not overly embarrass.)

_____

_____

_____

_____

_____

OR (Prepared joke, poem, quotation that is relevant. See Chapter XII Treasury of Wit and Wisdom).

_____

_____

_____

_____

_____

Now introduce next speaker or conduct next event.

Program Speaker Introduction

* *"Our next presentation is"* (name of program event ie. Toast To The Bride, etc.)

  _____

  _____

  _____

* (Brief, humorous, true anecdote or story about speaker. Should not overly embarrass guest or audience).

  _____

  _____

  _____

  _____

  _____

  _____

* (Reason speaker was asked to perform task and/or relationship to Bride & Groom & Family)

  _____

  _____

  _____

  _____

  _____

* (Restate speaking assignment)

  _____

* *"Please help me welcome"* (pronounce name correctly)

  _____   _____
         (First Name)   (Last Name)

  _____
              (Phonetic spelling)

Toll Free: 1-800-66-Speak
www.customlearning.com
copyright © 1988

Toast To The Bride

M.C. Closing Comments

(Acknowledge presenter(s) speaker(s)

_____

_____

_____

_____

_____

(Prepared joke, poem, quotation that is relevant)
(See Chapter XII, Treasury of Wit and Wisdom)

_____

_____

_____

_____

_____

OR (Brief, humorous anecdote or true story relevant to this topic or previous speaker. Do not overly embarrass.)

_____

_____

_____

_____

_____

The Notion Of: **Groom's Reply To: "The Toast to the Bride"**

Presented by: The Groom

Purpose: To accept the toast, thank the speaker and everyone involved and to express personal feelings about the bride and the event.

Suggested Content:

See Groom's Reply Presenter Outline, on next page.

Suggested Length: 1$^1/_2$ - 2 minutes.

Toll Free: 1-800-66-Speak
www.customlearning.com
copyright © 1988

Presenter Outline

Groom's Reply to: "The Toast To The Bride"

Presented by: The Groom

Please Note: The following is an outline of a few ideas you may wish to cover in your remarks. Feel free to add or delete anything you wish as long as it is in good taste and does not exceed 2 minutes.

"Mr./Madame Master of Ceremonies, Head Table Guests, Ladies and Gentlemen, and especially"

_____

(first name of Toast to the Bride Presenter)

(Acknowledge speaker for his/her good words and perhaps comment on one of his/her remarks):

_____

_____

_____

_____

(Thank Bride's parents for welcoming you to the family).

_____

_____

_____

_____

(Photocopy page and give to Presenter/Speaker)

Groom's Reply Presenter Outline

(express your sincere feelings about the way you have been received by the Bride's family)

_____

_____

_____

_____

(share a brief, humorous true anecdote about your relationship with bride, wedding preparation, how you met, etc.

_____

_____

_____

(specifically thank all who organized and were involved in the reception. Check with M.C. to avoid duplication).

- Flower Girl _____
- Ring Bearer_____
- Usher #1 _____
- Usher #2 _____
- Usher #3 _____
- Usher #4 _____
- Reception Host/Hostess _____
  #1_____
  _____
- Reception Host/Hostess _____
  #2 _____
- Photographer_____
  _____
- Video _____
- Bride's Parents/Family _____
  _____
- Groom's Parents/Family _____
  _____

- Cooks & Servers
  _____
  _____
- Groomsmen _____
  _____
- Bridesmaids_____
  _____
- Bartender_____
  _____
- Band - D.J. _____
  _____
- Officiant/Minister/Priest
  _____
  _____
- Other _____
- Guests _____
- M.C. _____
  _____

(Photocopy page and give to Presenter/Speaker)

Toll Free: 1-800-66-Speak
www.customlearning.com
copyright © 1988

Groom's Reply Presenter Outline

(Express romantic comment about your bride)

_____

_____

_____

_____

_____

(any other comment)

_____

_____

_____

_____

_____

(Thank all for attending and encourage them to enjoy the remaining program)

_____

_____

_____

_____

_____

(No need to say thank you . . . return to your seat)

(Photocopy page and give to Presenter/Speaker)

Toll Free: 1-800-66-Speak
www.customlearning.com
copyright © 1988

Groom's Reply

M.C. Opening Comments

(Transition comment from previous event.)

_____

_____

_____

_____

_____

(Brief, humorous anecdote or true story relevant to this topic or next speaker. Do not overly embarrass.)

_____

_____

_____

_____

_____

OR (Prepared joke, poem, quotation that is relevant. See Chapter XII Treasury of Wit and Wisdom).

_____

_____

_____

_____

_____

Now introduce next speaker or conduct next event.

Toll Free: 1-800-66-Speak
www.customlearning.com
copyright © 1988

Example: Opening Comments: Groom's Reply

- Agree on Anything

"_____, *in our* _____
    (Groom/husband name)   (# Months/Years)

of _____, *we haven't been able to agree on anything.*"
        (dating/marriage)

"*It's been* _____, *dear.*"
                        (Months/Years)

- Mutual Admiration

"*Both* _____ *and* _____
              (Bride/Wife)   (Groom/Husband)

realized they had something in common:

_____ *loved* _____
              (Bride/Wife)   (Groom/Husband)

and so did he/she."

- Say You Love Me

"*Overheard* _____ *last night say to*
                                (Bride)

_____ *most passionately,* "*Say you love me,*
        (Groom)

Say you love me!" _____ *said,* "*You Love Me?*"
                                (Groom)

- Post Wedding Work

"_____ *asked* _____
              (Bride)   (Groom)

if he would let her work after the wedding. "*Certainly not, you can stay at home and wash and clean and take care of the kids. No wife of mine is going to work!*" *(or how about reversing the roles?)*

Toll Free: 1-800-66-Speak
www.customlearning.com
copyright © 1988

217

Program Speaker Introduction

- *"Our next presentation is"* (name of program event ie. Groom's Interview, etc.)

  _____

  _____

  _____

- (Brief, humorous, true anecdote or story about speaker. Should not overly embarrass guest or audience).

  _____

  _____

  _____

  _____

  _____

  _____

- (Reason speaker was asked to perform task and/or relationship to Bride & Groom & Family)

  _____

  _____

  _____

  _____

  _____

- (Restate speaking assignment)

  _____

- *"Please help me welcome"* (pronounce name correctly)

  _____   _____

       (First Name)   (Last Name)

  _____

                 (Phonetic spelling)

Toll Free: 1-800-66-Speak
www.customlearning.com
copyright © 1988

The Groom's Interview

Purpose:	To add spontaneous humour to groom's reply.

Note:	This is an optional idea.
	Carefully select the Questions.

- M.C. calls the groom to the lectern.
- M.C. asks groom the selected questions:

  (No rehearsal. This is spontaneous.)

Questions

❑ When and how did you meet the bride?

❑ Why pick her? Does she remind you of your Mother? Is it true you've given up all your other girlfriends?

❑ How did you propose?

❑ Are you ready to be a Father?

❑ How many grandchildren have your parents requested?

❑ Where are you staying on your wedding tonight?

❑ What do you plan to do?

❑ Would you like your friends to drop by for a party tonight?

Other Questions:

_____

_____

_____

_____

_____

Following the interview, ask groom to proceed with reply to toast. . .

Groom's Reply

M.C. Closing Comments

(Acknowledge presenter(s) speaker(s))

_____

_____

_____

_____

_____

(Prepared joke, poem, quotation that is relevant)

(See Chapter XII, Treasury of Wit and Wisdom)

_____

_____

_____

_____

_____

OR (Brief, humorous anecdote or true story relevant to this topic or previous speaker. Do not overly embarrass.)

_____

_____

_____

_____

_____

Toll Free: 1-800-66-Speak
www.customlearning.com
copyright © 1988

The Notion Of: **Bride's Reply To: "The Toast to the Bride"**

Presented by: The Bride (optional.)

Purpose: Permit the Bride to express her feelings about the Wedding, her Family(s), her new Husband and the presenter of the Toast to the Bride speech.

Suggested Content:

See Bride's Reply Presenter Outline, on next page.

Suggested Length: 1$^1/_2$ - 2 minutes.

Presenter Outline

Bride's Reply to: "The Toast To The Bride"

Presented by: The Bride (Optional)

Please Note: The following is an outline of a few ideas you may wish to cover in your remarks. Feel free to add or delete anything you wish as long as it is in good taste and does not exceed 2 minutes.

"Mr./Madame Master of Ceremonies, Head Table Guests, Ladies and Gentlemen, and especially"

_____

(first name of Toast to the Bride Presenter)

(Acknowledge speaker for his/her good words and perhaps comment on one of his/her remarks):

_____

_____

_____

(Thank Groom's parents for a job well done, raising the Groom and for welcoming you to the family).

_____

_____

_____

_____

(Photocopy page and give to Presenter/Speaker)

Toll Free: 1-800-66-Speak
www.customlearning.com
copyright © 1988

Bride's Reply Presenter Outline

(express your sincere feelings about the way you have been received by the Groom's family)

_____

_____

_____

_____

(share a brief, humorous true anecdote about your relationship with groom, wedding preparation, how you met, etc.

_____

_____

_____

(specifically thank all who organized and were involved in the reception. Check with M.C. to avoid duplication).

- Flower Girl _____
- Ring Bearer _____
- Usher #1 _____
- Usher #2 _____
- Usher #3 _____
- Usher #4 _____
- Reception Host/Hostess _____
  #1 _____
  _____
- Reception Host/Hostess _____
  #2 _____
- Photographer _____
  _____
- Video _____
- Bride's Parents/Family _____
  _____
- Groom's Parents/Family _____
  _____

- Cooks & Servers
  _____
  _____
- Groomsmen _____
  _____
- Bridesmaids _____
  _____
- Bartender _____
  _____
- Band - D.J. _____
  _____
- Officiant/Minister/Priest
  _____
  _____
- Other _____
- Guests _____
- M.C. _____

(Photocopy page and give to Presenter/Speaker)

Toll Free: 1-800-66-Speak
www.customlearning.com
copyright © 1988

Bride's Reply Presenter Outline

(Express romantic comment about your groom)

_____

_____

_____

_____

_____

(any other comment)

_____

_____

_____

_____

_____

(Thank all for attending and encourage them to enjoy the remaining program)

_____

_____

_____

_____

_____

(No need to say thank you . . . return to your seat)

(Photocopy page and give to Presenter/Speaker)

Toll Free: 1-800-66-Speak
www.customlearning.com
copyright © 1988

Bride's Reply (to the toast)

M.C. Opening Comments

(Transition comment from previous event.)

_____

_____

_____

_____

_____

(Brief, humorous anecdote or true story relevant to this topic or next speaker. Do not overly embarrass.)

_____

_____

_____

_____

_____

OR (Prepared joke, poem, quotation that is relevant. See Chapter XII Treasury of Wit and Wisdom).

_____

_____

_____

_____

_____

Now introduce next speaker or conduct next event.

Program Speaker Introduction

- *"Our next presentation is"* (name of program event ie. *"Bride's Reply to The Toast to the Bride"*, etc.)

- (Brief, humorous, true anecdote or story about speaker. Should not overly embarrass guest or audience).

- (Restate speaking assignment)

- *"Please help me welcome"* (pronounce name correctly)

(First Name)	(Last Name)

(Phonetic spelling)

Toll Free: 1-800-66-Speak
www.customlearning.com
copyright © 1988

Bride's Reply To: "The Toast To The Bride"

M.C. Closing Comments

(Acknowledge presenter(s) speaker(s)

_____

_____

_____

_____

_____

(Prepared joke, poem, quotation that is relevant)
(See Chapter XII, Treasury of Wit and Wisdom)

_____

_____

_____

_____

_____

OR (Brief, humorous anecdote or true story relevant to this topic or previous speaker. Do not overly embarrass.)

_____

_____

_____

_____

_____

The Notion Of: **Special Guest Introductions**

Purpose: To properly recognize guests who may not yet have been
acknowledged.

Suggested Content:

- Special guests could include guests that were not introduced
during:

    - head table introductions

    - sub-head table introductions

    - out-of-town guest introductions

- Possible special guests might include:

    - immediate family

    - employer

    - local elected leaders

    - special close friend(s)

    - Godparents

    - individual(s) who introduced couple to each other

- Use the forms provided pages 232 to 239.

Toll Free: 1-800-66-Speak
www.customlearning.com
copyright © 1988

How To Use

Special Guest Introduction Form(s)

- **Explain why this person(s) is/are special**, ie. the relationship with Bride and Groom and/or family, e.g. "introduced Bride and Groom," or "local elected official" or "Bride's Boss."

- **Brief (humorous) anecdote or true story** - see page 62, "The Makings of a Great Story/Anecdote." Remember, it should be funny, but not overly embarrass.

- If you are unable to obtain an appropriate anecdote or story, then try a joke or quotation from the Treasury of Wit and Wisdom chapter and insert here.

- **Sincere, Positive Comment** to "balance" the previous story. Conclude with a sincere, positive comment, i.e. their nicest quality, personal achievement, etc.

- **Indicate whether you expect them** to stand and be recognized, or come forward and speak . . . and for what purpose.

- **Please help me welcome** - pronounce name correctly and lead the applause. If you're not absolutely certain, then spell it out phonetically in the space provided.

Don't Forget To:

- Meet each special guest beforehand in order to:
    - ensure that they are **actually** present
    - get to know them and their **feelings** about being introduced
    - learn the **correct spelling** and **pronunciation** of **both** their names
    - obtain their **approval** as to the **appropriateness** of the introduction you have prepared (if you're not certain it's true or in good taste, or might overly embarrass.)

- If guest is to speak, then:
    - let them know **when** they will be introduced
    - check if they have any **special** presentation **requirements**
    - **diplomatically** make them aware of time objective
    - shake hands with each presenter as they arrive and depart

- **Lead** the audience in applause

Suggested Length:

As quickly as possible - No longer than 30 seconds.

Special Guest Introduction - Example

• Explain why this person(s) is/are "special"

"Next I will introduce you to the lady who introduced Bob and Stacy."

• (Share a brief, humorous anecdote or true story about speaker. Should not overly embarrass guest or audience.)

"She's quite enthusiastic. In fact, she recently had another wedding to attend in Vancouver, and was so excited she and her husband arrived the WEEKEND BEFORE!"

_____

_____

_____

• Sincere, Positive Comment:

"She's been totally supportive of both the Bride and the Groom."

• Indicate whether you expect them to:

    • stand and be recognized or come forward and speak.... and for what purpose.

"I would like her and her husband to stand."

• *"Ladies and Gentlemen please help me welcome"*

Leslie	**Jones**
(First Name)	(Last Name)
Bill	**Castle**
(First Name Spouse/Escort)	(Last Name)

Toll Free: 1-800-66-Speak
www.customlearning.com
copyright © 1988

Special Guest Introduction

M.C. Opening Comments

(Transition comment from previous event.)

_____

_____

_____

_____

_____

(Brief, humorous anecdote or true story relevant to this topic or next speaker. Do not overly embarrass.)

_____

_____

_____

_____

_____

OR (Prepared joke, poem, quotation that is relevant. See Chapter XII Treasury of Wit and Wisdom).

_____

_____

_____

_____

_____

Now introduce next speaker or conduct next event.

Special Guest Introduction

- Explain why this person(s) is/are "special""

  _____

  _____

  _____

- (Share a brief, humorous anecdote or true story about speaker. Should not overly embarrass guest or audience).

  _____

  _____

  _____

  _____

- Sincere, Positive Comment:

  _____

  _____

  _____

- Indicate whether you expect them to:

  - stand and be recognized or come forward and speak.... and for what purpose.

  _____

  _____

- *"Ladies and Gentlemen please help me welcome"*

  _____   _____
  (First Name)   (Last Name)

  _____   _____
  (First Name Spouse/Escort)   (Last Name)

Toll Free: 1-800-66-Speak
www.customlearning.com
copyright © 1988

Special Guest Introduction

- Explain why this person(s) is/are "special""

  _____

  _____

  _____

- (Share a brief, humorous anecdote or true story about speaker. Should not overly embarrass guest or audience).

  _____

  _____

  _____

  _____

- Sincere, Positive Comment:

  _____

  _____

  _____

- Indicate whether you expect them to:

  - stand and be recognized or come forward and speak.... and for what purpose.

  _____

  _____

- *"Ladies and Gentlemen please help me welcome"*

| _____ | _____ |
| (First Name) | (Last Name) |

| _____ | _____ |
| (First Name Spouse/Escort) | (Last Name) |

Special Guest Introduction

- Explain why this person(s) is/are "special""

  _____

  _____

  _____

- (Share a brief, humorous anecdote or true story about speaker. Should not overly embarrass guest or audience).

  _____

  _____

  _____

  _____

- Sincere, Positive Comment:

  _____

  _____

  _____

- Indicate whether you expect them to:

  - stand and be recognized or come forward and speak.... and for what purpose.

  _____

  _____

- *"Ladies and Gentlemen please help me welcome"*

  _____   _____
  (First Name)   (Last Name)

  _____   _____
  (First Name Spouse/Escort)   (Last Name)

Toll Free: 1-800-66-Speak
www.customlearning.com
copyright © 1988

Special Guest Introduction

- Explain why this person(s) is/are "special""

  _____

  _____

  _____

- (Share a brief, humorous anecdote or true story about speaker. Should not overly embarrass guest or audience).

  _____

  _____

  _____

  _____

- Sincere, Positive Comment:

  _____

  _____

  _____

- Indicate whether you expect them to:
  - stand and be recognized or come forward and speak.... and for what purpose.

  _____

  _____

- *"Ladies and Gentlemen please help me welcome"*

  _____   _____
  (First Name)   (Last Name)

  _____   _____
  (First Name Spouse/Escort)   (Last Name)

Special Guest Introduction

- Explain why this person(s) is/are "special""

  _____

  _____

  _____

- (Share a brief, humorous anecdote or true story about speaker. Should not overly embarrass guest or audience).

  _____

  _____

  _____

  _____

- Sincere, Positive Comment:

  _____

  _____

  _____

- Indicate whether you expect them to:

  - stand and be recognized or come forward and speak.... and for what purpose.

  _____

  _____

- *"Ladies and Gentlemen please help me welcome"*

  _____   _____
  (First Name)   (Last Name)

  _____   _____
  (First Name Spouse/Escort)   (Last Name)

Toll Free: 1-800-66-Speak
www.customlearning.com
copyright © 1988

Special Guest Introduction

• Explain why this person(s) is/are "special""

_____

_____

_____

• (Share a brief, humorous anecdote or true story about speaker. Should not overly embarrass guest or audience).

_____

_____

_____

_____

• Sincere, Positive Comment:

_____

_____

_____

• Indicate whether you expect them to:

   • stand and be recognized or come forward and speak.... and for what purpose.

_____

_____

• *"Ladies and Gentlemen please help me welcome"*

_____   _____
(First Name)   (Last Name)

_____   _____
(First Name Spouse/Escort)   (Last Name)

Special Guest Introduction

- Explain why this person(s) is/are "special""

  _____

  _____

  _____

- (Share a brief, humorous anecdote or true story about speaker. Should not overly embarrass guest or audience).

  _____

  _____

  _____

  _____

- Sincere, Positive Comment:

  _____

  _____

  _____

- Indicate whether you expect them to:
    - stand and be recognized or come forward and speak.... and for what purpose.

  _____

  _____

- *"Ladies and Gentlemen please help me welcome"*

  _____   _____
  (First Name)   (Last Name)

  _____   _____
  (First Name Spouse/Escort)   (Last Name)

Toll Free: 1-800-66-Speak
www.customlearning.com
copyright © 1988

Special Guest Introduction

• Explain why this person(s) is/are "special""

_____

_____

_____

• (Share a brief, humorous anecdote or true story about speaker. Should not overly embarrass guest or audience).

_____

_____

_____

_____

• Sincere, Positive Comment:

_____

_____

_____

• Indicate whether you expect them to:

    • stand and be recognized or come forward and speak.... and for what purpose.

_____

_____

• *"Ladies and Gentlemen please help me welcome"*

_____	_____
(First Name)	(Last Name)

_____	_____
(First Name Spouse/Escort)	(Last Name)

Presenter Outline

The Notion of   **The Toast To The Maid of Honour & Bridesmaid(s)**

Presented by: The Best Man (if best man is the MC, then perhaps presented by another groomsman - should be presented by someone in the wedding party.)

Purpose: Acknowledge the involvement of the Maid or Matron of Honour (and Bridesmaids.)

Suggested Content:

See Toast to the Bridesmaids Presenter outline, on the next page

Suggested Length: $1^1/_2$ - 2 minutes.

Toll Free: 1-800-66-Speak
www.customlearning.com
copyright © 1988

Presenter Outline

Toast To The Bridesmaids

Presented by: The Best Man or a groomsman.

Please Note: The following is an outline of a few ideas you may wish to cover in your remarks. Feel free to add or delete anything you wish as long as it is in good taste and does not exceed 2 mins.

"Mr./Madame Master of Ceremonies, Head Table Guests, Ladies and Gentlemen, and especially"

_____

(first name of the Maid of Honour and Bridesmaids)

(Acknowledge the valuable role she/they have played in the Wedding and its preparations.)

_____

_____

_____

_____

Refer to brief, humorous, true story or anecdote about your (and other groomsmen's) involvement with them during planning, rehearsal, wedding ceremony or photographs, etc.

_____

_____

_____

_____

(Photocopy page and give to Presenter/Speaker)

Toast To Bridemaids Presenter Outline

- Optional - insert prepared joke, poem or quotation. See Chapter XII -Treasury of Wit and Wisdom.

_____

_____

_____

_____

_____

_____

- Acknowledge her/their beauty, special qualities

_____

_____

_____

_____

_____

_____

_____

_____

(Photocopy page and give to Presenter/Speaker)

Toll Free: 1-800-66-Speak
www.customlearning.com
copyright © 1988

Toast To Bridesmaids Presenter Outline

• Any other appropriate comments?

_____

_____

_____

_____

_____

_____

_____

_____

_____

_____

• Properly lead the guests through toast

"Ladies and Gentlemen

Would you please stand (pause till they do)

a***nd raise your glasses***

in a toast to

THE BRIDESMAIDS"

(audience will repeat "to the bridesmaids")

(no need to say thank you . . . return to your seat)

(Photocopy page and give to Presenter/Speaker)

Toast to the Bridesmaids

M.C. Opening Comments

(Transition comment from previous event.)

_____

_____

_____

_____

_____

(Brief, humorous anecdote or true story relevant to this topic or next speaker. Do not overly embarrass.)

_____

_____

_____

_____

_____

OR (Prepared joke, poem, quotation that is relevant. See Chapter XII Treasury of Wit and Wisdom).

_____

_____

_____

_____

_____

Now introduce next speaker or conduct next event.

Toll Free: 1-800-66-Speak
www.customlearning.com
copyright © 1988

Program Speaker Introduction

- *"Our next presentation is"* (name of program event ie. *"Toast to the Maid of Honour and Bridesmaids,* etc.)

  _____

  _____

  _____

- (Brief, humorous, true anecdote or story about speaker. Should not overly embarrass guest or audience).

  _____

  _____

  _____

  _____

  _____

  _____

- (Reason speaker was asked to perform task and/or relationship to Bride & Groom & Family)

  _____

  _____

  _____

  _____

  _____

- (Restate speaking assignment)

  _____

- *"Please help me welcome"* (pronounce name correctly)

  _____   _____

  (First Name)   (Last Name)

  _____

  (Phonetic spelling)

Toast to the Maid of Honour and Bridesmaids

M.C. Closing Comments

(Acknowledge presenter(s) speaker(s)

_____

_____

_____

_____

_____

(Prepared joke, poem, quotation that is relevant)

(See Chapter XII, Treasury of Wit and Wisdom)

_____

_____

_____

_____

_____

OR (Brief, humorous anecdote or true story relevant to this topic or previous speaker. Do not overly embarrass.)

_____

_____

_____

_____

_____

Toll Free: 1-800-66-Speak
www.customlearning.com
copyright © 1988

The Notion Of: **The Reply To: "The Toast To The Maid of Honour & Bridesmaids"**

Presented by: The Maid/Matron of Honour

Purpose: To permit the Maid/Matron of Honour to accept the toast, and acknowledge the Best Man (and Groomsmen)

Suggested Content:

See Reply to Toast to Bridesmaids Presenter Outline, on next page.

Suggested Length: $1^1/_2$ - 2 minutes.

Presenter Outline

Reply to: "The Toast To The Bridesmaids"

Presented by: Maid of Honour

Please Note: The following is an outline of a few ideas you may wish to cover in your remarks. Feel free to add or delete anything you wish as long as it is in good taste and does not exceed 2 mins.

"Mr./Madame Master of Ceremonies, Head Table Guests, Ladies and Gentlemen, and especially"

_____

(first name of Best Man and Groomsmen)

"On behalf of myself and

_____

(first names of fellow Bridesmaids)

I/we wish to acknowledge the kind toast"

(You may wish to respond to or comment on one of Best Man's specific remarks)

_____

_____

_____

_____

_____

_____

(Photocopy page and give to Presenter/Speaker)

Toll Free: 1-800-66-Speak
www.customlearning.com
copyright © 1988

Bridesmaids' Reply Presenter Outline

• Acknowledge the valuable role he/they have played in the Wedding and preparation.

_____

_____

_____

• Optional - refer to a brief, humorous true story or anecdote about your experience with him/them during the planning, rehearsal, wedding ceremony or photographs, etc.

_____

_____

_____

_____

_____

• Optional - insert prepared joke, poem, or quotation. See Chapter XII.

_____

_____

_____

_____

(Photocopy page and give to Presenter/Speaker)

Bridesmaids' Reply Presenter Outline

- Acknowledge his/their special qualities

  _____

  _____

  _____

  _____

  _____

- Any other appropriate comments?

  _____

  _____

  _____

  _____

- Properly lead guests through toast

> *"Ladies and Gentlemen, on behalf of myself*
> *and my fellow Bridesmaids,*
> *Would you please stand* (pause till they do)
> *and raise your glasses*
> *in a toast to*
> *THE GROOMSMEN"*

(Audience will repeat "to the Groomsmen")

(No need to say thank you . . . return to your seat)

(Photocopy page and give to Presenter/Speaker)

Toll Free: 1-800-66-Speak
www.customlearning.com
copyright © 1988

The Reply To The Toast To The Bridesmaids

M.C. Opening Comments

(Transition comment from previous event.)

_____

_____

_____

_____

_____

(Brief, humorous anecdote or true story relevant to this topic or next speaker. Do not overly embarrass.)

_____

_____

_____

_____

_____

OR (Prepared joke, poem, quotation that is relevant. See Chapter XII Treasury of Wit and Wisdom).

_____

_____

_____

_____

_____

Now introduce next speaker or conduct next event.

Program Speaker Introduction

- *"Our next presentation is"* (name of program event ie. *"Reply To The Toast to the Maid of Honour and Bridesmaids,* etc.)

  _____

  _____

  _____

- (Brief, humorous, true anecdote or story about speaker. Should not overly embarrass guest or audience).

  _____

  _____

  _____

  _____

  _____

  _____

- (Reason speaker was asked to perform task and/or relationship to Bride & Groom & Family)

  _____

  _____

  _____

  _____

  _____

- (Restate speaking assignment)

  _____

- *"Please help me welcome"* (pronounce name correctly)

  _____   _____
          (First Name)   (Last Name)

  _____
                 (Phonetic spelling)

Toll Free: 1-800-66-Speak
www.customlearning.com
copyright © 1988

The Reply To The Toast To The Bridesmaids

M.C. Closing Comments

(Acknowledge presenter(s) speaker(s)

_____

_____

_____

_____

_____

(Prepared joke, poem, quotation that is relevant)
(See Chapter XII, Treasury of Wit and Wisdom)

_____

_____

_____

_____

_____

OR (Brief, humorous anecdote or true story relevant to this topic or previous speaker. Do not overly embarrass.)

_____

_____

_____

_____

_____

The Reply To The Toast To The Groomsmen

M.C. Opening Comments

(Transition comment from previous event.)

_____

_____

_____

_____

_____

(Brief, humorous anecdote or true story relevant to this topic or next speaker. Do not overly embarrass.)

_____

_____

_____

_____

_____

OR (Prepared joke, poem, quotation that is relevant. See Chapter XII Treasury of Wit and Wisdom).

_____

_____

_____

_____

_____

Now introduce next speaker or conduct next event.

Toll Free: 1-800-66-Speak
www.customlearning.com
copyright © 1988

Program Speaker Introduction

- *"Our next presentation is"* (name of program event ie. *"Reply To The Toast to the Groomsmen,* etc.)

  _____

  _____

  _____

- (Brief, humorous, true anecdote or story about speaker. Should not overly embarrass guest or audience).

  _____

  _____

  _____

  _____

  _____

- (Reason speaker was asked to perform task and/or relationship to Bride & Groom & Family)

  _____

  _____

  _____

  _____

  _____

- (Restate speaking assignment)

  _____

- *"Please help me welcome"* (pronounce name correctly)

  _____   _____

         (First Name)   (Last Name)

  _____

                 (Phonetic spelling)

The Reply To The Toast To The Groomsmen

M.C. Closing Comments

(Acknowledge presenter(s) speaker(s)

_____

_____

_____

_____

_____

(Prepared joke, poem, quotation that is relevant)

(See Chapter XII, Treasury of Wit and Wisdom)

_____

_____

_____

_____

_____

OR (Brief, humorous anecdote or true story relevant to this topic or previous speaker. Do not overly embarrass.)

_____

_____

_____

_____

_____

The Notion of: **The Roving "Donahue"**

Presented by: The M.C. or an experienced speaker.

Purpose: To involve the audience and take advantage of their curiosity in order to create spontaneous humour and fun.

Suggested Content:

- Physical Set Up: Two Microphones
    - one that can be passed between members of the head table
    - a remote microphone or one with a cord long enough to reach anyone in the audience.
- Get the Audience Ready: (select 2 or 3 of these questions)
- "I know many of you are curious about. . .
    - what it's really like to be a member of the bridal party
    - or how the couple met
    - or what it cost to rent the tuxedos
    - or how the Best Man is getting along with the Maid of Honour
    - or where the couple is staying tonight
    - Or ANYTHING. . . (that is not overly embarrassing or in bad taste)"
- Ask the audience to signify by raising their hand
- Ask a few questions yourself... to get everyone started
- If necessary, repeat questions to make sure everyone can hear
- Serve notice you're wrapping up - I'll take 3 last questions
- Possibly recruit an assistant to move microphone at head table(s)

Suggested Length: 3-7 minutes.

Roving "Donahue"

M.C. Opening Comments

(Transition comment from previous event.)

_____

_____

_____

_____

_____

(Brief, humorous anecdote or true story relevant to this topic or next speaker. Do not overly embarrass.)

_____

_____

_____

_____

_____

OR (Prepared joke, poem, quotation that is relevant. See Chapter XII Treasury of Wit and Wisdom).

_____

_____

_____

_____

_____

Now introduce next speaker or conduct next event.

Toll Free: 1-800-66-Speak
www.customlearning.com
copyright © 1988

Roving "Donahue" - M.C. Notes

Roving "Donahue"

M.C. Closing Comments

(Acknowledge presenter(s) speaker(s)

_____

_____

_____

_____

_____

(Prepared joke, poem, quotation that is relevant)

(See Chapter XII, Treasury of Wit and Wisdom)

_____

_____

_____

_____

_____

OR (Brief, humorous anecdote or true story relevant to this topic or previous speaker. Do not overly embarrass.)

_____

_____

_____

_____

_____

Toll Free: 1-800-66-Speak
www.customlearning.com
copyright © 1988

The Notion Of   **The Father Of The Bride/Mother of the Bride - Address**

Presented by: The Father of the Bride (and Mother of the Bride).
Both parents can present together as opposed to just a presentation
by the Father of the Bride

Purpose: Thank guests for attending and welcome Groom's family into the
family.

Suggested Content:

See Father of the Bride/Mother of the Bride Presenter Outline, on
next page

Suggested Length: 1¹/₂- 2 minutes.

Presenter Outline

Father Of The Bride/Mother of the Bride - Address

Presented by: Father of the Bride/Mother of the Bride (or nearest relative)

Please Note: The following is an outline of a few ideas you may wish to cover in your remarks. Feel free to add or delete anything you wish as long as it is in good taste and does not exceed 2 mins.

"Mr./Madame Master of Ceremonies, Head Table Guests, Ladies and Gentlemen, and especially"

_____

(first names of the Bride and Groom)

(On behalf of your wife and/or family express appreciation to guests for attending):

_____

_____

_____

_____

(Welcome Groom into your Family)

_____

_____

_____

_____

_____

(Photocopy page and give to Presenter/Speaker)

Toll Free: 1-800-66-Speak
www.customlearning.com
copyright © 1988

Father of Bride/Mother of the Bride Presenter Outline

- (Share a brief, humorous true story or anecdote about your experience with the Groom and Bride)

  _____

  _____

  _____

  _____

  _____

  _____

- (Optional - insert joke, poem or quotation - see Chapter XII)

  _____

  _____

  _____

  _____

- (Express sincere feelings about your daughter)

  _____

  _____

  _____

- (Express sincere feelings about your new son-in-law)

  _____

  _____

  _____

(Photocopy page and give to Presenter/Speaker)

 Toll Free: 1-800-66-Speak
www.customlearning.com
copyright © 1988

Father of The Bride/Mother of the Bride Presenter Outline

- (Express sincere feelings about your son-in-law's parents, family)

  _____

  _____

- (Acknowledge your wife)

  _____

  _____

- (Perhaps offer friendly advice to groom on how to handle daughter)

  _____

  _____

  _____

- (Conclude by re-thanking guests for sharing in the event)

  _____

  _____

  _____

- (Optional Conclusion)
- (Properly lead guest through toast)

"Ladies and Gentlemen

Would you please stand (pause till they do)

and raise your classes

in a toast to

THE FAMILY OF THE GROOM"

(audience will repeat "to the Family of the Groom")

(no need to say thank you . . . return to your seat)

(Photocopy page and give to Presenter/Speaker)

Toll Free: 1-800-66-Speak
www.customlearning.com
copyright © 1988

Father of the Bride/Mother of the Bride - Address

M.C. Opening Comments

(Transition comment from previous event.)

_____

_____

_____

_____

_____

(Brief, humorous anecdote or true story relevant to this topic or next speaker. Do not overly embarrass.)

_____

_____

_____

_____

_____

OR (Prepared joke, poem, quotation that is relevant. See Chapter XII Treasury of Wit and Wisdom).

_____

_____

_____

_____

_____

Now introduce next speaker or conduct next event.

Father of the Bride/Mother of the Bride - Address

Example: M.C. Opening Comments

Father Defined

•   *"A father is a person who forks over several thousand dollars for his daughter's wedding, then reads in the paper that **he gave her away***!"

Daughter's Support

•   *"* _____ *(groom's name), do you think you can support*

my daughter on _____ *(small amount) dollars a week?"*

- I'm willing to try sir, if that's the best you can do."

Talk is Cheap

•   *"I've got a feeling that the guy who said 'talk is cheap' . . . never said, 'I do!'"*

Toll Free: 1-800-66-Speak
www.customlearning.com
copyright © 1988

Program Speaker Introduction

*   *"Our next presentation is"* (name of program event ie. *"Father of the Bride/Mother of the Bride - Address*, etc.)

    _____

    _____

    _____

*   (Brief, humorous, true anecdote or story about speaker. Should not overly embarrass guest or audience).

    _____

    _____

    _____

    _____

    _____

    _____

*   (Reason speaker was asked to perform task and/or relationship to Bride & Groom & Family)

    _____

    _____

    _____

    _____

*   (Restate speaking assignment)

    _____

*   *"Please help me welcome"* (pronounce name correctly)

    _____   _____

         (First Name)   (Last Name)

    _____

          (Phonetic spelling)

 Toll Free: 1-800-66-Speak
www.customlearning.com
copyright © 1988

Father of the Bride/Mother of the Bride - Address

M.C. Closing Comments

(Acknowledge presenter(s) speaker(s)

_____

_____

_____

_____

_____

(Prepared joke, poem, quotation that is relevant)
(See Chapter XII, Treasury of Wit and Wisdom)

_____

_____

_____

_____

_____

OR (Brief, humorous anecdote or true story relevant to this topic or previous speaker. Do not overly embarrass.)

_____

_____

_____

_____

_____

Toll Free: 1-800-66-Speak
www.customlearning.com
copyright © 1988

The Notion Of   **The Father Of The Groom/Mother of the Groom - Address**

Presented by: The Father of the Groom/Mother of the Groom (optional)

Purpose: To thank guests for attending and welcome Bride's family into the family.

Suggested Content:

See Father of the Groom/Mother of the Groom Presenter Outline, on next page

Suggested Length: 1^1/$_2$- 2 minutes.

Presenter Outline

Father Of The Groom/Mother of the Groom- Address

Presented by: Father of the Groom/Mother of the Groom(optional)

Please Note: The following is an outline of a few ideas you may wish to cover in your remarks. Feel free to add or delete anything you wish as long as it is in good taste and does not exceed 2 mins.

"Mr./Madame Master of Ceremonies, Head Table Guests, Ladies and Gentlemen, and especially"

_____

(first names of the Bride and Groom)

(On behalf of your wife and/or family express appreciation to guests for attending):

_____

_____

_____

_____

(Welcome Bride into your Family)

_____

_____

_____

_____

_____

(Photocopy page and give to Presenter/Speaker)

Toll Free: 1-800-66-Speak
www.customlearning.com
copyright © 1988

Father of Groom/Mother of the Groom Presenter Outline

* (Share a brief, humorous true story or anecdote about your experience with the Groom and Bride)

  _____

  _____

  _____

  _____

  _____

  _____

* (Optional - insert joke, poem or quotation - see Chapter XII)

  _____

  _____

  _____

  _____

* (Express sincere feelings about your son)

  _____

  _____

  _____

* (Express sincere feelings about your new daughter-in-law)

  _____

  _____

  _____

(Photocopy page and give to Presenter/Speaker)

Father of The Groom/Mother of the Groom Presenter Outline

- (Express sincere feelings about your daughter-in-law's parents, family)

  _____

  _____

- (Acknowledge your wife)

  _____

  _____

- (Perhaps offer friendly advice to bride on how to handle son)

  _____

  _____

  _____

- (Conclude by re-thanking guests for sharing in the event)

  _____

  _____

  _____

- (Optional Conclusion)
- (Properly lead guest through toast)

"Ladies and Gentlemen

Would you please stand (pause till they do)

and raise your classes

in a toast to

THE FAMILY OF THE BRIDE"

(audience will repeat "to the Family of the Bride")

(no need to say thank you . . . return to your seat)

(Photocopy page and give to Presenter/Speaker)

Toll Free: 1-800-66-Speak
www.customlearning.com
copyright © 1988

Father of the Groom/Mother of the Groom - Address

M.C. Opening Comments

(Transition comment from previous event.)

_____

_____

_____

_____

_____

(Brief, humorous anecdote or true story relevant to this topic or next speaker. Do not overly embarrass.)

_____

_____

_____

_____

_____

OR (Prepared joke, poem, quotation that is relevant. See Chapter XII Treasury of Wit and Wisdom).

_____

_____

_____

_____

_____

Now introduce next speaker or conduct next event.

Father of the Groom/Mother of the Groom - Address

Example: M.C. Opening Comments

Black Eye

*   *"I suppose you're still angry because I came home late last night with a black*
    eye?" said _____ *(the husband). "Maybe you've forgotten, replied*
    _____ *,(the wife) but when you came home, you didn't have*
    that black eye."

Strong Minded

*   " _____ *(groom's name), is strong minded like his father*
    _____ *, who runs everything . . . the vacuum, toaster,*
    dishwasher, floor polisher."

Toll Free: 1-800-66-Speak
www.customlearning.com
copyright © 1988

Program Speaker Introduction

- *"Our next presentation is"* (name of program event ie. *"Father of the Groom/Mother of the Groom - Address,* etc.)

  _____

  _____

  _____

- (Brief, humorous, true anecdote or story about speaker. Should not overly embarrass guest or audience).

  _____

  _____

  _____

  _____

  _____

  _____

- (Reason speaker was asked to perform task and/or relationship to Bride & Groom & Family)

  _____

  _____

  _____

  _____

  _____

- (Restate speaking assignment)

  _____

- *"Please help me welcome"* (pronounce name correctly)

  _____   _____

  (First Name)   (Last Name)

  _____

  (Phonetic spelling)

Father of the Groom/Mother of the Groom - Address

M.C. Closing Comments

(Acknowledge presenter(s) speaker(s))

_____

_____

_____

_____

_____

(Prepared joke, poem, quotation that is relevant)

(See Chapter XII, Treasury of Wit and Wisdom)

_____

_____

_____

_____

_____

OR (Brief, humorous anecdote or true story relevant to this topic or previous speaker. Do not overly embarrass.)

_____

_____

_____

_____

_____

Toll Free: 1-800-66-Speak
www.customlearning.com
copyright © 1988

The Notion Of: **Optional Toasts**

Presented by: Anyone noted below

Purpose: To permit friends/family member(s) to propose toasts that are not always planned.

Suggested Content:

- Remember the golden rule of wedding receptions is. . . THERE ARE NO RULES, so anyone toasting anyone else because they want to is ABSOLUTELY OK! !

- Toasts could be to:
    - the wedding couple
    - the grandparents
    - the godparents
    - the couple's parents - to their health both Mothers - reply by fathers

Suggested Length: 1- 1$^1/_2$ minutes.

- Replies to these toasts are optional.

Optional Toasts

M.C. Opening Comments

(Transition comment from previous event.)

_____

_____

_____

_____

_____

(Brief, humorous anecdote or true story relevant to this topic or next speaker. Do not overly embarrass.)

_____

_____

_____

_____

_____

OR (Prepared joke, poem, quotation that is relevant. See Chapter XII Treasury of Wit and Wisdom).

_____

_____

_____

_____

_____

Now introduce next speaker or conduct next event.

Toll Free: 1-800-66-Speak
www.customlearning.com
copyright © 1988

Program Speaker Introduction

* *"Our next toast is by:"*

  _____

  _____

* (Brief, humorous, true anecdote or story about speaker. Should not overly embarrass guest or audience).

  _____

  _____

  _____

  _____

  _____

  _____

* (Reason speaker was asked to perform task and/or relationship to Bride & Groom & Family)

  _____

  _____

  _____

  _____

  _____

* (Restate speaking assignment)

  _____

* *"Please help me welcome"* (pronounce name correctly)

  _____   _____

  (First Name)   (Last Name)

  _____

  (Phonetic spelling)

Program Speaker Introduction

- *"Our next toast is by:"*

  _____

  _____

- (Brief, humorous, true anecdote or story about speaker. Should not overly embarrass guest or audience).

  _____

  _____

  _____

  _____

  _____

  _____

- (Reason speaker was asked to perform task and/or relationship to Bride & Groom & Family)

  _____

  _____

  _____

  _____

  _____

- (Restate speaking assignment)

  _____

- *"Please help me welcome"* (pronounce name correctly)

  _____   _____
  (First Name)   (Last Name)

  _____
  (Phonetic spelling)

Toll Free: 1-800-66-Speak
www.customlearning.com
copyright © 1988

Program Speaker Introduction

* *"Our next toast is by:"*

  _____

  _____

* (Brief, humorous, true anecdote or story about speaker. Should not overly embarrass guest or audience).

  _____

  _____

  _____

  _____

  _____

  _____

* (Reason speaker was asked to perform task and/or relationship to Bride & Groom & Family)

  _____

  _____

  _____

  _____

  _____

* (Restate speaking assignment)

  _____

* *"Please help me welcome"* (pronounce name correctly)

  _____   _____
       (First Name)   (Last Name)

  _____
                      (Phonetic spelling)

Optional Toasts

M.C. Closing Comments

(Acknowledge presenter(s) speaker(s)

_____

_____

_____

_____

_____

(Prepared joke, poem, quotation that is relevant)

(See Chapter XII, Treasury of Wit and Wisdom)

_____

_____

_____

_____

_____

OR (Brief, humorous anecdote or true story relevant to this topic or previous speaker. Do not overly embarrass.)

_____

_____

_____

_____

_____

Toll Free: 1-800-66-Speak
www.customlearning.com
copyright © 1988

The Notion of: **"Open" Toast Opportunity**

Presented by: Anyone who would like to.

Purpose: To provide every guest who may wish to participate in expressing best wishes to the couple or family an opportunity to do so.

Suggested Content:

- serve advance notice before the meal begins and a reminder just when the main program starts.

- announce "anyone who feels inclined, to propose a short toast may do so now."

- emphasize short (sober) presentations.

- if no one comes forward, then do not drag it out.

- these toasts do not necessarily require a reply.

Suggested Length: one (1) minute per toast

"Open" Toast Opportunity

M.C. Opening Comments

(Transition comment from previous event.)

_____

_____

_____

_____

_____

(Brief, humorous anecdote or true story relevant to this topic or next speaker. Do not overly embarrass.)

_____

_____

_____

_____

_____

OR (Prepared joke, poem, quotation that is relevant. See Chapter XII Treasury of Wit and Wisdom).

_____

_____

_____

_____

_____

Now introduce next speaker or conduct next event.

Toll Free: 1-800-66-Speak
www.customlearning.com
copyright © 1988

"Open" Toast Opportunity

M.C. Closing Comments

(Acknowledge presenter(s) speaker(s)

_____

_____

_____

_____

_____

(Prepared joke, poem, quotation that is relevant)
(See Chapter XII, Treasury of Wit and Wisdom)

_____

_____

_____

_____

OR (Brief, humorous anecdote or true story relevant to this topic or previous speaker. Do not overly embarrass.)

_____

_____

_____

_____

_____

The Notion of: **Acknowledgments**

Presented by: The M.C.

Purpose: To thank and recognize key wedding and reception participants.

Suggested Content:

- Consult with bride and groom as to the extent they intend to personally acknowledge individuals in their reply to the Toast to the Bride.

- Do your homework by acquiring a brief, humorous anecdote or true story about the person that does not overly embarrass them or the audience.

- Follow the format provided in the "Acknowledgment Introduction" forms.

- Acknowledgments could include:

  Name

  - Flower Girl   _____
  - Ring Bearer   _____
  - Ushers   _____
  - Reception Hosting   _____
  - Photographer   _____
  - Video Recorder   _____
  - Cooks, Caterers   _____
  - Band/D.J./Entertainer _____
  - Anyone else (see list on Presenter Outline - Reply To Toast to the Bride)

_____

_____

_____

Suggested Length: as fast as possible

Toll Free: 1-800-66-Speak
www.customlearning.com
copyright © 1988

Acknowledgements

M.C. Opening Comments

(Transition comment from previous event.)

_____

_____

_____

_____

_____

(Brief, humorous anecdote or true story relevant to this topic or next speaker. Do not overly embarrass.)

_____

_____

_____

_____

_____

OR (Prepared joke, poem, quotation that is relevant. See Chapter XII Treasury of Wit and Wisdom).

_____

_____

_____

_____

_____

Now introduce next speaker or conduct next event.

Acknowledgment Introductions

"Next, I'd like to recognize our:"

_____

_____

(Share a brief, humorous, true anecdote or story about person that does not overly embarrass them or audience).

_____

_____

_____

_____

_____

(Sincerely compliment them for a job well done)

_____

_____

_____

_____

_____

_____

"Folks, would you please join with me in a round of applause to thank:"

_____   _____

(First Name)   (Last Name)

Toll Free: 1-800-66-Speak
www.customlearning.com
copyright © 1988

Acknowledgment Introductions

"Next, I'd like to recognize our:"

_____

_____

(Share a brief, humorous, true anecdote or story about person that does not overly
embarrass them or audience).

_____

_____

_____

_____

_____

(Sincerely compliment them for a job well done)

_____

_____

_____

_____

_____

_____

"Folks, would you please join with me in a round of applause to thank:"

_____   _____

(First Name)   (Last Name)

Acknowledgment Introductions

"Next, I'd like to recognize our:"

_____

_____

(Share a brief, humorous, true anecdote or story about person that does not overly embarrass them or audience).

_____

_____

_____

_____

_____

_____

(Sincerely compliment them for a job well done)

_____

_____

_____

_____

_____

_____

"Folks, would you please join with me in a round of applause to thank:"

_____   _____

(First Name)   (Last Name)

Toll Free: 1-800-66-Speak
www.customlearning.com
copyright © 1988

Acknowledgment Introductions

"Next, I'd like to recognize our:"

_____

_____

(Share a brief, humorous, true anecdote or story about person that does not overly embarrass them or audience).

_____

_____

_____

_____

_____

(Sincerely compliment them for a job well done)

_____

_____

_____

_____

_____

_____

"Folks, would you please join with me in a round of applause to thank:"

_____ _____

(First Name) (Last Name)

Acknowledgment Introductions

"Next, I'd like to recognize our:"

_____

_____

(Share a brief, humorous, true anecdote or story about person that does not overly embarrass them or audience).

_____

_____

_____

_____

_____

_____

(Sincerely compliment them for a job well done)

_____

_____

_____

_____

_____

_____

"Folks, would you please join with me in a round of applause to thank:"

_____   _____

(First Name)   (Last Name)

Toll Free: 1-800-66-Speak
www.customlearning.com
copyright © 1988

Acknowledgment Introductions

"Next, I'd like to recognize our:"

_____

_____

(Share a brief, humorous, true anecdote or story about person that does not overly embarrass them or audience).

_____

_____

_____

_____

_____

(Sincerely compliment them for a job well done)

_____

_____

_____

_____

_____

_____

"Folks, would you please join with me in a round of applause to thank:"

_____   _____

       (First Name)   (Last Name)

Acknowledgment Introductions

"Next, I'd like to recognize our:"

_____

_____

(Share a brief, humorous, true anecdote or story about person that does not overly embarrass them or audience).

_____

_____

_____

_____

_____

_____

(Sincerely compliment them for a job well done)

_____

_____

_____

_____

_____

_____

"Folks, would you please join with me in a round of applause to thank:"

_____   _____
(First Name)   (Last Name)

Toll Free: 1-800-66-Speak
www.customlearning.com
copyright © 1988

Acknowledgment Introductions

"Next, I'd like to recognize our:"

_____

_____

(Share a brief, humorous, true anecdote or story about person that does not overly
embarrass them or audience).

_____

_____

_____

_____

_____

(Sincerely compliment them for a job well done)

_____

_____

_____

_____

_____

_____

"Folks, would you please join with me in a round of applause to thank:"

_____   _____

(First Name)   (Last Name)

Acknowledgment Introductions

"Next, I'd like to recognize our:"

_____

_____

(Share a brief, humorous, true anecdote or story about person that does not overly embarrass them or audience).

_____

_____

_____

_____

_____

_____

(Sincerely compliment them for a job well done)

_____

_____

_____

_____

_____

_____

"Folks, would you please join with me in a round of applause to thank:"

_____   _____

          (First Name)   (Last Name)

Toll Free: 1-800-66-Speak
www.customlearning.com
copyright © 1988

Acknowledgment Introductions

"Next, I'd like to recognize our:"

_____

_____

(Share a brief, humorous, true anecdote or story about person that does not overly embarrass them or audience).

_____

_____

_____

_____

_____

(Sincerely compliment them for a job well done)

_____

_____

_____

_____

_____

_____

"Folks, would you please join with me in a round of applause to thank:"

(First Name)	(Last Name)

Acknowledgment Introductions

"Next, I'd like to recognize our:"

_____

_____

(Share a brief, humorous, true anecdote or story about person that does not overly embarrass them or audience).

_____

_____

_____

_____

_____

_____

(Sincerely compliment them for a job well done)

_____

_____

_____

_____

_____

_____

"Folks, would you please join with me in a round of applause to thank:"

_____   _____

(First Name)   (Last Name)

Toll Free: 1-800-66-Speak
www.customlearning.com
copyright © 1988

Acknowledgment Introductions

"Next, I'd like to recognize our:"

_____

_____

(Share a brief, humorous, true anecdote or story about person that does not overly embarrass them or audience).

_____

_____

_____

_____

_____

(Sincerely compliment them for a job well done)

_____

_____

_____

_____

_____

_____

"Folks, would you please join with me in a round of applause to thank:"

_____   _____
(First Name)   (Last Name)

Toll Free: 1-800-66-Speak
www.customlearning.com
copyright © 1988

299

Acknowledgment Introductions

"Next, I'd like to recognize our:"

_____

_____

(Share a brief, humorous, true anecdote or story about person that does not overly embarrass them or audience).

_____

_____

_____

_____

_____

(Sincerely compliment them for a job well done)

_____

_____

_____

_____

_____

_____

"Folks, would you please join with me in a round of applause to thank:"

_____   _____

(First Name)   (Last Name)

Toll Free: 1-800-66-Speak
www.customlearning.com
copyright © 1988

Acknowledgment Introductions

"Next, I'd like to recognize our:"

_____

_____

(Share a brief, humorous, true anecdote or story about person that does not overly embarrass them or audience).

_____

_____

_____

_____

_____

_____

(Sincerely compliment them for a job well done)

_____

_____

_____

_____

_____

_____

_____

"Folks, would you please join with me in a round of applause to thank:"

_____   _____

(First Name)   (Last Name)

Acknowledgement Introductions

M.C. Closing Comments

(Acknowledge presenter(s) speaker(s)

_____

_____

_____

_____

_____

(Prepared joke, poem, quotation that is relevant)

(See Chapter XII, Treasury of Wit and Wisdom)

_____

_____

_____

_____

_____

OR (Brief, humorous anecdote or true story relevant to this topic or previous speaker. Do not overly embarrass.)

_____

_____

_____

_____

_____

Toll Free: 1-800-66-Speak
www.customlearning.com
copyright © 1988

The Notion of: **Ceremonial Cake Cutting**

Presented by: The M.C. or Best Man/Maid of Honour

Purpose: Symbolizes the successful conclusion of the Wedding Reception.

Suggested Content:

- (M.C.) announces it is time for the ceremonial cutting of the cake

- Cake should be set off to one side of the head table

- Invite the Wedding Couple to move towards the cake

- While all are getting ready, this is an excellent time to tell how the bride and groom met or some other interesting story about their courtship

Note:

- The groom places his right hand over the bride's hand and they together cut the first slice from the bottom tier, divide it and then eat it!!

- Estimate five full servings per pound of cake.

- Upon completion, ask everyone to take their seats for the conclusion of the program.

Suggested Length: 3-5 minutes.

Note: May take place after the program.

Ceremonial Cake Cutting

M.C. Opening Comments

(Transition comment from previous event.)

_____

_____

_____

_____

_____

(Brief, humorous anecdote or true story relevant to this topic or next speaker. Do not overly embarrass.)

_____

_____

_____

_____

_____

OR (Prepared joke, poem, quotation that is relevant. See Chapter XII Treasury of Wit and Wisdom).

_____

_____

_____

_____

_____

Now introduce next speaker or conduct next event.

Toll Free: 1-800-66-Speak
www.customlearning.com
copyright © 1988

The Notion of: **Closing Announcements**

Presented by: The M.C.

Purpose: To inform the audience as to details of the remaining program.

Suggested Content:

•   see Outline as follows on the next page.

Suggested Length: 1¹/₂ minutes

Closing Announcements Outline

- (Wedding Couple will deliver Wedding Cake)

_____

_____

- (Require volunteer(s) to - clear tables, clear dance floor, etc.)

_____

_____

- (Bar opening and closing time)

_____

_____

- (In the case of a no-host bar explain ticket or cash arrangement)

_____

_____

- (If table centerpieces are for guests to keep, explain method of choosing who should keep them, i.e., tape under plate or chair - or let table decide)

_____

_____

- (How long before dance begins (and where). If no dance, then what happens next?)

_____

_____

- (Explain how first 3-4 dances will be conducted)

_____

_____

Toll Free: 1-800-66-Speak
www.customlearning.com
copyright © 1988

Announcements

- (Possibly announce when couple plan to change from formal clothes (if applicable), as often guests remain until then)

  _____

  _____

- (Invite guests to remain - at least until after the first dance by the bridal party)

  _____

  _____

- (Announce details of next day's Open House if there is or is not one)

  _____

  _____

- (Introduce name of the band or disc jockey)

  _____

  _____

- (Acknowledge your audience)

  _____

  _____

- (Other Announcements)

  _____

  _____

  _____

  _____

  _____

  _____

The Notion of: **M.C.'s Final Advice**

Presented by: The M.C.

Purpose: To conclude the program on an entertaining note.

Suggested Content:

- see example of closing advice on next page
- create your own advice
- select a closing poem, quotation or song, (see Treasury of Wit and Wisdom, Chapter XII).

Suggested Length: 1 - 1¹/₂ minutes.

    maximum three (3) acts

Toll Free: 1-800-66-Speak
www.customlearning.com
copyright © 1988

Final Advice to
Bride and Groom - Example Only

To the Bride:

"Congratulations, you now have the latest gadget for housework . . . it's called a husband!"

OR

_____

_____

_____

_____

_____

To the Groom:

"Never contradict anything your wife says, it's only your word against thousands of hers!"

OR

_____

_____

_____

_____

_____

To Both:

"May all your troubles be little ones!"

OR

_____

_____

_____

ADJOURN

CHAPTER XI

Organizing The Dance Program

How to Use This Dance Chapter   313

Dance Program Planner   314

Dance Program Event Options   315

M.C. Dance Program Notes   322

Wedding Dance Music Selection   323

How To Use This Dance Chapter

- The objective of this chapter is that it be used as a planner in consultation with whatever band or disc jockey service you have selected.

- For information on hiring a D.J. service, network with friends and relatives for advice.

- Remember, all items are optional, so pick and choose to suit your own preferences.

- Decide whether the program is to be M.C.'d by your program's M.C. or the D.J. or band leader, or both.

- Quickly review chapter's ideas first, then check off preferences.

- After deciding on the program, make sure all the key players know the details, ie:

(Name)

Band/D.J. Service _____

Master of Ceremonies _____

Facility Manager/Volunteer _____

Food Service _____

Bartender _____

Other _____

_____

- The order the events appear in this chapter is recommended, but feel free to rearrange as desired.

Dance Program Planner

Event Option		Time Est.	Page #
❑	1. Post program break	_____	315
❑	2. Bar Details: Open _____ Close: _____	_____	315
❑	3. Band/D.J. Details:		316

Begins Playing _____ Concludes _____ _____

Breaks/Details _____

| ❑ | 4. Wedding Cake Delivery | _____ | 316 |
| ❑ | 5. Ceremonial First Dance(s) | _____ | 316 |

Dancers   Music (see list, pages 323 - 324)

❑ #1 _____ _____

❑ #2 _____ _____

❑ #3 _____ _____

❑	6. Opening Dance - "Paul Jones"	_____	317
❑	7. Bingo Dance:		
	(Optional alternative to "Paul Jones" Starts with)	_____	318
❑	8. Bouquet Toss	_____	318
❑	9. Garter Toss	_____	318
❑	9. Dance Options Notes: _____	_____	319

❑ bunny hop   ❑ butterfly   ❑ polka   ❑ hokey-pokey

❑ cha-cha   ❑ schottische   ❑ waltz   ❑ two step

❑ bird dance   ❑ fox trot   ❑ jive - rock & roll

❑	11. Entertainment		319
	Act #1 _____ Act #2 _____	_____	319
❑	12. Breaks: 1st Break from _____ to _____		
	2nd Break from _____ to _____		
	3rd Break from _____ to _____		
❑	13. Bride & Groom Change Clothes	_____	319
❑	14. Spot Dance: Prize(s) _____ Spotter _____	_____	319
❑	15. Evening Snack	_____	320
	Buffet Set Up Time	_____	
	Take Down Time	_____	
❑	16. Ladies' Choice	_____	320
❑	17. "Duty" Dance	_____	320
❑	18. London Bridge	_____	320
❑	19. Last Dance	_____	320
❑	20. For They Are Jolly Good Fellows	_____	321
❑	21. Bar Closing	_____	321
❑	22. Hall Cleared and Closed	_____	321

314

Dance Program Event Option

1. **Post-Program Break**
    The post-program break time is an opportunity for:
    *   bride and groom to deliver their wedding cake
    *   bar to open
    *   servers to finish clearing the tables
    *   guests to:
        *   leave for the evening
        *   and/or freshen up
        *   and/or get some fresh air
        *   volunteers to clear the dance floor
    *   Should be no longer than 15-20 minutes

2. **Bar Details**
    Bar will serve the following:_____

    _____

    _____

    Liquor ticket prices (if any) _____

    _____

    Bar Hours:

Before Meal:	From _____	To _____
After Meal:	From _____	To _____
Close:	From _____	To _____

    Special Instructions (ie. Wine Service, etc.) _____

    _____

    _____

    Liquor License details _____

    *   Be certain to serve non-alcoholic punch, soft drinks and coffee./tea
    *   Consumption estimates
        *   1-1½ ounces of liquor per drink
        *   3 ounces of wine per drink
    *   The average guest consumes one drink every half hour when the bar is open.
    *   Estimate one bottle of wine/champagne for every two people.
    *   Avoid leaving the bar open longer than one hour prior to the meal as it may result in excessive consumption that can detract from the program.

Dance Program Event Option

3. **Band/D.J. Details**

    Begins playing ———————— Concludes ——————————
    Breaks, details ——————————————————————————————

    Note: A D.J. Service does not take breaks unless specifically instructed to. Be
    sure to check the time by which hotel or hall would like you to vacate.

    If live band is playing

Suggested	Wedding	4:00 p.m.	Picture	5:00 p.m.
timing:	Reception	6:00 p.m.	Meal/Program	6:30 p.m.
	First Dance	8:00 p.m.	Breaks	9,10,11 p.m.

4. **Wedding Cake Delivery**

    *   It is recommended that the Bride and Groom deliver the cake immediately after
        the reception program, as some guests leave right away.

    *   Or cake may be delivered during band breaks.

    *   During the break, the couple visit guests, beginning at one end of the room and
        ending at the other.

    *   Couple should take the time to visit and thank guests for attending.

5. **Ceremonial First Dance**

    *   M.C. should announce in advance, ie. "will begin in 5 minutes"

    *   M.C. stimulates and interrupts with applause:

        "Let's hear it for —————— & ——————————"

    *   Order of Dances (suggested) (time - approx. 3 ½ minutes)

    *   Song #1   Bride & Groom

        Then Father with Bride, Mother with Groom (It is traditional for the
        Bride's Father to cut in on the Groom, and the Groom then dances with
        the Bride's Mother)

        Then two (2) sets of parents (after dancing with each other, the Bride's
        parents exchange dances with the Groom's parents.)

Toll Free: 1-800-66-Speak
www.customlearning.com
copyright © 1988

Dance Program Event Option

- Song #2   Then entire Wedding Party (The Best Man dances with the Bride and the Groom with the Maid of Honour.)

- Then entire audience may join in (we suggest going immediately to the "Paul Jones")

Please Note   The Bride and Groom should make every effort to dance with as many guests as possible.

The Best Man and Groomsmen should have courtesy dances with each of the Bridesmaids.

6. **Opening Dance - "Paul Jones"**
   - Song #3

       - preferably upbeat, fun dances (3 songs in a row)

       - M.C. or D.J. announces the "Paul Jones," ask everyone seated to "please stand up" and. . . "please take their places on the dance floor" women on the outside - facing in, men on the inside - facing out

       - invite everyone to meet, shake hands and introduce themselves to those on each side of them

       - all join hands - outside circles one way, inside the other

       - when the music stops, "dance with the partner you are facing"

       - suggested music for the circles: The Happy Wanderer/Polkas

       - suggested music for the dances: The Shadow of Your Smile
                                            Blue Spanish Eyes

       - bride and groom stay in the middle or participate with all

       - repeat 5 or 6 times

Dance Program Event Option

7. **Bingo Dance** (Optional Alternative to Paul Jones)
   The M.C.:
   * asks either the wedding couple or bridal party or whoever is on the dance floor to begin First Dancers

   _____

   _____

   * announces in advance that he/she fully expects EVERYONE to be up on the dance floor -- NO HOLD OUTS! ! !
   * allows couple(s) to dance for a short time then calls BINGO
   * after each bingo call, encourages dancers already on the floor to "break up" and find other partners
   * continues calling Bingo until everyone is up
   * should choose relatively popular music that everyone likes, regardless of age
   * when everyone is up, maintains music momentum to keep dancers on their feet

8. **Bouquet Toss**
   Bouquet and Garter Toss should take place:
   * Just before the bride and groom leave to change, or midway during the dance.
   * The bride's garter was considered a token of good luck in 14th Century France. To prevent the scrambling for this item, a creative bride substituted her bouquet.
   * M.C. invites all the single females in the audience to come forward.
   * M.C. plays music in the background - or a drum roll.
   * Bride stands on stage, chair, staircase, etc.
   * Counts 1- 2 - 3 with back to audience.
   * Tosses bouquet over her shoulder to a "Future Bride."

9. **Garter Toss**
   * M.C. invites all the single males in the audience to come forward (or why not . . . all the gentlemen?)
   * M.C. plays "provocative" music in the background (The Stripper)
   * Groom places a stool for the Bride to place garter leg on.
   * Groom slowly slides garter off.
   * Hands garter to bride who tosses it over her shoulder to a "Future Groom."
   * Possibly have fun interviewing the winner?

Toll Free: 1-800-66-Speak
www.customlearning.com
copyright © 1988

Dance Program Event Option

10. **Dance Options**
    The M.C. should endeavour to coordinate a variety of dance specialties in order to satisfy all age groups.

• Bunny Hop	• Butterfly	• Cha-Cha
• Schottische	• Bird Dance	• Fox Trot
• Hokey-Pokey	• Jive	• Two Step
• Waltz	• Rock & Roll	• Polka

11. **Entertainment** (Optional)
    * Here is an excellent place and time to schedule volunteer entertainment. (See Page 197)

    Entertainment #1 _____

    Entertainment #2 _____

12. **Breaks**
    * For band, schedule a 10-15 minute break every hour.

13. **Bride and Groom Change Clothes** (Optional)
    * About half way through the evening it was traditional for the Bride and Groom to change out of their formal clothes into more comfortable travel attire. This is now considered optional. After all, how many opportunities will they have to wear their wedding clothes?

    * It is suggested the M.C. either announce their temporary departure and/or their return.

    "Ladies and Gentlemen, please help me welcome back Mr. & Mrs."

    _____

14. **Spot Dance** (Optional)
    The M.C.
    * announces as soon as possible that the next dance will be a spot dance

    * announces the prize _____

    * announces who will select the SPOT: Name _____

    * encourages everyone to participate

    * selects music that will stimulate all to dance at the end of the music tells everyone to "freeze". The "spotter" either:

        * walks to obvious spot (under or near something), paces out some pre-determined number of steps (eg. 10 forward, 5 sideways, 2 back)

        * spotter either presents the prize or takes winner to receive prize from M.C. or other designated person

Dance Program Event Option

15. **Evening Snack**
    - This tradition is based on providing a snack or limited meal to guests half way through the dance program.

    - If you have a professional band, we suggest after midnight.
      Suggested menu: _____

      _____

      _____

      Buffet set up time _____ take down time _____

      M.C. announces the snack.

16. **Ladie's Choice**
    - Suggest this takes place two or three times.

    - M.C. announces next dance is "Ladie's Choice."

    - Adds that no male is permitted to turn down a ladies' request to dance.

    - Challenges every lady to get up and ask a gentlemen to dance. "Would all the ladies please stand and go get one . . ."

17. **"Duty" Dance**
    - This is recommended to encourage mixing.

    - During this dance, husbands and wives do not dance with each other, but should find another partner.

18. **London Bridge**
    - Guests assemble in two lines facing each other, holding hands to create an archway.

    - Bride and Groom start at one end.

    - D.J./Band plays "fun" music.

    - Couple start running, hand in hand, up the middle of the lines.

    - Guests closest to couple lower their hands to "catch" the couple when the music stops.

    - Successful guests let go in order to allow bride and groom to carry on down the line.

    - As soon as bride and groom pass by, guests move to the front of the line to continue the process (for up to 2 songs)

19. **Last Dance**
    - Do so just prior to "Jolly Good Fellow/Auld Lang Syne."

    - We recommend "Could I Have This Dance For The Rest Of My Life" - Anne Murray

Toll Free: 1-800-66-Speak
www.customlearning.com
copyright © 1988

Dance Program Event Option

20. **For They Are Jolly Good Fellows/Auld Lang Syne**
    - Often this is used as a farewell event for the couple, either
        - prior to departing
        - or end of the evening
    - Begin by saying "This is your opportunity to say Goodbye."
    - Ask Groom to escort Bride to her Father.
    - Father dances with daughter to "Daddy's Little Girl."
    - Father escorts daughter to Husband.

        (M.C. - Now that they're married_____ (Groom) is just a domesticated wolf.)
    - Bride and Groom then dance together.
    - "He's Got The Whole World In His Hands) "
    - Wedding party and parents form inner circle.
    - Guests hold hands (possibly with arms crossed) and form a circle surrounding them.
    - M.C. leads guests in "For They Are Jolly Good Fellows" and/or "Auld Lang Syne."
    - Guests move back and forth, changing the formation of the circle as they weave in and out.

21. **Bar Closing**
    - We strongly recommend that you do not announce the bar is about to close. Just do it.
    - Make sure large amounts of coffee, tea and juice are readily available all evening.
    - Close bar - 1 hour prior to when band or D.J. is scheduled to stop playing music.
    - Close up hall 1 hour after music stops.

22. Hall Cleared & Closed

    The objective is

    _____

    _____

    _____

    _____

M.C. Dance Program Notes

Toll Free: 1-800-66-Speak
www.customlearning.com
copyright © 1988

Wedding Dance Music Selection

Always	Atlantic Star
Always and forever	Heatwave
Beautiful in My Eyes	Joshua Kadison
Because	Dave Clark 5
Because You Loved Me	Celine Dion
Butterfly Kisses	Bob Carlisle
Can You Feel the Love Tonight	Elton John (Lion King)
Can't Help Falling in Love	Elvis Presley
Could I Have This Dance	Anne Murray
Don't Know Much	Linda Ronstadt & Aaron Neville
Endless Love	Vandross & Carey/Richey & Ross
Everything I do	Bryan Adams
Finally Found Someone	Barbara Streisand & Bryan Adams
Forever and Ever Amen	Randy Travis
Give Me Forever	James Ingram & John Tesh
Glory of Love	Peter Cetera
Have I Told You Lately	Rod Stewart/Van Morrison
I Cross My Heart	George Straight
I Love the Way You Love Me	John Michael Montgomery
I Love You Because	Al Martino
I Swear	John Michael Montgomery/All-4-One
I Will Always Love You	Whitney Houston
In This Life	Colin Raye
It Had to Be You	Harry Connick, Jr.

Wedding Dance Music Selection (continued)

It's Your Love	Tim McGraw & Faith Hill
Just the Way You Are	Billy Joel
Just You & I	Eddie Rabbit & Crystall Gayle
Keeper of the Stars	Tracy Byrd
On Bended Knee	Boys II Men
Only Wanna Be With You	Hootie & The Blowfish
Open Arms	Journey
Perhaps Love	Placido Domingo & John Denver
Power of Love	Celine Dion
Someone Like You	Van Morrison
Suddenly	Billy Ocean
The Way You Look Tonight	Frank Sinatra
Tonight I Celebrate My Love	Peabo Bryson/Roberta Flack
True Companion	Marc Cohn
Truly, Madly, Deeply	Savage Garden
Unchained Melody	Righteous Brothers
Unforgettable	Nat King & Natalie Cole
When a Man Loves a Woman	Percy Sledge/Michael Bolton
When I Fall in Love	Celene Dion & Clive Griffin
	Nat King & Natalie Cole
When Love Finds You	Vince Gill
Wind Beneath My Wings	Bette Midler
Wonderful Tonight	Eric Clapton
You Mean the World to Me	Toni Braxton
Your Love Amazes Me	John Berry

Toll Free: 1-800-66-Speak
www.customlearning.com
copyright © 1988

CHAPTER XII

Treasury of Wit and Wisdom

How to Use This Chapter	327
How to Tell a Really Funny Joke Everytime	328
Nine (9) Humour Techniques and Resources	332

Section	Page	Section	Page
Anniversaries	333	Love	355
Bachelors	333	Marital Harmony	372
Best Man	335	Marriage	381
Brides	336	Marriage Quotations	394
Bridesmaids	338	Marriage Definitions	395
Dating	339	Mothers	396
Engagement	340	Parents	396
Fathers	344	Single Females	397
Grooms	345	Sex	399
Husbands	347	Weddings	401
Jealousy	354	Wives	408

Treasury of Wit and Wisdom

How To Use This Chapter

- First, quickly review the introduction to humour pages including:

   How To Tell A Really Funny Joke Everytime

   How NOT To Use Humour

   Nine (9) Humour Techniques and Resources

- Next, as you prepare your M.C. Opening and Closing Comments, Introductions, etc., wherever possible use a true humourous story, provided it does not overly embarrass.

However

- When you do require a joke or quotation, simply consult the table of contents (page 325) for the appropriate category(ies), and

   - Review the various joke-quotation options available.

   THEN, either:

   ❑ Photocopy page, circle selected joke and insert the entire page directly where it is needed.

      or

   ❑ Cut out joke or quotation and tape or staple to the portion of the page designated "Prepared Humour."

How To Tell A Really Funny Joke Everytime

Carefully Choose Your Jokes

• Select only those jokes that you feel comfortable about, and that are your style . . . that are you.

• Write them down as you hear them. Avoid choosing or telling a joke just to get a laugh. It should contribute to your message.

The 5 Golden Rules Of Great Joke Selection

A Great Joke:

1. Should be clean enough to tell in a church
   • why offend anyone unnecessarily?

2. Should be really funny
   • choose jokes you enjoy.
   • test it out in advance to be certain it "works".

3. Should not overly embarrass
   • the best "target" for a joke is yourself.
   • never pick on the "defenseless".
   • when in doubt about a remark about someone else, ask them beforehand.

4. Should be appropriate
   • ask yourself - why would this audience find this joke funny?
   • ethnic jokes are a "no-no" (unless it's your own group.)

5. Should preferably make fun of yourself (rather than others)
   • shows you don't take yourself too seriously.

Toll Free: 1-800-66-Speak
www.customlearning.com
copyright © 1988

How To Tell A Really Funny Joke Everytime

"Customize" The Joke By:

- modernizing to today's context, jargon, etc.

- using real names, e.g. yourself and especially people in the audience.

- making it believable - use real dates and occasions.

- giving it the "ring of truth" without deliberately misleading.

- practicing the punch line. . . word for word!

When Beginning a Joke

- Avoid being trite, e.g.

  "Which reminds me of a great story."

  "As the story goes"

  "It seems there were two Irishmen"

  "Seriously though"

Approach Strategy

- Practice beforehand - if you cannot get a laugh from three individuals one on one, then don't try it on an audience.

- Do not use notes as a resource. Know the joke.

- Use smiles with caution.

- Don't seek audience approval.

Delivery Strategy

- Speak in pictures, not words.

- Use as few words as possible.

- Be animated. Live the story and create the characters. Become the story.

- Turn your head to change character roles.

- Don't get diverted.

- Maintain suspense - never telegraph punchlines.

- Focus on the punchline and know it word for word.

- Develop your own style.

Toll Free: 1-800-66-Speak
www.customlearning.com
copyright © 1988

How To Tell A Really Funny Joke Everytime

After The Punchline

- After delivering the punchline, wait. Don't smile. Don't move. Stare at the audience as if non-verbally saying "OK audience, now you can laugh."

- Timing is important.

  Betty Rogers said about Will Rogers

  "He makes a statement, then another, then a third . . .

  After a pause, an explosion goes off."

- Watch timing after delivery of punchline. Let laughter live as long as it can. Use a "bell" curve. When audience laugh is "half way down" the other side, get going again. Don't let it die.

- Avoid laughing at your own joke.

Read Your Audience Reaction

- Be aware of the variety of ways people "laugh" at a joke. i.e. wild roar, belly laugh, giggle, silent "snorters". If punchline doesn't work, start talking, run with it. Audience may never know they were supposed to laugh.

- "Read" the type of laughter you're getting. i.e. groans and awkward or embarrassed laughs are a message that it's time to change your material.

- If the joke bombs, don't go back to explain. Don't try to buy it back!

Transition

- Plan your transition from the joke to your point . . . carefully.

Toll Free: 1-800-66-Speak
www.customlearning.com
copyright © 1988

How To Tell A Really Funny Joke Everytime

How NOT To Use Humour

- When in doubt

- If it is a written joke

- If your friends don't laugh at it privately

- All the time - let the occasion and subject determine the amount and kind of humour

- If audience isn't ready for it

    "The first law of humour is that things can be funny only when we are in fun." - Mal Eastman "Enjoyment of Laughter"

- If it is not relevant

    - an opening joke must fit the occasion and audience

    - relate all humour to your main theme

    - an unrelated joke will divert your audience's attention.

Nine (9) Humour Techniques and Resources

1. **Wit:**
   - *"Wisdom in tight harness"*
     - Josh Bukings
   - strike twice 1. obvious 2. underlying truth
   - *"He is a modest man and has much to be modest about"*
     - Churchill

2. **Satire:**
   - holding folly to ridicule
   - is biting and sarcastic
   - Will Rogers - To American Bankers' Association
     "You're the funniest looking bunch of shylocks that ever foreclosed a mortgage on a poor widow's home."

3. **Irony:**
   - speak one thing and mean another
   - is playful and may be directed against oneself
   - *"An egotist is a person of low taste more interested in himself than me."*

4. **Exaggeration:**
   - extend an idea past reason
   - *"Pedestrians have the right of way only after the ambulance has picked them up"*

5. **Understatement:**
   - reduce a situation beyond reason
     A pig ate three sticks of dynamite. Farmer: "We had a mighty sick pig for a few days."

6. **The Pun:**
   - play on words
   - use with care, as normal audience response is to groan
   - "One man's pun is another man's punishment"

7. **Parody:**
   - either poetry or prose
   - the unexpected or ridiculous imitation of a well known story, essay or poem

8. **Burlesque:**
   - the treating of absurd things seriously or serious things absurdly

9. **Personal Anecdotes:**
   - can be personal, dramatic, enlightening or humourous
   - collect and write them down

Toll Free: 1-800-66-Speak
www.customlearning.com
copyright © 1988

Anniversaries ★★★

★ **Fat Chickens**

Freda: *"You know, Fred, tomorrow will be our 25th Wedding Anniversary."*

Fred: *"You don't say. So what."*

Freda: *"Well, to observe the day, I thought we could kill those two fat chickens out in the coop."*

Fred: *"Now just how can you go blaming those two poor chickens for what happened 25 years ago?"*

★ **Rough Places**

Said husband Joe to wife Mary on their 25th Anniversary:

"Well, my dear, I've carried you safely over all the rough places of life, haven't I?"

Mary: *"Yes, you sure did. I don't think you missed one of them."*

★ **Quote from Homer**

The women of Greece counted their age from their marriage, not from their birth.

Bachelors ★★★

★ **Bachelor's Disease**

Marriage is a kind of graduation ceremony in which a fellow loses his Bachelor's degree without acquiring a Masters.

• **Fools**

Fools rush in where bachelors fear to wed.

• **Kipling**

Down to Gehavva or up to the Throne, He travels the fastest who travels alone.

- Kipling (The Winners)

Bachelors ★★★

★ **Genesis**

It is not good that man should be alone.

- Old Testament, Genesis 11, 18

★ **Torriano**

Before thy marry, get thy habitation ready.

- Piazza Universale: Torriano, 1600

★ **Advice**

Marry the Boss's daughter.

- Advice to the class of 1929, Massachusetts
Institute of Technology, Robert Roger

★ **An Interlude**

O love, O lover, lose or hold me fast, I had thee first, whoever have thee last.

- An Interlude, Charles Swinburne, 1866

★ **Precious Possession**

The most precious possession that ever comes to a man in this world is a woman's heart.

- Holland

Toll Free: 1-800-66-Speak
www.customlearning.com
copyright © 1988

Best Man ★★★

★ **Best Man**

The Best Man is the one chosen to keep the Groom from escaping before the ceremony.

★ **Being Best**

The trouble with being Best Man is that you get no chance to prove it.

★ **As Good As You Are**

Here's to you as good as you are,
And here's to me, as bad as I am;
As bad as I am, as good as you are,
I'm as good as you are as bad as I am.

- Old Scottish Toast

Brides ★★★

★ **Stunning**

A wedding is where the bride looks stunning and the groom looks stunned.

★ **Well Groomed**

At a wedding, the bride is usually well-groomed and the groom is well-bridled.

★ **Night Hawk**

"The Lady, who turned _____ from a night hawk - into a homing pigeon."

★ **Inspiration**

"She may very well have been the inspiration for Charley Rich when he wrote the words, 'Hey, did you happen to see the most beautiful girl in the world.'"

★ **Never Above**

"Never above you. Never below you. Always beside you.""

- Walter Winchell

★ **Grow Old With Me**

"Grow old along with me. The best is yet to be. The last of life, for which the first is made."

- Robert Browning

★ **Hesperides**

I sing of brooks, of blossoms, birds and bowers of April, May, of June, and July flowers.
I sing of maypoles, hock-harts, wassails, wakes
Of Bridegrooms, Brides, and of their bridal cakes.

- Hesperides: Robert Herrick, 1648

Toll Free: 1-800-66-Speak
www.customlearning.com
copyright © 1988

Brides ★★★

★ A Wedding Gown

There is something about a wedding gown prettier than any other gown in the world.

- Douglas Jerolds Wit: A Wedding Gown:
Douglas Jerold, 1859

★ Prospect

Bride: a woman with a fine prospect behind her.

- The Devil's Dictionary: Ambrose Bierce,
1906

★ Gnomologia

As your wedding ring wears,
You'll wear off your cares.

- Gnomologia No. 6146: Thomas Fuller, 1642

★ 10,000 Words

One picture is worth more than ten thousand words.

- Ancient Chinese Proverb: date unknown

★ Ask Advice

A woman seldom asks advice before she has bought her wedding clothes.

- The Spectator: Joseph Addison, 1771

Brides ★★★

★ **All Thy Joys**

Let all thy joys be as the month of May, and all thy days be as a Marriage Day:
Let sorrow, sickness, and a troubled mind
Be a stranger to thee.

- To A Bride: Francis Quarles, 1635

★ **Possess Me Forever**

Possess me forever
  O Sweet delirium!
Sweep through my restless blood
  O delicious fever!
Intoxicate my mind
  O surging madness!
Fill utterly my being
  O mystic joy!
And spur me to great deeds
  O soul's ferment!

Bridesmaids ★★★

★ **Bridesmaids**

A happy bridesmaid makes a happy bride.

- Alfred Lord Tennyson

★ **Soon Be Brides**

Bridesmaids may soon be brides; one wedding brings on another.

- Salt cellars: C.H. Spurgeon, 1919

Toll Free: 1-800-66-Speak
www.customlearning.com
copyright © 1988

Dating ★★★

★ Evenings

"You know," said the lovely blonde, *"for months I just couldn't figure out where my husband was spending his evenings."*

"What did you do about it?" asked her friend.

"Oh, nothing. I just went home early one night, and there he was."

★ Advertising

A lonesome man advertised for a wife. He got over 200 replies, most saying, *"You can have mine."*

★ Fork and Spoon

Courtship makes a man spoon -- but marriage makes him fork over.

★ Billing and Cooing

Marriage starts with billing and cooing, but only the billing lasts.

★ Controversy

All this started. . . in the Garden of Eden
and great controversy ever since
Trouble with Adam and Eve was not the
     - first apple in tree, it was the
     - pear (pair) on the ground
There was controversy even then
     - Eve asked Adam *"Do you still love me?"*
     - Adam replied, ***"Who else?"***

Engagement ★★★

★ Receiver

A popular Southern belle, whose beauty had made her one of the most sought-after women in the state, finally accepted the proposal of one of the more persistent suitors.

"How does it feel to be engaged?" asked a close friend.

"I feel just like a man must feel after he has built up his business and then finds himself about to go into the hands of a receiver," Debbie replied.

★ Practice

Two co-eds were discussing their boyfriends. *"Your fiance is graduating from medical school this June, isn't he?"* asked the first.

"Yes he is," replied Heather.

"Then, I guess you'll be getting married right away."

"Oh, no," Heather replied, *"I want him to practice for at least a year first."*

★ The Proposal

_____ and _____ had been dating for quite a while and one evening they went out for dinner to a Chinese restaurant. They began studying the menu and _____ asked *"How would you like your rice - fried or steamed?"* _____ looked at him and said, *"Thrown."*

Toll Free: 1-800-66-Speak
www.customlearning.com
copyright © 1988

Engagement ★★★

★ Fast and Loose

Two young girls were talking about their boyfriends. "Are you really going to marry Sam?" asked one.

"I can't make up my mind," replied her friend. *"I know he's fast and loose now, but he says if I marry him, he'll be just the opposite."*

"Well, then what are you waiting for?" asked her friend.

"Don't you believe him?"

"Oh, I believe him all right," replied Sally. *"But, I'm not sure I want to be married to someone who is slow and tight."*

★ Phrenologist

A young man and his bride-to-be went to a carnival one summer evening. They decided to have their palms read and ask the gypsy what the future held for them. The old gypsy looked deep into her crystal ball and slowly shook her head. They bent closer to hear, but she would say nothing. This infuriated the young woman, and she stormed out of the tent, leaving her fiance alone with the fortune teller.

"My son," she said, *"I can do nothing for you, but if you would heed my words, go into the next tent and let Zoltan advise you."*

"Who is Zoltan?" asked Brian

"Zoltan is the greatest phrenologist in the world," she replied.

"And why do I need a phrenologist, old woman?"

"Because, my son, if you persist in this marriage, you need your head examined!"

Engagement ★★★

★ **Myron Stevens**

"I'm not rich, I don't own a yacht and a lot of fancy cars like Myron Stevens, but I love you dearly, Terri," said John.

"I love you too, dear," replied Terri, *"but tell me more about Myron Stevens."*

★ **Right Man**

Father: *"I will not have you rushing Ruth into marriage! Give her time. She can wait until the right man comes along."* Mother: *"Why should she? I didn't when I was her age!"*

★ **Someone Else**

"Why don't you marry me?" demanded the ardent, if somewhat conceited suitor. *"There can't be someone else."*

"Oh, Frank, there must be."

★ **Permission**

"I know, sir, that it is a mere formality, but I would like your permission to marry your daughter, Elaine."

"And what makes you think getting my permission to marry Elaine is a 'mere formality', young man?" demanded the irate father.

"Elaine's mother," was his calm reply.

★ **Announcement**

From an engagement announcement in the Edmonton Journal: *"No fate has been set for the wedding."*

Toll Free: 1-800-66-Speak
www.customlearning.com
copyright © 1988

Engagement ★★★

★ **Marriage is Adventure**

To a woman at 18, marriage is an adventure, at 22 it's a career, at 30 a goal, and at 40 - heaven.

★ **Eyes and Ears**

One should choose a wife with his ears, instead of his eyes!

★ **Postpone**

Don: *"Do you think it's unlucky to postpone a wedding?"*

Ron: *"Not if you keep on doing it!"*

★ **Authority**

Two friends were discussing the upcoming marriage of a fraternity brother. *"What a shame Jane and George aren't nearly good enough for each other,"* said the first with a grin.

"Whatever makes you say that?" asked his surprised friend.

"I have it on the best authority. I've been talking to HIS mother and HER father."

★ **A Happy Age**

It was a happy age when a man might have wooed his woman with a pair of kid gloves, a silver thimble, or a tawdry lace; but now a velvet gown, a chain of pearl, or a coach with four horses will scarcely serve the turn.

- Barnaby Rich, 1600

★ **Triumph of Hope**

Alas! Another instance of the triumph of hope over experience.

- comment on a friend's second marriage:
Samuel Johnson, 1770

Fathers ★★★

★ **Paying**

After paying for the wedding, about the only thing a father has left to give away is the bride.

★ **Giving Away**

A father is the person who forks over several thousand dollars for his daughter's wedding, only to read in the paper that he gave her away.

★ **Exchange**

A wedding is a put-and-take exchange where the groom takes your daughter off your hands while you put him on his feet.

★ **Talk is Cheap**

"I've got a feeling that the guy who said 'talk is cheap'. . . never said, 'I do.'"

★ **Attention**

I am the Father of the Bride.

Nobody's paying much attention to me today. But I can assure you that I am getting my share of attention - for the banks and several business firms are watching me very closely.

Toll Free: 1-800-66-Speak
www.customlearning.com
copyright © 1988

Grooms ★★★

★ **Groom's Presence**

Among Those Present:

The bridal veil was fragile net, The bridal gown was lace.

The bride wore slippers on her feet, A smile upon her face.

The bride wore gloves of softest silk, And garlands in her hair.

The bride's bouquet was white.

P.S. The groom was also there.

★ **Best You Can Do**

"_____(grooms name) , do you think you can support my daughter on _____ (small amount) dollars a week?"

"*I'm willing to try sir, if that's the best you can do.*"

★ **Strictly Honourable**

His designs were strictly honourable, as the phrase is, that is to rob a lady of her fortune by way of marriage.

- Tom Jones: Fielding, 1749

★ **Harvest Moon**

My Lord Denbigh is going to marry a fortune, I forget her name: my Lord Gower asked him how long the honey-moon would last? He replied, "*Don't tell me of the honey-moon; it is the harvest moon with me.*"

- from a letter by Horace Walpole, 1756

Grooms ★★★

* **What A Finish**

  It has been said *"Man is not complete until he's married. . . and then he's finished."* But, boy, what a finish!

---

* **Advice To The Groom**

  Boy: *"Did you know, Dad, that in some parts of Africa a man doesn't know his wife until he marries her?"* Dad: *"Why single out Africa?"*

---

* **Don't Ask**

  To the Groom: Don't try to find out who is boss in the house - you'll be happier not knowing.

---

* **Old Testament**

  "It is not good that man should live alone; I will make him a help mate."

  - Old Testament

---

* **Qualities**

  I chose my wife, as she did her wedding gown, not for a fine glossy surface, but such qualities as would wear well.

  - The Vicar of Wakefield: Oliver Goldsmith,1766

---

* **Both are Thine**

  Look, how my ring encompasseth thy finger; Even so thy breast encloseth my poor heart; Wear both of them, for both of them are thine.

  - Richard the Second: William Shakespeare, 1593

Toll Free: 1-800-66-Speak
www.customlearning.com
copyright © 1988

Husbands ★★★

★ Training

"Mother, that dog is vicious! I don't think you'll ever train him."

"Nonsense, you should have seen your father when I first married him!"

★ The Ideal

Two secretaries were discussing the attributes of their ideal husbands. The first one insisted that her ideal mate be musically inclined, sing, dance, tell jokes, and above all, stay home with her every night.

Her friend thought it over for a minute and said, *"Are you sure you want to get married? You'd be better off with a new TV set."*

★ Eating Again

A sick man got well, and his wife was overheard telling a friend, *"It would do your heart good just to hear him eat again."*

★ Parakeet

"If you were to lose your husband," aked the eager-beaver insurance salesman, *"what would you get?"*

After thinking seriously about it for a moment, the lady replied, *"A parakeet."*

★ Husband's Fortune

A wife read her husband's fortune card to him: *"You are a leader of men. You are brave, handsome, strong and popular with the ladies."*

She paused and said, *"It has your weight wrong, too."*

Husbands ★★★

★ **Slim**

A year ago a girl we know went on a diet to keep slim - and she's been keeping the lazy bum ever since.

★ **Retirement**

Retirement is twice as much husband around all the time, and half as much income.

★ **Apologizing**

Overheard a man telling his friends, *"I guarantee you, gentlemen, I always have the last word in any argument with my wife. - I apologize."*

★ **Mistakes**

The man who claims he never made a mistake in life, usually has a wife who did.

★ **Longevity**

"And another thing," Sharon fumed. *"Married men live longer than single men. You should be grateful that you married me."*

Toll Free: 1-800-66-Speak
www.customlearning.com
copyright © 1988

Husbands ★★★

★ **Advice**

Advice to Husbands Around the House:

If you want a thing done well, don't do it yourself - unless you know how.

★ **Finding Way Home**

There was a fellow who took his wife with him everywhere he went. But no matter where he went, or how far, she always managed to find her way back home.

★ **Grumpy**

A lady said to her friend, *"Do you ever wake up grumpy?"* The friend replied, *"Sometimes I do and sometimes I just let him sleep."*

★ **Sense of Humour**

The man who says a wife can't take a joke forgets that she took him.

★ **Paint and Wallpaper Store**

Did you see the sign in a paint and wallpaper store window? It says, *"Any husband choosing colours must have a note from his wife."*

★ **Man Can**

Man can climb the highest mountain, swim the widest ocean, fight the strongest tiger, but once he's married, mostly he takes out the garbage.

Husbands ★★★

★ **Nursery Rhyme**

An Anonymous Nursery Rhyme: Needles and pins, needles and pins, When a man marries, his trouble begins.

★ **Wills and Wishes**

Married men can't make a will; they're lucky if they can make a wish.

★ **Husband's Diary**

Most women can write their husband's diary a week in advance.

★ **Crying at Weddings**

Women cry at weddings; men afterwards.

★ **Born Equal**

All men are born free and equal. If they go and get married, that's their own fault.

★ **Affluence**

Affluence reaches equilibrium when the husband spends all his leisure time repairing the wife's labor-saving devices.

Toll Free: 1-800-66-Speak
www.customlearning.com
copyright © 1988

Husbands ★★★

★ **Liking Things**

Wife: *"My husband and I like the same things - but it took him 16 years to learn them."*

★ **Tweed Aprons**

Recommended for hen-pecked husbands wanting to maintain a semblance of masculinity: Tweed aprons!

★ **Married 20 Years**

The man who has been married twenty years knows more about marriage than the man who has been married many times.

★ **Self Starters**

If more husbands were self-starters, fewer wives would have to be cranks.

★ **Foolish**

George Eliot said: *"I'm not denying the women are foolish: God Almighty made them to match the men."*

★ **Runs Everything**

_____ is strong minded like his father

_____ - who runs everything. . . the vacuum, toaster,

dishwasher, floor polisher.

Husbands ★★★

★ **Going to Work**

The bride (groom) asked her (his) husband (wife)_____(name) if he (she) would let her (him) work after the wedding.

"Certainly not, you can stay home and wash and clean and take care of the kids. No wife (husband) of mine is going to work."

★ **Goodness**

Two women were discussing the recently deceased husband of a mutual acquaintance. *"You know, he really was a wonderful man. So good to his family,"* said the first.

"Yes, he was," agreed the second, *"Why, he was hardly ever home."*

★ **Cheap Shoes**

Customer: *"I want a pair of cheap shoes."*

Sarcastic Clerk: *"To go with what?"*

Customer: *"My cheap husband."*

★ **Trading Places**

Harry and Sue had just arrived at the movies.

Harry: *"Can you see all right?"*

Sue: *"Just fine."*

Harry: *"Not too drafty for you in that seat?"*

Sue: *"No, it's just fine."*

Harry: *"Seat isn't broken is it?"*

Sue: *"Of course not, this is just fine."*

Harry: *"In that case, let's trade seats."*

Toll Free: 1-800-66-Speak
www.customlearning.com
copyright © 1988

Husbands ★★★

★ **Never Criticize**

"Never criticize your wife. It may just have been those same failings which prevented her from getting a better husband."

★ **Congreve**

Man's best possession is a sympathetic wife.

- Congreve

★ **Table Talk**

Of all actions of a man's life, his marriage does least concern other people; yet of all actions of our life, 'tis most meddled with by other people.

- Table Talk

★ **Loving Wife**

A man's best possession is a loving wife.

- Anatomy of Melancholy: Robert Burton, 1641

Jealousy ★★★

★ **Men are Peculiar**

Men are peculiar, just as women have long suspected. For instance, a fellow who hadn't kissed his wife for two years shot a fellow who did!

★ **Upstairs Maid**

"I didn't like the looks of that girl you hired as the upstairs maid, Richard," said his wife. *"I fired her this afternoon."*

★ **Jealous Wives**

Fred and Jake were discussing their jealous wives. *"My wife is so jealous,"* said Fred, *"She goes over all my shirts looking for traces of lipstick."*

"You think that's bad," said Jake, *"my wife goes over all my clothes looking for long blonde hair."*

"Does she ever find any?" asked Fred.

"No, but that doesn't mean she trusts me," said Jake, *"Last night she accused me of going out with bald-headed women."*

Toll Free: 1-800-66-Speak
www.customlearning.com
copyright © 1988

Love ★★★

★ Lovesick Couple

The only one who can cure a lovesick couple is a Doctor of Divinity.

★ Behind Every Wedding

Love should be behind every wedding, but not too far behind.

★ Loving Your Wife

Better to have loved your wife than never to have loved.

★ Love at First Sight

Love at first sight is easy to understand. It's when two people have been looking at each other for years that it becomes a miracle.

★ If it Doesn't Rain

"Darling," he murmured into the phone, *"I love you, I adore you. I'd climb Mount Everest in my bare feet for you. I'd slay dragons for you. I'd walk on hot coals for you. I would endure any hardship for you."*

"Oh, Henry, I love you too. When will I see you again?"

"Well," replied Henry, *"I'll pick you up on Saturday if it doesn't rain."*

★ Rich

Judy was telling Julie about her new boyfriend. *"Julie, it was love at second sight."*

"Wait a minute, Judy. Don't you mean love at first sight?"

"No, how could it be? I didn't know he was rich when we first met."

★ Puppy Love

"Daddy," said young David, *"what's puppy love?"*

"The beginning of a dog's life, my boy."

Love ★★★

★ Her Money

Peter and Rosie had been married for six months when they moved into their new house. *"I just want you to know,"* she said, *"that if it weren't for my money, we wouldn't be here."* A few months later when the last of their new furniture was being delivered, she said, *"You know, if it weren't for my money, this furniture wouldn't be here."*

The day the new color TV was delivered, again she said, *"If it weren't for my money, this TV wouldn't be here."*

"Rosie," said Peter wearily, *"I think you ought to know something. If it weren't for your money, I wouldn't be here."*

★ Love

Love does not consist in gazing at each other - but in looking together in the same direction.

- Antoinne de Saint Exupery

★ Taking Advantage

A love-struck young man gazed upon his beloved and sighed,

"Harriet, I have loved you more than you will ever know." With that Harriet drew herself up and slapped him right across the face.

"You rat!" she cried. *"You did take advantage of me when I was drunk last night."*

★ Say You Love Me

Overheard _____ last night said to

_____ most passionately, *"Say you love me/Say you love me."* _____ said, *"You love me?"*

Toll Free: 1-800-66-Speak
www.customlearning.com
copyright © 1988

Love ★★★

★ Conceit

Both _____(bride) and _____(groom)

realized they had something in common: _____(bride) loved

_____ (groom) and so did he.

★ From The Prophet

You were born together, and together you shall be forevermore.

You shall be together when the white wings of death scatter your days.

But let there be spaces in your togetherness,

And let the winds of the heavens dance between you.

Love one another, but make not a bond of love:

Let it rather be a moving sea between the shores of your souls

Fill each other's cup but drink not from one cup.

Give one another of your bread but eat not from the same loaf.

Sing and dance together and be joyous, but let each one of you be alone,

Even as the strings of a lute are alone though they quiver with the same music.

Give your hearts, but not into each other's keeping.

For only the hand of Life can contain your hearts.

And stand together yet not too near together;

For the pillars of the temple stand apart,

And the oak tree and the cypress grow not in each other's shadow.

- Kahlil Gibran

Love ★★★

✶ From Paradise Lost

With thee conversing I forget all time,
All seasons and their change, all please alike.
Sweet is the breath of morn, her rising sweet,
With charm of earliest birds; pleasant the sun
When first on this delightful land he spreads
His orient beams on herb, tree, fruit, and flower,
Glist'ning with dew; fragrant the fertile earth
After soft showers; and sweet the coming on
Of grateful ev'ning mild; then silent night
With this her solemn bird and this fair moon
And these the gems of heav'n her starry train:
But neither breath of morn when she ascends
With charm of earliest birds, nor rising sun
On this delightful land, nor herb, fruit, flower,
Glist'ning with dew, nor fragrance after showers,
Nor grateful ev'ning mild, nor silent night
With this her solemn bird, nor walk by moon
Or glittering star-light without thee is sweet.

- John Milton

✶ Love-Song

How can I hinder or restrain my soul
So that it does not yearn for yours? And how
Can it be lured to life apart from you?
Gladly would I (had I complete control)
Transport it, a dark secret thing, to new
And untried depths of silence. But I know
How everything that stirs me, stirs you too;
How you and I are like a bow that's bound,
Though with two strings, to give a single sound.
Upon what instrument have we been spanned?
And what strange player plays us, heart and hand? O long, sweet song!

Rainer Maria Rilke
(Translated by Louis Untermeyer)

Toll Free: 1-800-66-Speak
www.customlearning.com
copyright © 1988

Love ★★★

★ **Sonnets from the Portuguese,14**

If thou must love me, let it be for naught
Except for love's sake only. Do not say,
I love her for her smile - her look - her way
Of speaking gently - for a trick of thought
That falls in well with mine, and certes brought
A sense of pleasant ease on such a day
For these things in themselves, Belov'd, may
Be changed, or change for thee - and love, so wrought,
May be unwrought so. Neither love me for
Thine own dear pity's wiping my cheeks dry
A creature might forget to weep, who bore
Thy comfort long, and lose thy love thereby!
But love me for love's sake, that evermore
Thou may'st love on, through love's eternity.

- Elizabeth Barrett Browning

★ **A Time for Everything (popularized by the Birds in Turn! Turn! Turn)**

To everything there is a season, and a time to every purpose under the heavens;
A time to be born, and a time to die; a time to plant,
　　and a time to pluck up that which is planted.
A time to kill, and a time to heal; a time to break down, and a time to build up.
A time to weep, and a time to laugh; a time to mourn, and a time to dance.
A time to cast away stones, and a time to gather stones together; a time to embrace,
　　and a time to refrain from embracing.
A time to get, and a time to lose; a time to keep silence, and a time to speak.
A time to love, and a time to hate; a time of war, and a time of peace.
To everything there is a season, and a time to every purpose under the heaven.

- Ecclesiastes 3:1-8, KJV.

Love ★★★

✴ Desiderata

Go placidly amid the noise and haste, and remember what peace there may be in silence. As far as possible, without surrender, be on good terms with all persons. Speak your truth quietly and clearly; and listen to others, even the dull and ignorant, they too have their story. Avoid loud and aggressive persons, they are vexations to the spirit. If you compare yourself with others, you may become vain and bitter, for always there will be greater and lesser persons than yourself. Enjoy your achievements as well as your plans.

Keep interested in your own career, however humble; it is a real possession in the changing fortunes of time. Exercise caution in your business affairs; for the world is full of trickery. But let this not blind you to what virtue there is, many persons strive for high ideals; and everywhere life is full of heroism. Be yourself. Especially, do not feign affection. Neither be cynical about love; for in the face of all aridity and disenchantment it is perennial as the grass. Take kindly the counsel of the years, gracefully surrendering the things of youth. Nurture strength of spirit to shield you in sudden misfortune. But do not distress yourself with imaginings. Many fears are born of fatigue and loneliness. Beyond a wholesome discipline, be gentle with yourself. You are a child of the universe, no less than the trees and the stars; you have a right to be here. And whether or not it is clear to you, no doubt the universe is unfolding as it should. Therefore be at peace with God, whatever you conceive him to be, and whatever your labours and aspirations, in the noisy confusion of life, keep peace with your soul. With all its sham and drudgery and broken dreams, it is still a beautiful world. Be cheerful. Strive to be happy.

- Max Ehrmann, 1927

Toll Free: 1-800-66-Speak
www.customlearning.com
copyright © 1988

Love ★★★

★ How Do I Love Thee?

How do I love thee? Let me count the ways.
I love thee to the depth and breadth and height
My soul can reach, when feeling out of sight
For the ends of Being and ideal Grace.
I love thee to the level of every day's
Most quiet need, by sun and candle-light.
I love thee freely, as men strive for right;
I love thee purely, as they turn from praise.
I love thee with the passion put to use
In my old griefs, and with my childhood's faith.
I love thee with a love I seemed to lose
With my lost saints - I love thee with the breath,
Smiles, tears, of all my life! - and, if God choose,
I shall but love thee better after death.

- Elizabeth Barrett Browning,
"Sonnets from the Portuguese"

★ Love Is Sweet

All love is sweet,
Given or returned. Common as light is love,
And its familiar voice wearies not ever. . .
They who inspire it most are fortunate,
As I am now; but those who feel it most
Are happier still.

- Percy Bysshe Shelley

Love ✫✫✫

✫ If Ever Two Were One

If ever two were one, then surely we;
If ever man were loved by wife, then thee;
If ever wife was happy in a man,
Compare with me, ye women, if you can.
I prize thy love more than whole mines of gold,
Or all the riches that the East doth hold.
My love is such that rivers cannot quench,
Nor aught but love from thee give recompense.
Thy love is such I can no way repay;
The heavens reward thee manifold, I pray.
Then while we live in love let's do so persevere
That when we live no more we may live ever.

- Anne Bradstree
To My Dear and Loving Husband"

✫ The Nature of True Love

Let me not to the marriage of true minds
Admit impediments. For love is not love
Which alters when it alteration finds
Or bends with the remover to remove.
O, no! It is an ever-fixed mark
That looks on tempests and is never shaken;
It is the star to every wand'ring bark,
Whose worth's unknown although his height be taken.
Love's not Time's fool, though rosy lips and cheeks
Within his bending sickle's compass come.
Love alters not with his brief hours and weeks,
But bears it out even to the edge of doom.
If this be error, and upon me proved, I never writ, nor no man ever loved.

- From a Midsummer Night's Dream
by William Shakespeare

Toll Free: 1-800-66-Speak
www.customlearning.com
copyright © 1988

Love ★★★

★ Endymium

A thing of beauty is a joy forever.

- Endymium: John Keats, 1818

★ The Distaff

A great love goes here with a little gift.

- The Distaff, Theocritus, 280 B.C.

★ Le Menterur

The manner of giving is worth more than the gift.

- Le Menterur: Pierre Corneille, 1642

★ The Rose

Loveliest of lovely things are they,
On earth, that soonest past away.
The rose that lives its little hour,
Is prized beyond the sculptured flower.

- A Scene On The Banks Of The Hudson:

William Bryant, 1832

★ Drink To Me

Drink to me only with thine eyes
And I will pledge with mine;
Or leave a kiss but in the cup,
And I'll not ask for wine.
The thirst that from the soul doth rise
Doth ask a drink divine,
But might I of Jove's nectar sup,
I would not change for thine.

Love ★★★

★ **Say It With Flowers**

Say it with flowers from love's sweetest bowers
And you'll find her waiting, waiting for you.

- Say It With Flowers; Neville Fleeson, 1919

★ **Sacred Flame**

All thoughts, all passions, all delights.
Whatever stirs this mortal frame,
Are all but ministers of Love,
And feed his sacred flame.

- Coleridge

★ **Sonnet XCI**

Some glory in their birth, some in their skill,
Some in their wealth, some in their body's force
Some in their garments, though new-fangled ill;
Some in their hawks and hounds, some in their horse;
And every humour hath his adjunct pleasure,
Wherein it finds a joy above the rest;
But these particulars are not my measure;
All these I better in one general best.
They love is better than high birth to me,
Richer than wealth, prouder than garments cost
Of more delight than hawks or horses be;
And having thee of all men's pride I boast;
Wretched in this alone, that thou mayest take
All this away, and me most wretched make.

- William Shakespeare

Toll Free: 1-800-66-Speak
www.customlearning.com
copyright © 1988

Love ★★★

★ The Temple

Only the flower sanctifies the vase.

- The Temple: Robert Johnson, 1883

★ I Wish You Love

I do not wish you joy without a sorrow,
Nor endless day without the healing dark,
Nor brilliant sun without the restful shadow,
Nor tides that never turn against your back.
I wish you love, and strength, and wisdom,
And gold enough to help some needy one,
I wish you songs, but also blessed silence,
And God's sweet peace when every day is done.

- author unknown

★ The Night Has A Thousand Eyes

The night has a thousand eyes,
And the day but one;
Yet the light of the bright world dies
With the dying sun.
The mind has a thousand eyes,
And the heart but one;
Yet the light of a whole life dies
When love is done.

- Francis William Bourdillon

★ De Flagello Myrteo

Perfect love casts out prudery together with fear.

- De Flagello Myrteo: Fichard Garnett, 1905

Love ★★★

★ **What Is Love?**

What is love? It is the ardent outflow of the whole being - the yearning of one human heart to lavish all its treasures upon another.

- James de Mille

★ **Loved**

The greatest happiness of life is the conviction that we are loved, loved for ourselves, or rather loved in spite of ourselves.

- Victor Marie Hugo

★ **Joys**

May your joys be as deep as the ocean, and your sorrows as light as its foam.

- Anonymous

★ **To be Loved, be loveable.**

- Ovid

★ **Happiness**

There is only one happiness in life, to love and to be loved.

- George Sand

★ **All mankind loves a lover.**

-Ralph Waldo Emerson

Toll Free: 1-800-66-Speak
www.customlearning.com
copyright © 1988

Love ★★★

★ Those who love have all.

- Anonymous

★ The only gift is a portion of thyself.

- Ralph Waldo Emerson

★ Small kindnesses, small courtesies, give a great charm to the character, and great comfort to others.

- Kelty

★ The small courtesies sweeten life; The greater ennoble it.

- Bovee

★ **Rue des Vents, VIII**

Your body's beauty is an air that blows
Out of some garden where the Spring has come
Where never yet has faded any rose
And never any singing bird is dumb.
You are white waterfalls in piney woods
Touched by the freshness of October wind.
You are the slim young silver moon that broods
Over a dusk where lovers wander blind.
And how shall these eyes ever have their fill
Of you, alight with loveliness and love
My starlight water, tremulous or still,
Across which music wakens as you move!
Over the floor laughing and white you pass. . .
I see all April light that ever was.

- Arthur Davison Ficke

Love ★★★

★ **From Heritage**

What fills the heart of man
Is not that his life must fade,
But that out of his dark there can
A light like a rose be made,
That seeing a snow-flake fall
His heart is lifted up,
That hearing a meadow-lark call
For a moment he will stop
To rejoice in the musical air
To delight in the fertile earth
And the flourishing everywhere
Of spring and spring's rebirth.
And never a woman or man
Walked through their quickening hours
But found for some brief span
An intervale of flowers,
Where love for a man or woman
So captured the heart's beat
That they and all things human
Danced on rapturous feet.

- Theodore Spencer

Toll Free: 1-800-66-Speak
www.customlearning.com
copyright © 1988

Love ★★★

★ From The Good Morrow

And now good morrow to our waking souls
Which watch not one another out of fear;
For love all love of other sights controls,
And makes one little room an everywhere.
Let sea-discoverers to new worlds have gone,
Let maps to other, worlds on worlds have shown;
Let us possess one world, each hath one, and is one.
My face in thine eye, thine in mine appears,
And true plain hearts do in the faces rest;
Where can we find two better hemispheres
Without sharp north, without declining west?
Whatever dies was not mixed equally;
If our two loves be one, or thou and I
Love so alike that none do slacken, none can die.

- John Donne

★ Sonnet

Love is the simplest of all earthly things.
It needs no grandeur of celestial trust
In more than what it is, no holy wings;
It stands with honest feet in honest dust,
And is the body's blossoming in clear air
Of trustfulness and joyance when alone
Two mortals pass beyond the hour's despair
And claim that Paradise which is their own.
Amid a universe of sweat and blood,
Beyond the glooms of all the nations' hate,
Lovers, forgetful of the poisoned mood
Of the loud world, in secret ere too late
A gentle sacrament may celebrate
Before their private altar of the good.

- Arthur Davison Ficke

Love ✰✰✰

✰ **The Passionate Shepherd to His Love**

Come live with me and be my Love
And we will all the pleasures prove
That hills and valleys, dales and fields,
Or woods or steepy mountain yields.
And we will sit upon the rocks,
And see the shepherds feed their flocks
By shallow rivers, to whose falls
Melodious birds sing madrigals.
And I will make thee beds of roses
And a thousand fragrant posies;
A cap of flowers, and a kirtle
Embroider'd all with leaves of myrtle.
A gown made of the finest wool
Which from our pretty lambs we pull;
Fur-lined slippers for the cold,
With buckles of the purest gold.
A belt of straw and ivy-buds
With coral clasps and amber studs;
And if these pleasures may thee move,
Come live with me and be my Love.
The shepherd swains shall dance and sing
For thy delight each May morning;
If these delights thy mind may move,
Then live with me and be my Love.

- Christopher Marlowe

Toll Free: 1-800-66-Speak
www.customlearning.com
copyright © 1988

Love ★★★

★ **Poem 94**

Being to timelessness as it's to time,
love did no more begin than love will end;
where nothing is to breathe to stroll to swim
love is the air the ocean and the land
(do lovers suffer? all divinities
proudly descending put on deathful flesh:
are lovers glad? only their smallest joy's
a universe emerging from a wish)
love is the voice under all silences,
the hope which has no opposite in fear;
the strength so strong mere force is feebleness:
the truth more first than sun more last than star
- do lovers love? why then to heaven with hell.
Whatever sages say and fools, all's well.

-E.E. Cummmgs

★ **From Song of Solomon, Chapter IV**

Behold, thou art fair, my love; behold, thou art fair;
Thou hast doves' eyes within thy locks:
Thy hair is as a flock of goats,
That appear from Mount Gilead.
Thy teeth are like a flock of ewes that are newly shorn,
Which are come up from the washing:
Whereof every one hath twins,
And none is barren among them.
Thy lips are like a thread of scarlet,
And thy speech is comely:
Thy temples are like a piece of pomegranate within thy locks.
Thy neck is like the tower of David builded for an armoury,
Whereon there hang a thousand bucklers,
All shields of mighty men.
Thy two breasts are like two young roes that are twins,
Which feed among the lilies.

Marital "Harmony" ★★★

✶ Mourning

"Mr. Brown, I really don't understand this provision in your will," said the puzzled lawyer.

"Which provision is that?"

"The one that stipulates that your wife must remarry before receiving any part of your estate. Why do you insist she remarry?"

"Well," replied Mr. Brown. *"It's a pity for a man to go unmourned. I want somebody to be sorry I died."*

✶ Two Kinds of Couples

There are only two kinds of married couples. The compatible and the combatible.

✶ Disaster

"Miss Johnson, please draw a red circle around the twenty-seventh of the month on the calendar."

"Certainly, sir, but what day is that?"

"That is the day my marriage occurred."

"Excuse me, sir", said Miss Johnson, *"I don't mean to be rude, but a marriage 'takes place'. A disaster or a catastrophe 'occurs'"*.

"As I said, Miss Johnson, that is the day my marriage occurred."

✶ Earning and Spending

Matrimony is a popular form of disagreement where the husband thinks that the wife should spend less, and the wife thinks the husband should earn more.

Toll Free: 1-800-66-Speak
www.customlearning.com
copyright © 1988

Marital "Harmony" ★★★

★ **Infatuation**

"*I was a fool when I married you, Moe,*" snapped his shrewish wife.

"*I know, I know,*" moaned Moe, "*but I was too infatuated to notice at the time.*"

★ **Private Detective**

"*I want you to follow my husband day and night,*" demanded Mrs. Jones. "*I'm sure there's another woman.*"

"*I understand completely,*" replied the private eye. "*I'll do up a full report on her.*"

"*Never mind her, I want a full report on what it is she sees in him.*"

★ **Standing in Line**

The bride asked the marriage counselor, "*Isn't there some way I can keep my husband in line?*"

Counselor: "*Young lady, your husband shouldn't have to stand in line.*"

★ **Last Words**

We all asked the grieving widow, "*What were your husband's last words?*"

Said she: "*That gun doesn't scare me, you couldn't hit the side of a barn.*"

Marital "Harmony" ★★★

✷ Complete Rest

A weary man dragged himself to his doctor's office, and complained of sleepless nights, loss of appetite, fatigue and constant tension.

"My good man," said the doctor, *"I'm going to call your wife and tell her that you must go to the seashore for a complete rest."*

"Well, Doc," said the patient with a weary sigh, *"if you want me to get a complete rest, you'd better tell her to go to the mountains."*

✷ Snoring

Two women were talking. One complained bitterly about her husband's snoring. She said it was driving her crazy and that she was at her wit's end. Her friend was completely sympathetic.

"I know how you must feel, my dear. Only think of my poor sister."

"What's your sister got to do with it?"

"Well, you see, my sister's husband was a very heavy snorer. And it finally did drive her mad. You see, he was a ventriloquist, and he snored on her side of the bed."

✷ Too Much

A rather grouchy businessman attended a lecture on married life. He was so taken by some of the lecturer's ideas and so ashamed of himself for being such an insensitive husband that he decided to start making amends right away. He arrived home that evening with roses for his wife, told her he was going to take her to dinner, and began nuzzling her neck.

"Oh, for heaven's sake," cried the wife, *"This is too much. First the baby fell out of his crib, the washing machine broke and blew every fuse in the house, and tonight of all nights, you come home drunk!"*

Toll Free: 1-800-66-Speak
www.customlearning.com
copyright © 1988

Marital "Harmony" ★★★

★ **Changing Status**

When a man likes a girl, he likes her just as she is, but the girl always wants to alter his status.

★ **Things You Haven't Got**

Wife: *"John, I've got a lot of things I want to talk to you about."*

Husband: *"That's a switch. Usually you want to talk to me about the things you haven't got."*

★ **Escape**

A henpecked husband finally managed to lie his way out of the house one evening. He joined a few friends for a poker game that went on far into the night. When the game finally broke up, he was horrified to learn it was 4 a.m. He was sure his wife would murder him, but a sudden flash of genius saved his neck. He called his home and roused his sleepy wife.

"Don't pay the ransom", he shouted jubilantly. *"I've escaped."*

★ **Uh Huh**

Wife to husband reading newspaper: *"You can stop saying 'uh, huh' every 30 seconds, Harry, I quit talking ten minutes ago."*

★ **Winning an Argument**

After winning an argument with your wife, the safest thing you can do is apologize.

Marital "Harmony" ★★★

★ **Tough Dinner**

Two young men were discussing a mutual friend's marriage.

"You know," said Jack, *"I had dinner with old George and his new bride last week."*

"Really, how was it?"

"Not so bad, I'm sending them a new carving set. As a matter of fact, I'm going to stop off at the hardware store and pick it up tonight."

"You're buying a carving set in a hardware store?" asked his disbelieving friend.

"Of course, where else would I buy a mallet and chisel?"

★ **Jilted**

"You mean you've been jilted twice?"

"Well, not exactly," said Dan. *"I married the second one."*

★ **Town Gossip**

"Mabel, I hear that you and your husband aren't getting along these days," said the town gossip.

"Well, I wouldn't exactly say that," said Mabel. *"It's true that we had a fight and I stabbed him, but that's as far as it went."*

★ **Ran off with Wife**

A man called the local mental hospital and demanded to know if anyone had escaped the previous night.

"Not that I know of," asked the doctor who answered the phone, *"why do you ask?"*

"Because," replied the caller, *"some poor guy just ran away with my wife."*

Toll Free: 1-800-66-Speak
www.customlearning.com
copyright © 1988

Marital "Harmony" ★★★

★ Twenty Odd Years

"How long have you been married, Mr. Green?"

"Twenty-odd years, my friend, twenty-odd years."

"Why do you say twenty-odd years?"

"Just wait till you meet my wife," came the weary reply.

★ Dodging the Draft

One member of the local draft board claims he has finally seen everything. A young man insisted he was not eligible for the draft due to defective eyesight, and he brought his wife along to prove the point.

★ Tall, Dark and Handsome

A woman came into the police station to report her husband missing. She described him as *"30 years old, tall, dark and handsome."*

"I know your husband," said the desk sergeant. *"He's fat, bald and forty."*

"I'm well aware of that," she replied, *"but who wants him back?"*

★ Bad Cook

"I didn't imply my wife was a bad cook - I merely said our garbage disposal had an ulcer."

Marital "Harmony" ✲✲✲

✲ Niagara Falls

Sally had married the dreariest bore in town and they went off to Niagara Falls (where else?) for their honeymoon. Two weeks later, she was back in town looking positively radiant. *"It was just wonderful,"* she gushed to a group of girl friends who had dropped in. *"You just can't imagine how exciting it was."*

Since every one of her friends knew perfectly well what a bore she'd married, that was difficult to imagine. So difficult, that one of them was moved to say, *"Why, what did you do? Go over the Falls in a barrel?"*

✲ Lewis and Clark

A modern-day Lewis and Clark exploration team had returned from a two-year expedition of the upper Amazon. Having bravely gone where no man had gone before, they were greeted by members of the press from every nation.

"Tell us, sir," asked a reporter of one of the explorers, *"what made you go?"*

"I had to go," he replied. *"I had to meet the challenge, to test my mettle, to meet the unknown, to face hardship, and to ponder the real meaning of life."*

"And you, sir," he inquired of the second explorer, *"why did you go?"*

"You should meet my wife," came the weary reply.

✲ Trouble

"Son, I just know you'll do the right thing by this little girl," said the preacher, *"You just marry her, and you'll be at the end of your troubles."* So the young fellow did the right thing, and he married the girl, and about six months later when he saw the preacher again, he tried to murder him.

"You miserable liar!" shouted the young man. *"You told me if I married her, I would be at the end of my troubles. Well, I married her, and she has made my life miserable."*

"That may be true, son, but you can't blame me," replied the minister. *"I said you'd be at the end of your troubles, but I never said which end."*

Toll Free: 1-800-66-Speak
www.customlearning.com
copyright © 1988

Marital "Harmony" ★★★

★ Burglar

"Wake up, Joe," she whispered. *"There's a burglar going through your pants pockets."*

"For heaven's sake, Ethel, leave me out of it!", Joe replied sleepily.

"You two will just have to fight it out between you."

★ Victim

Two ladies met in the hospital one day. *"Tell me,"* said the first, *"how is your husband? I hear he was in an accident. Is he all right?"*

"Well," replied the second, *"he ain't all right, but he's just like he was before."*

★ Six - Seven

Husband: *"In our six years of marriage, we haven't been able to agree on anything."*

Wife: *"It's been seven years, dear."*

★ Multi-Millionaire

Seems that a man told one of his buddies. *"My wife made a millionaire out of me."*

The buddy wanted to know, *"What were you before?"*

"A multi-millionaire," replied the man.

★ Stand Sideways

"Just tell me one thing, Ethel," demanded the outraged husband. *"Where does all that money I give you for food go?"*

"Stand sideways and look in the mirror!" snapped the wife.

Marital "Harmony" ★★★

★ **Football**

The wife complained, *"You love football more than you love me."*

"Maybe so," replied her husband. *"But I love you more than I love basketball."*

★ **Wife's Dreams**

Two friends were talking. *"My wife had a funny dream last night. She dreamed that she was married to a millionaire."*

"That's not funny, my friend, that's lucky," replied his friend.

"How do you mean lucky?"

"I mean it's lucky you aren't married to my wife. She dreams that in the daytime."

★ **Late Last Night**

"I suppose you're still angry because I came home late last night with a black eye?" said _____. *"Maybe you've forgotten,"* replied _____ *"but when you came home, you didn't have that black eye."*

★ **To Be Wronged**

To be wronged is nothing unless you continue to remember it.

- Confucius

Toll Free: 1-800-66-Speak
www.customlearning.com
copyright © 1988

Marriage ★★★

★ Blessings For a Marriage

May your marriage bring you all the exquisite excitements a marriage should bring.

May life grant patience, tolerance and understanding.

May you always need one another - not so much to fill your emptiness as to help you to know your fullness.

A mountain needs a valley to be complete; the valley does not make the mountain less but more; and the valley is more a valley because it has a mountain towering over it.

So let it be with you and you.

May you need one another - but not out of weakness.

May you want one another - but not out of lack.

May you entice one another - but not compel one another.

May you embrace one another but not encircle one another.

May you succeed in all important ways with one another, and not fail in the little graces.

May you look for things to praise, often say, "I love you" and take no notice of small faults.

If you have quarrels that push you apart,

May both of you hope to have good sense enough to take the first step back.

May you enter into the mystery which is the awareness of one another's presence - no more physical than spiritual; warm and near when you are side by side; and warm and near when you are in separate rooms or even distant cities.

May you have happiness, and may you find it making one another happy.

May you have love, and may you find it loving one another.

May the passing of time only enhance and accentuate this joyful sense of wonder on the journey you are beginning today.

- Anonymous

★ Endless Conversation

Marriage is an endless conversation, in which the more the wife talks, the less the husband listens.

Marriage ★★★

★ **Population Explosion**

Know what is setting off the population explosion? - MATCHES.

★ **Success and Failure**

It takes two to make a marriage a success and only one to make it a failure.

★ **Neighbours Talk**

Married life is a mistake: first he talks, then she talks, then the neighbours talk.

★ **Working for Us**

Daddy was showing "Junior" the family album and came across the picture of himself and his wife on their wedding day.

"Was that the day Mom came to work for us?" Junior asked.

★ **Marriage Dues**

Marriage is a union where the husband's dues for the rights of membership amount to the whole of his take-home pay.

★ **No Draft**

Sign posted in an Army recruiting station after the announcement was made that married men would not be drafted:

"Better for two years than for life."

Toll Free: 1-800-66-Speak
www.customlearning.com
copyright © 1988

Marriage ★★★

★ **Biking the Boss**

Experience teaches that being a good husband is about the same as achieving success in any other job - it's much easier if you like the boss.

★ **Ways and Means**

Marriage is a committee of two on ways and means with the right to add to their number.

★ **Trouble with Matrimony**

The trouble with matrimony is not with the institution, it's with the personnel.

★ **Happy Marriage**

There's only one way to make a happy marriage, and most husbands and wives would like to know what it is.

★ **Fifty-Fifty Proposition**

Whoever said marriage is a fifty-fifty proposition, doesn't know the half of it.

★ **Knowing the Reason**

Before Herman got married, he always said he would be the boss or know the reason why. And now that Herman is married, what does he say? He knows the reason why.

Marriage ★★★

★ **Happiness**

Two men where discussing their marriages. *"I never knew what real happiness was until I got married,"* said Bob.

"Yeah, I know what you mean," said his friend. *"But then it's too late."*

★ **Lottery Chance**

Two old cronies were having a drink one evening. *"Tell me Dick, do you believe that marriage is like a lottery?"*

"Heck, no!" said Dick. *"At least in a lottery a man has a chance."*

★ **Like a Melody**

"Why is a pretty girl like a melody?" asked Johnny.

"Well, son," replied his dad, *"I guess it's because when you marry her, you've got to face the music."*

★ **Marriage Animal**

Marriage brings out the animal in some men - usually the chicken.

★ **Convincing**

"I really do love Sam," wailed Sue, *"but I could never marry an atheist! Why, he doesn't believe in anything - not even in hell!"*

"Don't worry dear," soothed her mother, *"You marry him, and we'll convince him."*

Toll Free: 1-800-66-Speak
www.customlearning.com
copyright © 1988

Marriage ★★★

★ Roof Over Her Head

To many a girl, all that marriage means is a roof over her head and a man under her thumb.

★ Reform and Education

The only thing worse than marrying a man to reform him is marrying a woman to educate her.

★ Marriage is a Gamble

Marriage is a gamble - that's why we speak of winning a husband or wife.

★ Sitting in the Bathtub

Married life is like sitting in the bathtub; once you get used to it, it's not so hot.

★ Carping Critic

Marriage is an unfailing method of turning an ardent admirer into a carping critic.

★ Some Like it Cold

Some like it cold, some like it hot, some freeze while others smother. And by some fiendish, fatal plot, they marry one another.

★ A Necessary Evil

Marriage, if one will face the truth, is an evil; but a necessary evil.

- Menander, 300 B.C.

Marriage ★★★

★ **Ups and Downs**

Marriage is a matter of ups and downs, keeping up appearances and keeping down expenses.

★ **Marriage License**

Husband-hunting is the only time in which the animal that gets caught has to buy a license.

★ **Men's Success**

The secret of many men's success is application - for a marriage license.

★ **Advice**

Some advice: Don't get married on a shoe string or you may find it hard to keep it tied.

★ **Marriage is a Game**

Marriage is a game where the husband tries to be as fast on the deposit as the wife is on the draw.

★ **Vacation Planning**

Why is planning a vacation always easy for a married man? Because the boss tells him when, and the wife says where.

Toll Free: 1-800-66-Speak
www.customlearning.com
copyright © 1988

Marriage ★★★

★ **Violin**

Marriage is like a violin. . .

- after the beautiful music

- strings are still attached.

★ **Millionaire**

"No," cooed the much-married international beauty. *"It is definitely not true that I married my last husband because he was a millionaire. Actually, I made him one."*

"Really? What was he before?"

"A multi-millionaire," she replied.

★ **Finished**

A long-married couple were having dinner with a pair of newly-weds. *"You know,"* said the older wife, *"a man is not complete until he is married. Isn't that right, Henry?"* Her husband smiled and replied, *"Quite right, my dear. Once a man is married, he's really finished."*

★ **Fool and Money**

A fool and his money are soon married.

★ **Credit Cards**

Grow old along with me,
The best is yet to be,
I've got a credit card
And you've got three.

- Herbert V. Prochnow

Marriage ★★★

★ Good Marriage

A good marriage would be between a blind wife and a deaf husband.

★ Optimists

The best place to find optimists is at a marriage license bureau.

★ Thomas Fuller "of Marriage"

Deceive not thyself by overexpecting happiness in the married estate. Remember the nightingales which sing only some months in the spring, but commonly are silent when they have hatched their eggs.

★ Hunting Permit

A marriage license is a hunting permit that entitles you to one animal at a time.

★ Hail the Bridegroom

Hail the Bridegroom - hail the Bride! When the nuptial knot is tied.

★ Compass

No compass was ever invented for the high seas of matrimony.

Toll Free: 1-800-66-Speak
www.customlearning.com
copyright © 1988

Marriage ★★★

★ **Marriage is Singular**

Marriage is singular. You add one and one and make one.

★ **Staying Married**

Marriage wouldn't be so bad if men and women were as anxious to stay married as they are to get married.

★ **Bossed**

In marriage, he who hesitates is bossed!

★ **Defying Management**

Matrimony was probably the first union to defy management.

★ **Yearning and Earning**

Marriage is a union brought on by yearning, and maintained by earning.

★ **The Ideal**

They're telling this everywhere in Hollywood these days: A man finds his ideal woman is one who possesses virtue, beauty, amiability, loyalty, affection, domesticity, comradeship and patience. . . A woman finds her ideal man is one who possesses cash, dough, coin, currency and money!

Marriage ★★★

★ **Friends of Youth**

"May the friends of our youth be the companions of our old age."

★ **All Our Friends**

"May our house always be too small to hold all our friends."

- Myrtle Reed

Second Marriages ★★★

★ **Highest Compliment**

Were a man not to marry a second time, it might be concluded that his first wife had given him a disgust for marriage; but by taking a second wife he pays the highest compliment to the first.

- Samuel Johnson

★ **Sweets of Life**

A happy marriage has in it all the pleasures of friendship, all the enjoyments of sense and reason and, indeed, all the sweets of life.

- Joseph Addison

★ **Temptation**

Marriage is popular because it combines the maximum of temptation with the maximum of opportunity.

- Man and Superman: G.B. Shaw, 1903

Toll Free: 1-800-66-Speak
www.customlearning.com
copyright © 1988

Marriage ★★★

★ **End Bargain**

A world-without-end bargain.

- Love's Labour's Lost: Shakespeare, 1595

★ **Spaces**

Let there be spaces in your togetherness.

- The Prophet, on Marriage: Kahlil Gibran, 1923

★ **Sinew of Love**

Money is the sinew of love as well as of war.

- Gnomologia 3442: Thomas Fuller, 1642

★ **Treaty of Marriage**

You are embarked on a treaty of marriage, a work of such consequences that it may make you or mar you.

- Letter: James Howell, 5 Feb., 1625

★ **Honourable**

Marriage is honourable in all.

- New Testament

★ **Sanctity**

A nation stands or falls with the sanctity of it's domestic ties.

- Robertson

Marriage ★★★

★ **Love's History**

Love's history is not ended by marriage.

- Bayard Taylor

★ **First Bond**

The first bond of society is marriage.

- De Officüs: Cicero, 29 B.C.

★ **Money**

There is only one thing for a man to do who is married to a woman who enjoys spending money; and that is to enjoy earning it.

- Country Town Sayings: E.W. Howe, 1911

★ **Devotion**

There's nothing like the devotion of a married woman. It's a thing no married man knows anything about.

- Lady Windermere's Fan: Oscar Wilde, 1892

★ **Don't**

Advice to persons about to marry, "Don't".

- Punch, 1845

This is generally regarded as Punch's most famous and oft repeated quip.

Toll Free: 1-800-66-Speak
www.customlearning.com
copyright © 1988

Marriage ★★★

★ No Enemies

Marriage has no enemies that can survive a happy night.

> - Ancient Chinese Proverb: Date unknown

★ Dwell Together

Nothing is greater or better than this; that a man and wife dwell together in accord.

> - Odyssey: Homer, 850 B.C.

★ Infinite Debt

The sum which two married people owe to one another defies calculation. It is an infinite debt, which can only be discharged through all eternity.

> - Elective Affinities: Johann Van Goethe, 1808

★ Ideal Marriage

The ideal marriage is not one in which two people marry to be happy, but to make each other happy.

> - Roy L. Smith, 1886

★ Life together

Now you will feel no rain, for each of you will be shelter for the other.
Now you will feel no cold, for each of you will be warmth to the other.
Now there is no more loneliness.
Now you are two persons, but there is only one life before you.
Go now to your dwelling to enter into the days of your life together.
And may your days be good, and long upon the earth.

Marriage Quotations ★★★

★ One should believe in marriage as in the immortality of the soul.

- Honore de Balzac

★ If there is such a thing as a good marriage, it is because it resembles friendship rather than love.

- Michel E. de Montaign

★ Here's to marriage, that happy estate that resembles a pair of scissors: "So joined that they cannot be separated; often moving in opposite directions, yet punishing anyone who comes between them."

- Sydney Smith

★ In the opinion of the world, marriage ends all, as it does in a comedy. The truth is precisely the reverse, it begins all.

- Mme. Swetchine

★ Matrimony - the high sea for which no compass has yet been invented.

- Heinrich Heine

★ For in what stupid age or nation, was marriage ever out of fashion?

- Samuel Butler

★ To marry is to halve your rights and double your duties.

- Arthur Schopenhauer

★ Keep your eyes wide open before marriage, half shut afterwards.

- Benjamin Franklin

★ A man's friendships are, like his will, invalidated by marriage - but they are also no less invalidated by the marriage of his friends.

- Samuel Butler

Toll Free: 1-800-66-Speak
www.customlearning.com
copyright © 1988

Marriage Definitions ★★★

★ **Marriage:**Requires falling in love many times - always with the same person.

★ **Marriage:**Is the only known example of the happy meeting of the immovable object and the irresistible force.

- Ogden Nash

★ **Marriage:**Is that relation between man and woman in which the independence is equal, the dependence mutual and the obligation reciprocal.

★ **Marriage:**Is a mutual admiration society in which one person is always right and the other is always the husband.

★ **Happy Marriage**

There was a couple who had an outstandingly happy and successful marriage, and the husband was once asked to what he attributed this remarkable situation.

"It's simple," he said, *"Division of labour. My wife makes all the small, routine decisions. She decides what house we buy, where we go on vacation, whether the kids go to private schools, if I should change my job, etc."*

"And You?"

"I make the big fundamental decisions. I decide if Canada should have free trade with the U.S., if Petro Canada should be sold, and so on."

Mothers ★★★

★ Whose Mother?

A couple had been married for 20 years, and were to celebrate by taking a trip. While talking over their plans one evening, the husband now and then glanced into the next room where an old lady was sitting doing her knitting. *"The only thing,"* he finally said in a hushed voice, *"is that for once, I'd like to be by ourselves. I'd like to take this trip without your mother."*

"My mother," exclaimed the wife. *"I thought she was your mother."*

★ Giving the Daughter Away

At a wedding, a father gives his daughter up with reluctance, and a mother gives her up with relief!

Parents ★★★

★ Happiest Couple

At a wedding, the happiest couple is sometimes the Bride and Groom: But most often, it is the Bride's parents.

★ True Love; True Joy

"It is written: 'When children find true love, parents find true joy.' Here's to your 'joy' and ours, from this day forward."

Toll Free: 1-800-66-Speak
www.customlearning.com
copyright © 1988

Single Females ★★★

★ Goddess Athena

"Professor Peabody," inquired a young thing, *"was the goddess Athena married?"*

"My dear," replied the sage professor, *"Athena was the goddess of wisdom. Naturally, she remained single."*

★ Reaching 30

No woman ever reaches thirty without having been asked to marry - at least by her parents.

★ Nobody Loves Her

Miss Henshaw, a spinster lady, was invited to chaperone a sleigh ride. The other chaperone was to be the eligible minister of a nearby church. As they were racing through the winter night, Miss Henshaw heaved a great sigh.

"Why, whatever is the matter?" asked the minister.

"Oh, it's just that nobody loves me, and besides, my hands are cold."

"Nonsense," replied the minister. *"God loves you, and you can sit on your hands."*

★ Wedding Music

A woman of sixty, like a girl of six, runs at the sound of wedding music.

- Babylonian Talmud: Jebamoth, 450 B.C.

★ Masterpiece

Nature intended that woman would be her masterpiece.

- Lessing

Single Females ★★★

★ **No Need for Husbands**

"Tell me, Aunt Ada, why is it you never married?" inquired Mary.

"Well Mary, I have a dog that snarls, a parrot that swears, a chimney that smokes, and a cat that stays out all night. I just never needed a husband."

★ **Marry Again**

For I'm not so old, and I'm not so plain, and I'm quite prepared to marry again.

- Iolanthe: W.S. Gilbert, 1882

★ **Deliberate**

The woman that deliberates is lost.

- Addison

Toll Free: 1-800-66-Speak
www.customlearning.com
copyright © 1988

Sex ★★★

★ Garlic

Italians have had a birth control pill for hundreds of years. It's called garlic.

★ Phony

A disenchanted husband was watching his wife get undressed. She removed her wig, her false eyelashes, her makeup, her padded bra, and her girdle, and what was left prompted her spouse to say, *"You know, Mary you're not the girl I married. In fact, you never were."*

★ Could Be Fatal

A man of 95 informed his doctor that he was planning on marrying a 22 year old nightclub entertainer.

"I hope you realize that this could be fatal," warned the doctor.

"I wish you hadn't said that, Doc," said the old man. *"I'd feel real bad now if she dies."*

★ Bouncing Cheque

A gorgeous young girl got into the elevator and asked to be taken to the penthouse home of the very rich and eccentric Mr. Green. About three hours later the elevator operator got a call from the penthouse and arrived just in time to hear this tender parting: *"Good night; Mr. Green, I've had a wonderful time - unless the cheque bounces."*

★ Adult Movies

After viewing some of the new "adult" movies Joan asked her husband why he never made love to her the way the men in the movies made love.

"Are you serious?" replied the husband. *"Do you know how much they pay those guys to do that?"*

Sex ★★★

★ **Great Temptation**

The Dean of Women at a small college was lecturing her students on moral virtues.

"In moments of great temptation," she said, *"just ask yourself one question: Is this hour of sinful pleasure worth a lifetime of disgrace?"* Having said her piece, the Dean then asked if there were questions.

One pretty young girl raised her hand and asked quietly,

"Can you really make it last an hour?"

★ **Wise Union**

The sexes were made for each other and only in the wise and loving union of the two is the fullness of health and duty and happiness to be expected.

- William Hall

★ **Shy and Honorable**

This fellow was so shy and honorable

- his wife went on their honeymoon by herself

- because he didn't believe in sleeping with a married woman.

Toll Free: 1-800-66-Speak
www.customlearning.com
copyright © 1988

Weddings ★★★

★ Acquiring a Mind of her Own

A wedding is a ceremony at which a woman acquires another mind of her own.

★ Wedding Ritual

A wedding is a ritual marking the time when a woman stops dating and starts intimidating.

★ Far From Broke

"You can't be serious!" gasped Amy. *"You aren't really going to marry that crazy old man even if he is supposed to be a millionaire."*

"Oh yes, I am," replied her friend firmly. *"He may be cracked, but he's far from broke."*

★ Customs

Customs may not be as wise as laws, but they are always more popular.

- Speech, House of Commons: Disraeli, 1870

Weddings ★★★

★ **Love Your Enemies**

It may be hard for a girl to love her enemies, but she usually sends them an announcement of her wedding.

★ **Listening to Wife**

A wedding is a ceremony at which a man chooses the woman he wants to spend the rest of his life listening to.

★ **Before the Wedding**

Before the wedding, you expect too much of marriage; after the wedding, you get too much of it.

★ **"I Do"**

There are no words in the English language that lead to as many arguments as "I do."

★ **Movie Stars**

The happiest days in a movie stars life are her wedding days.

★ **Wedding Happiness**

Every wedding leads to happiness, if not for the couple, then for their enemies.

Toll Free: 1-800-66-Speak
www.customlearning.com
copyright © 1988

Weddings ★★★

★ Book of Common Prayer

1. *"To have and to hold from this day forward, for better, for worse, for richer, for poorer, in sickness, and in health, to love and to cherish, 'till death do us part."*

2. *"With this ring I thee wed, with my body I thee worship, and with all my worldly goods I thee endow."*

★ Up the Aisle

A little girl, at her first church wedding, suddenly whispered loudly to her mother: *"Mummy, has the lady changed her mind?"*

"Why, what do you mean?" the mother asked.

"Well, she went up the aisle with one man and came back with another."

★ Elopement

If it weren't for the presents, an elopement would be preferable.

★ W.S. Gilbert

Happiness untold awaits them When the parson consecrates them.

- W.S. Gilbert

★ Surrendering

A wedding is a ceremony at which a woman surrenders before she proceeds to dictate her own terms.

Weddings ★★★

★ **In Las Vegas**

Sign on Las Vegas lawyer's door: "Satisfaction guaranteed or your honey back."

★ **J.G. Saxe**

I asked of Echo t'other day
    (Whose words are few and often funny),
What to a novice she could say
    Of courtship, love and matrimony.
    Quoth Echo, plainly, - "Matter-o-money."

★ **Matthew**

"What therefore God hath joined together, let no man put asunder."

                - Matthew, XIX, 6

★ **Genesis**

Therefore shall a man leave his father and his mother, and shall cleave unto his wife; and they shall be one flesh.

                - Genesis II, 24

★ **The Altar**

The altar is the place where many a man and woman are mispronounced man and wife.

Toll Free: 1-800-66-Speak
www.customlearning.com
copyright © 1988

Weddings ★★★

★ **Leading a Man to the Halter**

A wedding is the bridal day when a woman leads a man to the halter.

★ **We Before I**

Every bride and groom would do well to remember that in the wedding, the we comes before the I.

★ **Without a Hitch**

The only wedding that is sure to go off without a hitch is when the groom doesn't show up.

★ **Life and Liberty**

A wedding is a ceremony that alters a man's life, liberty and pursuit of happiness.

★ **Going Steady**

Many a wedding takes place when a man can't afford to go steady with a girl any longer.

★ **Games of Chance**

Ministers who are opposed to games of chance somehow don't object to performing wedding ceremonies.

Weddings ★★★

★ Easier Said Than Done

A good many things are easier said than done - including the marriage vows.

★ Wedding Formality

A wedding is a formality a man has to go through before going to work for a new boss.

★ Arguments Forever

A wedding takes only a few hours, the arguments can go on forever.

★ Silver Sixpence

Something old, something new,
Something borrowed, something blue,
And a silver sixpence in her shoe.

- Wedding Rhyme - Anonymous

★ Pop the Question

"We're all delighted to join with _____(bride) and _____ (groom) on this special occasion, but I know you're all dying to find out how it happened. Well, at great danger to myself, I obtained a transcript of how _____ popped the question. He said, "You know _____, I'm thinking of asking some girl to marry me. What do you think of the idea? To which _____ replied, "It's a great idea, if you ask me!" and _____ did, and that's why we're all here."

Toll Free: 1-800-66-Speak
www.customlearning.com
copyright © 1988

Weddings ★★★

★ **Lifetime of Love**

To the Bride and Groom - may they have a lifetime of love, and an eternity of happiness.

- Anonymous

★ **Sunlight of Love**

Here's to the Bride and Groom - may their joys be as bright as the morning, and their sorrows but shadows that fade in the sunlight of love.

- Anonymous

★ **Eden**

The voice that breathed o'er Eden
That earliest wedding day,
That primal marriage blessing,
It hath not passed away.

- Holy Matrimony: John Deble,1869

★ **Wedding Gifts:**

People seldom think alike until it is time to buy a wedding gift.

★ **Invitation**

An invitation to a wedding invokes more trouble than a summons to a police court.

- William Feather, Date Unknown

Wives

★ **Foot Down**

A wedding marks the time when a woman stops putting her best foot forward and starts putting her foot down.

★ **Take It Away**

Two vacationing merchants from the garment centre were reclining in Miami. Their conversation turned to a beautiful movie star who was staying at their hotel.

"Look," said one, *"If you take away that gorgeous figure, that beautiful blonde hair, those expensive clothes, and that perfect face, then what's left?"*

"My wife," came the grim reply.

★ **His Birthday**

Jane: *"Today's your birthday, and have I got a wonderful surprise for you."*

Jack: *"Great, I can hardly wait to see it."*

Jane: *"Just a minute and I'll put it on."*

Toll Free: 1-800-66-Speak
www.customlearning.com
copyright © 1988

Wives ★★★

★ Plastic Surgery

One businessman to another: *"My wife had plastic surgery yesterday. - I cut off her credit cards."*

★ Financial Wizard

"Daddy," said little Mary, *"what's a financial wizard."*

"Well, darling," replied her Dad, *"that's a guy who has discovered some magic for making more money than his wife can spend."*

★ Definition of Wife

Continual buzzing in a man's ear.

★ Not Mad

Wife to newspaper-reading husband: *"You couldn't have been listening, or you would be mad."*

★ Listen

The best way to get along happily with your wife is to go home every evening and give her a thorough listening to.

Wives ✳✳✳

✳ Piece of Mind

"You can tell me the truth, Doc," said Harry.

"Well," replied the doctor, *"then I must tell you that your wife is insane. Her mind is completely gone."*

"I'm not really surprised, Doc. After all, she's given me a piece of it every day for the last fifteen years."

✳ Gardening for Her

Some advice to a husband planning a garden
Here's some advice
It'll pay you to heed.
Don't plant more
Than your wife can weed.

✳ Tax Forms

"Why have I been feeding my wife six meals a day?"

"Well, my tax accountant said I had to fill out my wife's form this year."

✳ Interrupting

"I haven't spoken to my wife in two weeks! Don't want to interrupt her."

✳ Private and Personal

Betty: *"I'm sorry to phone you at the office, dear, but you have a special delivery letter which just arrived marked, 'private and personal.'"*

Bob: *"Okay, what does it say?"*

Toll Free: 1-800-66-Speak
www.customlearning.com
copyright © 1988

Wives ★★★

★ Criticizing

Before you criticize your wife's faults, consider that it may have been those very same defects that prevented her from marrying a better man.

★ Marrying Well

The man who marries well seldom has a wife who does.

★ Good Spouse

In order to have a good spouse, you have to be one.

★ Depend on a Woman

The only time you can depend upon a woman not to change her mind is at her wedding.

★ Getting a Raise

Nothing makes a woman's clothes go out of style faster than her husband getting a raise.

★ Superior

He used to subscribe to the theory that men are superior to women. That was until his wife canceled the subscription.

Wives ★★★

★ Doing Dishes

The best way for an overworked housewife to have a few minutes to herself at the end of the day is to begin to do dishes.

★ No Matter Who Left It

They say he married her because her uncle left her a million dollars! But he claimed he'd have married her no matter who left it to her.

★ Marrying For Looks

Marrying a girl for her looks is like buying a house for its paint.

★ Four Letter Words

My wife admits that she often feels repelled by four letter words, such as cook, wash, iron, dust, work.

★ His and Hers

His wife is leading a double life complains one husband - hers and his.

★ Co-Pilot

The sweet wife riding in the car with her husband said to him,

"Try not to think of me as a back seat driver, darling. Think of me as your co-pilot."

Toll Free: 1-800-66-Speak
www.customlearning.com
copyright © 1988

Wives ★★★

★ **Beautiful Clothes**

By the time a man is in shape to buy his wife beautiful clothes, she isn't.

★ **Different**

"I married my wife because she was different from the other women I had met."

★ **Fine Meals**

His wife prepares the finest meals you ever thaw.

★ **Support**

Said one wife to another: *"I wish I had waited to get married until I was able to support a husband."*

★ **Waiting**

Every girl waits for the right man to come along, but in the meantime she gets married.

★ **Saving Money**

A wife was busy convincing her husband that she really did need the new dress she had just bought. *"Look at it this way, darling,"* she reasoned. *"The dress was originally $100. I bought it when it was marked down to $50. So I really bought the dress with the $50 I saved."*

Wives ★★★

★ Dressing Now

"Good news, dear," called the husband as he came into the house. *"I picked up two tickets for the theater on the way home from work."*

"Oh, that's wonderful," said the wife. *"I'll start dressing right away."*

"That's a good idea," he said. *"The tickets are for tomorrow night."*

★ Alert Driver

"My wife happens to be a very alert driver," the husband stated proudly. *"In fact yesterday, she stopped on a dime. Unfortunately, it was in a parking meter."*

★ Advice to Husbands

Some more advice for husbands: Never contradict your wife, it's only your word against thousands of hers.

★ Listening to Wife

Said one husband to another: *"My wife talks to herself."* Second husband: *"So does mine, but she doesn't know it, she thinks I'm listening."*

★ William Cooper

What is there in the value of life
Half so delightful as a wife,
When friendship, love and peace combine
To stamp the marriage-bond divine?

- William Cooper

Toll Free: 1-800-66-Speak
www.customlearning.com
copyright © 1988

Wives ★★★

★ Outspoken

I admit my wife is outspoken, but by whom?

★ Proverbs

Who so findeth a wife findeth a good thing.

- Proverbs XVIII, 22

★ Thinking Alike

A man and his wife may think alike, but she gets the first crack at the think.

★ Diplomacy

DIPLOMACY is telling your wife that her beauty makes time stand still, instead of saying that her face would stop a clock.

★ Marriage is a Drag

The young wife complained to her friend: *"Marriage is such a drag. You wash dishes, make beds and vacuum, and then, two weeks later, you have it to do all over again."*

★ Rose Pastor Stokes

Some pray to marry the man they love, My prayer will somewhat vary:

I humbly pray to Heaven above That I love the man I marry.

- Rose Pastor Stokes

Wives ★★★

★ **No Life on Mars**

My neighbor says he is sure there is no life on Mars. No call there has ever shown up on his wife's phone bill.

★ **Strikes Like Lightning**

At lunch the other day a fellow said he was worried about his wife because she drove like lightning. And I said, *"I didn't know that she drove fast."*

He said: *"She doesn't, she strikes trees."*

★ **No Shopping**

"Boss, can I take tomorrow off?" asked poor, meek Roger. *"My wife wants me to go shopping with her."*

"You cannot! What do you think I'm running here - a resort?"

"Thanks, boss," was his reply. *"You don't know how much I appreciate this."*

★ **Advice**

There are two ways to handle a woman, and nobody knows either of them.

★ **Propose**

A woman might as well propose: Her husband will claim she did.

★ **Bigamy**

Bigamy is having one wife too many. Monogamy, in certain instances, is the same thing.

- London Opinion: Unknown

Toll Free: 1-800-66-Speak
www.customlearning.com
copyright © 1988

Wives ★★★

★ **Living Arrows**

You are the bows from which your living children as living arrows are sent forth.

- The Prophet, on Children: Kahlil Gibran, 1923

★ **Seven Years**

If a man stays away from his wife for seven years, the law presumes the separation to have killed him; yet according to our daily experience, it might well prolong his life.

- Scinticae Jones: Charles Darling, 1879

★ **Useless Each Without**

As unto the bow the cord is,

So unto the man is woman;

Though she bends him, she obeys him,

Though she draws him yet she follows

Useless each without the other!

- Longfellow

★ **Great Longevity**

A wife is essential for great longevity; she is the receptacle of half a man's cares and two-thirds of his ill-humour.

- Charles Reade

Toll Free: 1-800-66-Speak
www.customlearning.com
copyright © 1988

Addendum

Speech Master – A Short Course on Public Speaking   421

    Speech Writing   422

    Physical Delivery   424

    Vocal Delivery   426

    Speech Types   427

    Graceful Speeches (and responding to them)   429

    Professional Insights   431

    One Minute Name Memory   435

    The L.I.S.T.E.N. Name Memory Formula   438

Dress for Speaking Success   439

Speech Master
A Short Course on Public Speaking

Note: To Wedding M.C.'s

The following ten pages is a condensed summary of our "Speech Master" effective speaking course.

It is included in The Wedding M.C. as a "bonus".

While some of the material is relevant to the task at hand, most of the content is applicable to non-wedding speaking assignments.

We trust you will find it useful for future events in the development of your speaking career.

Speech Writing — 422
- Speech Structure
- The Salutation
- Topic Selection and Research
- Audience Participation

Physical Delivery — 424
- Nervousness
- Use of Notes
- Eye Contact
- Posture and Timing
- Hand Gestures
- Use of Microphone

Vocal Delivery — 426
- Voice Inflection
- Pauses & Pace
- Vocabulary & Grammar
- Breathing
- Diction & Articulation

Speech Types — 427
- Evaluation
- The Persuasive Speech
- The Informative Speech
- Speaker Introduction
- The Entertaining Speech

Graceful Speeches — 429
- The Welcome
- The Installation Speech
- The Presentation & Acceptance Speech
- The Toast & Reply
- The Retirement Speech

Speech Writing

Speech Structure

The Title should create curiosity and drama. It must be personalized for each audience.

Your Mission is to identify and communicate the basic idea, feeling or information you want your audience to take away when they leave.

The Opening - Your opening is vital. Assume your audience is about to fall asleep. Get their attention now or you may never get it at all. Build a bridge by involving each person. Techniques include appropriate humour, shocking fact, striking quotation, personal anecdote, thought provoking question or brief human interest story. Above all the opening should answer the question, **"Why should I listen?"**

The Outline - Tell your audience what you're going to tell them, ie. where you're going to take them.

The Body - Tell them. . . take them there: never make a point without a story, or tell a story without a point. Use facts sparingly and translate them so the audience can relate to them. Be fair and present to both points of view. Quote sources. Use sizzle and be unusual. Avoid personal opinions. Focus on personal experiences and success stories of others to illustrate ideas.

The Summary - Tell them what you told them. . . ie. where you took them.

The Close - Your objective is to build a climax, drive the point home and leave the audience wanting more. Be certain to relate the close to your opening. Acknowledge your audience. Remember, the degree to which you acknowledge them, they'll acknowledge you. Some closing techniques: use a moving quotation or excerpt from a song. Issue a challenge. Know your final sentence word for word.

Toll Free: 1-800-66-Speak
www.customlearning.com
copyright © 1988

Speech Writing (continued)

Topic Selection and Research

Apply two tests: Does it fit (1) the group? (2) the occasion? Write down ideas as you go and test the ideas on others. Obtain research from businesses, friends, library, T.V., newspaper, history, professionals, internet, etc.

The Salutation "The Act of Greeting" Correct pronunciation of names and titles is extremely important. Begin with the Chairman and with "Ladies and Gentlemen," Then address the most important to least. i.e.

1) Gathering chairmen,

2) Clergy,

3) Elected representatives,

4) Non-host group special guests,

5) Host group special guests,

6) Members,

7) Guests.

Audience Participation

Your primary concern is to know how your audience is thinking, feeling or reacting.

Physical Delivery

Nervousness

To be nervous is normal, healthy and causes adrenaline to bring out your best. The key is to put nervousness to work for you. It is overcome by self-confidence which comes from experience. There are three sources of nervousness:

1)   failure to control speech content;

2)   failure to control yourself;

3)   failure to control the audience.

With proper training and preparation, all 3 are completely controllable.

Posture and Timing

Get to the lectern quickly by the easiest route. Stand erect, feet six inches apart, one foot forward, hands at your sides. Establish eye contact with the entire audience before beginning. Always start and end on time. Rehearsing your speech will give you a good estimate of its time.

Use of Notes

Collect ideas and sort them into sequence. Write them out in longhand. Then select key points and transpose onto 4" x 6" cards. Practice three times, and privately review three times just before delivery. Trust yourself. Don't memorize.

Hand Gestures and Eye Contact

Be aware that only 7% of communication is verbal, then use your hand gestures to describe (size, height, shape), to locate (closeness, distance, certain objects and people) and to emphasize (importance, urgency, special words and phrases). Gestures can also enhance the expression of emotion. Use neither too many nor too few gestures and when not gesturing, leave your hands at your sides.

Three keys to remember: simplicity, appropriateness and variety. Begin by systematically establishing eye contact with the entire audience, ie. right, centre, left. Don't stare at shoes, at the ceiling, above heads, at your notes or at one person. Don't be distracted. "Read" your audience while effecting eye contact.

Toll Free: 1-800-66-Speak
www.customlearning.com
copyright © 1988

Physical Delivery (continued)

Use of Microphone

Every microphone is different, so check it out in advance. Treat it as your friend. You need it! Keep the microphone at a distance of approximately 15" and don't shout. Talk naturally. Don't forget to coach other speakers on the use of the microphone for height, speaking, etc.

Vocal Delivery

Voice Inflection

The use of voice inflection (modulation, variation) can make the difference between an average and a great speaker. An effective voice motivates. You can vary the following components of your voice: pitch, volume and rate of speaking. Sincerity, enthusiasm, joy, anger, and a host of other emotions are reflected in a speaker's competent use of his/her voice. Your voice is a powerful tool - Use It Well!!

Breathing

Practice deep breathing beforehand to relax. With normal inhalation, it doesn't work to raise your shoulders.

Pauses & Pace

Use a pause to make or emphasize a point and let the audience absorb it. A pause can be an opportunity to think, breathe, change pitch or rate of delivery, regain audience attention or to change ideas. Plan your pauses and vary their length. Use the time to refer to notes, to change facial expression or hand gestures.

Diction & Articulation

Your objective is to speak in accordance with the approved practice of the audience. The dictionary is the best guide for pronunciation. Poor enunciation comes from slurred or slovenly speech. Reading aloud daily (10 - 30 mins.) is excellent practice. Good pronunciation is putting the accent on the proper syllables. Good articulation occurs when every sound in every word is distinctly audible.

Vocabulary & Grammar

Words are labels. They can identify facts or be wrongly interpreted. They act as incitements and create attitudes. Select your words carefully. . . avoid being trite, eg. "unaccustomed as I am to public speaking" etc. An audience may not talk back, but they do "react back" with facial features, body language, laughter, snoring or attentiveness. Communication needs to be two-way. If you ignore your audience's response, you're not communicating, but unloading. Above all, approach the subject from the point of view of your listener. **Read, Read, Read** your audience.

Toll Free: 1-800-66-Speak
www.customlearning.com
copyright © 1988

Speech Types

The Speaker Introduction

Be brief, never more than 90 seconds. Answer these audience questions: Why this subject? For this audience? At this time? By this speaker? Avoid using stale phrases, exaggerating speakers achievements, stealing the spotlight. (Don't give the speech.) Be sure the last 2 words you say are the speaker's name - this is the audience's cue to applaud. As an MC, you would give a brief introduction to who you are and your relation to the bride and groom when you announce the program is about to begin in 5 minutes, or when people have taken their seats and the program is beginning.

The Persuasive Speech

The purpose is to win over, to convince and to overcome objections. Your strategy should be - put yourself in the position of your most articulate opponent. Anticipate every objection, acknowledge it and answer it. Appeal to emotions. We make decisions with emotion and defend them with logic. Be sincere, use humour, be fair. Relate your arguments so the audience can feel them personally. Tie in your views to fundamental human values. eg. peace, freedom. Don't open with hostile remarks, be flippant, play win/lose, be dogmatic or compromise your views.

The Entertainig Speech

The objective is to entertain. The perfect formula: 98% laughter, 2% message. A rule of thumb you should follow is: one hour preparation for one minute of delivery. Be brief, use personal experiences. Humour is a tension relief mechanism that is caused by surprise. Test out your presentation as much as possible. (See The Treasury of Wit and Wisdom, pages 390 to 394).

Speech Types (continued)

The Informative Speech

The objective is to inform in order to create understanding. Obstacles to clarity include not fully knowing the subject, attempting to impress rather than inform, being too general, picking too broad a topic and losing your objectivity. Here are some keys to accuracy:

1. interpret your facts from the audience's point of view, taking into consideration their education and background;

2. define terms;

3. clarify categories;

4. present both points of view;

5. be honest and don't ignore reality.

Always relate large facts (and numbers) to something with which the audience is familiar. Use idea transitions. eg. *"Now that we have -- ---, let us turn to ----."*

The Evaluation

The genius of great speakers is their desire to consistently seek constructive feedback and evaluation. Always "sandwich" criticisms between positive comments. Always focus on useful recommendations for improvement.

Toll Free: 1-800-66-Speak
www.customlearning.com
copyright © 1988

Graceful Speeches
(and responding to them)

The Welcoming Speech

Refer to the occasion and express goodwill on behalf of all. Acknowledge the achievement(s) of visitor(s) and be brief. Accept a welcome simply. Reverse the spotlight to your audience.

The Toast & Reply

Proposing a toast is a great honour. It is a mini-speech. Prepare it with care. State who is being toasted, why, and how they are relevant to the audience. Express goodwill on behalf of all. Always conclude with: "Ladies and Gentlemen please join me, stand and charge your glasses in a toast to(ie.) The Bride." "To the Bride".

Thanking a Speaker

Acknowledge the speaker for his/her preparation, useful information, special news, entertainment, long journey, etc. Avoid personal comments on speech content. Be sincere and use humour with caution. Unless there is a special reason, don't insist the gift be opened in public. Express appreciation on behalf of the audience.

The Reply.

Avoid one unless "forced to." Acknowledge audience, express your thanks and keep it short.

The Presentation Speech

Be sure to clearly identify the occasion. Express goodwill on behalf of the group and instruct the recipient on how to receive the award. Present the award, shake hands and pose for a photo (optional). Determine ahead of time the appropriateness of the recipient opening the gift on stage and/or their making public remarks.

Graceful Speeches (continued)

The Acceptance.

Express your sincere thanks and acknowledge debt to the group. Keep it short!

The Installation Speech

Express your appreciation of the honour conferred. Recognize the preceding holder of the office. You may refer briefly to your policy objectives. Some appropriate themes are service, humility and challenge.

The Retirement Speech

Acknowledge kind remarks and any gift(s). Express your thanks for support from your employer and/or co-worker(s). Summarize (briefly) your career, using a few humourous anecdotes. Offer your successor support and ask the audience to do likewise.

Toll Free: 1-800-66-Speak
www.customlearning.com
copyright © 1988

Professional Insights

I have studied and taught effective speaking for over twenty years. Since 1984 I have been a professional speaker, motivating and educating audiences throughout Canada and the United States.

In 1985 I delivered a keynote speech, which had all the right basic ingredients, but didn't work!

A week later, in preparation for another professional speaking appearance, I sat in a hot tub and attempted to analyze what had gone wrong and to summarize the insights gained from almost two decades of speaking to over 350,000 people. The following 35 speaking insights resulted, and I frequently review them prior to a major speaking event.

I am pleased to present them to you, with the hope you won't need to repeat the same mistakes, but rather learn from another's successes.

While these insights relate to overall excellence in presentation skills, they are just as applicable to everything you will be doing as an M.C.

General Strategy

1. The shorter the better. **Less is more**. Nice guys finish fast.

2. Encourage **audience participation** and involvement through questions and actions.

3. You **can't please everyone,** so don't try.

4. **Humility** beats ego 100 to 1.

5. Approach every speech as if it were your **first and last**.

6. Remember - **an audience** is nothing more than a group of individuals who think, feel and react exactly like you do.

7. An audience will acknowledge you to the degree you **acknowledge them**

Professional Insights (continued)

Speech Preparation

8. Know the audience beforehand. One handshake before is worth 10 after.

9. Always review notes 3 times prior to delivery. Never read a speech.

Your Mission

10. A speech without a clear objective, purpose or mission is a waste of time.

Speech Outline

11. Tell the audience what you're going to tell them. Tell them. Then tell them what you told them.

Delivery

12. Body language, enthusiasm and sincerity are 9 times more effective than words.

13. Silent pauses are more powerful than noisy screams.

14. A whisper carries more weight than a scream.

15. Voice variety is the spice of a speech.

Opening

16. If you don't get the audience's attention with the opening, you may never!

Body of The Speech/Content

17. One hour of research and preparation is worth one minute of delivery.

18. Content must relate to and identify with the audience.

19. Use humour in the beginning, middle and end. The perfect speech is 14 minutes laughter and 1 minute "the point."

20. A good quotation, story, anecdote or joke is worth 1000 pictures.

21. The most effective source of knowledge, wisdom or ideas is your personal experience.

22. An audience thinks about facts, but remembers an emotional experience. **Appeal** to emotions.

Toll Free: 1-800-66-Speak
www.customlearning.com
copyright © 1988

Professional Insights (continued)

23. Facts outweigh opinions 10 to 1.

24. To make a point
    - state the point
    - support it with fact
    - use an example
        - humour - anecdote
        - story - quotation

    In order to demonstrate its truth

    - re-state the point

25. One prop may be worth 100 facts.

26. Anticipating one objection is worth 2 positive arguments.

27. The amount of energy you place on a negative issue, will equate directly to the amount of energy your audience does.

28. Stating what unites us is twice as effective as stating what divides us.

29. Right/Wrong results in Win/Lose.

30. Never criticize or attack - "He who throws dirt loses ground."

31. Suggest - don't tell.

32. If your argument is based on "need", your audience will mirror that attitude.

Closing

33. The close is more important than the opening and body.

34. The close must relate to and support the opening.

35. What you say last, is what your audience will remember first.

Toll Free: 1-800-66-Speak
www.customlearning.com
copyright © 1988

One Minute Name Memory™

How to Remember Names
Putting Your Memory to Work for You

by Brian Lee, CSP

Embarrassment is a powerful motivator. I will never forget the moment I knew I had to do something about remembering names. I failed to recognize a woman who had worked **40** long days on my Legislative Assembly campaign. *"Brian, don't you REMEMBER me?"* she asked. It turned out she had helped every day of my campaign.

I attempted to apologize by sending drinks to her table all evening, but one can never really make up for that kind of oversight. And that's when I decided to make it a priority to remember people and their names. I created a technique which, over the years, developed into a formula to help me link names and faces.

It works for me and, after teaching it to dozens of people from many walks of life, I've found that it works for anyone who really wants it to work. Belva Goede, the mayor of Chauvin, Alberta, for example, reports after using the technique for four months, *"I have a lot of snakes and rabbits running around in my head now and I can always link them with the name. The technique's definitely improved my memory."*

The secret to remembering anything, not only names, is in moving the item from your short-term memory (which lasts up to a minute), into your long-term memory (which can last for years). Scientists call this process "consolidation" in the brain. Consolidation is believed to result in a memory trace: an actual alteration in the structure of the brain.

The **"L.I.S.T.E.N."** formula I have designed helps your brain move what you want to remember from your short-term memory to your long-term memory. **L.I.S.T.E.N.** stands for the six simple steps to follow when introduced to a person.

L. is for "LISTEN." Often when we're being introduced we do not focus on the name we're hearing for the first time but instead, on our own name. That is because our own names constitute the two most powerful words in our vocabulary. But we can be much more effective if we master the two most powerful words in the other person's vocabulary. So listen carefully to the name.

I. is for "INITIATE questions". Showing an interest in a person's name is showing an interest in him or her. People like that. So ask how the name is spelled, where it came from, what it means or the country of its origin. This will not only give you extra "hooks" for your memory, but also prevent you from getting the name wrong. Studies show that once you begin repeating a mistake, you will have it engraved on your brain and find it very difficult to unlearn.

S. is for "SAY it often". The key to memory and learning is "spaced repetition," which means that when you're studying for an exam or attempting to remember something for your line of work, the best thing to do is study it, go away from it, return and study it again. Research shows repetition seems to cause anatomical and chemical changes in the brain that fix learned material in the memory and provide easy access to it.

When you meet people, you have a chance to repeat their names - both names - three times; at the beginning, in the middle and at the end of the conversation, so grab that opportunity.

T. is for "TRANSLATE the name into a silly picture." Memory is related primarily to what we see, not to what we hear, which is why most people "know the face but can't remember the name." In fact, where visual perception is concerned, the average person has almost total recall, a fact that leads scientists to believe the brain has separate systems for storing pictorial and linguistic memories. Visual images are taken in and preserved directly, while words have a much more complex route of decoding and recoding before being stored. So make a picture in your mind out of the person's name - the more ridiculous the better because we remember the extraordinary much better than the ordinary.

For example, take my name, Brian Lee. Brian is often misspelled as "Brain", so visualize a brain lying on the ground. Lee may make you think of the Confederate army, so visualize a Confederate flag and, just to make it memorable, stick that flag into the brain and have a little blood ooze out. Got it? It is effective because the more silly and emotional the picture, the more memorable.

Toll Free: 1-800-66-Speak
www.customlearning.com
copyright © 1988

E. is for "ETCH the picture in key facial features." Look at the person and decide what is more unforgettable - the cute dimples or the chipped tooth, whatever it may be for you - and incorporate it into the silly picture step. For Brian Lee, a brain with a Confederate flag in it, bleeding into my dimples.

Many names automatically suggest a picture, like Winter, Wall, Stone, Hart and Fox, but most names are more abstract. Many of those, however, can conjure up an association and a picture - Graham may make you think of the cracker or the evangelist, Campbell the soup, Mantle the baseball player.

For even more abstract names, you have to use your imagination. Willene becomes Will lean; Tabatha, to bath ya; Gillespie, kills peas; Nestransky, nest across (trans) a ski. Or you can use rhyming nicknames like sad Ladd or poor Moore or cryin' Brian. It's a challenge that never gets boring.

When it comes to etching the picture to a facial feature, it's fortunate that every person's face is unique. Everyone has something memorable - look for bushy eyebrows, protruding ears, a scar, sunken cheeks, full lips, flaring nostrils. This attention to detail will also ensure that you do have total recall on faces you want to remember. Voices, too, can act as a memory aid: Is the voice high, low, squeaky, screeching, accented or sexy?

N. is for "NOTE it." If you can, obtain a business card and then on the front of the card write down the date and place of meeting, the most obvious facial feature and the subject most important to him or her. This will serve as an important memory jogger when you come across a business card you have no memory of receiving. If you can't obtain a business card from the person, use the back of one of yours to note all the information.

And that's it - the **L.I.S.T.E.N.** formula for remembering names. It may seem bothersome, but it quickly becomes a usable technique that takes a matter of seconds and, after awhile, most people are not even consciously aware they are using it. They simply find that when they see a face, a name appears with it.

We all have 18 billion brain cells, but we use only about 5 percent of them. **L.I.S.T.E.N.** helps call a few more into action. The brain can store up to 100 trillion items; most computers can only hold up to one billion.

When you choose to remember people's names, you're saying, "It's important to me." And the rewards of that choice range from increased confidence to more acquaintances. If you choose not to remember names, you pay the price - not only in dollars for drinks all evening - but in credibility and self-esteem.

At-A-Glance

One Minute Name Memory™
The L.I.S.T.E.N. Name Memory Formula

L   LISTEN carefully. Pronounce BOTH names correctly.

_____

_____

I   INITIATE questions - Origin? Meaning? Related to?

_____

_____

S   SAY both names three (3) times.

    1. Greeting   2. Conversing   3. Parting

_____

_____

T   TRANSLATE name into a silly PICTURE.

_____

_____

E   ETCH the picture into key facial features.

_____

_____

N   NOTE four (4) F.A.C.T.s

    F   Facial Feature (& name picture):

_____

    A   Activity & facility: (what event you were at, and building)

_____

    C   Contact date and city:

_____

    T   Topic of their greatest interest:

_____

Toll Free: 1-800-66-Speak
www.customlearning.com
copyright © 1988

Dress For Speaking Success

A. Introduction

- Your objective is to dress for **acceptance.**
- A Master of Ceremony's appearance should **complement** his/her message and not **distract** from it.
- Your overall appearance contributes to the **impact** of the message.
- 83% of a first impression is determined through the eye. eg. trust, attitude, authority, credibility & capability.
- Not only does appearance impact how others feel about you, it contributes to your **own** sense of **self** confidence.
- Above all, clothes should be **comfortable** and fit right.
- Flamboyant clothes are not recommended.

B. Tips For Both Men & Women

1. Consultation:
   - Find out what is being worn by the bridal party.
   - Check with the couple as to their preference.
   - Match bridal party or not? Formal or Semi Formal? Tuxedo or Long Gown?
2. **Personal Cleanliness:**
   - Bad breath is inexcusable. Brush your teeth and gargle.
   - Make sure cologne, hair application, etc. does not overpower.
   - Avoid using a toothpick in public.
   - Do not smoke in front of audiences, or when meeting guests prior to the event.

C. For Men Only:

1. **Suits**
   - Should be a suit, not sports jacket.
   - Should be in style, eg. width of lapels, pant cuffs or no cuffs?
   - Color - wear a darker color, ie. Navy Blue, Black, Dark Grey.
   - Avoid brown, or light grey.
   - Tuxedo - we suggest black only.

Dress for Speaking Success (Continued)

2. **Jackets**

   - Always button front of jacket. . . top button only unless double-breasted.
   - Do not remove jacket when speaking.
   - Wear jacket a little longer to add height.
   - Remove unnecessary items, ie. cigarettes, diary, keys, etc. before speaking.
   - Wear double-breasted to add width.
   - Double-breasted should be kept buttoned.

3. **Trousers**

   - Length of trousers is important.
   - Hem should be angled, slightly towards heel.
   - Cuff on pants is OK when in style.

4. **Vests**

   - Wearing a vest allows you to leave your jacket open.
   - Vest must fit exactly. . . not too tight.
   - Leave bottom button open.
   - Do not wear belt. . . use suspenders if necessary.

5. **Shirts**

   - Ideal color is white.
   - Plain white is better than white on white.
   - Size should fit exactly.
   - If color is preferred, very pale blue or soft yellow.
   - Avoid pink, solid red or pale lavender.
   - Should be lighter in color than your suit.
   - Long-sleeved only.
   - Nothing in shirt pocket (use suit pocket).
   - Collar length should be moderately stylish.
   - Button-down is OK.
   - Last button should be 3 inches below waist band of pants.

6. **Ties**

   - If you have a choice, wear a quality (well made) tie.
   - Must complement your outfit and not stand out.
   - Keep on the simple side.
   - Understate rather than overstate.
   - Stripes, paisley or plain tie with small pattern.

Toll Free: 1-800-66-Speak
www.customlearning.com
copyright © 1988

Dress For Speaking Success (Continued)

- Bow tie is acceptable only with tuxedo, unless it is your everyday practice.
- Length of tie should be to belt buckle unless wearing a vest. . . when it should be shorter and not show at the bottom.
- Should be darker in color than your suit.
- Avoid short ties, black ties, purple or any pattern that is hard to look at.
- When in doubt as to pattern, ask "will this distract?"
- Should match or contrast with shirt.
- Should not clash with suit.
- Do not wear if stained.

7. **Handkerchiefs**
- Must be clean.
- Could match tie color.

8. **Belts**
- Don't wear suspenders and a belt.
- Should match color of suit.
- Width should be in harmony with suit lapel.

9. **Shoes**
- Should look as if they are new or polished.
- Should be in style.
- Coordinate with clothing and socks, stockings.
- Heels should be of reasonable height and be in good repair.

10. **Socks**
- Never wear white.
- Mid calf or full executive length OK.
- Color should coordinate with suit.

11. **On Coordinating Clothes**
- Never put 2 patterns next to each other.
- Solid suit - pattern shirt - solid tie - O.K.
- Always separate pattern by a solid.
- Pinstripe suit OK with solid shirt.

Dress For Speaking Success (Continued)

12. **Jewelry**

    - A gold watch chain is OK.
    - Only one ring on each hand. . . the less the better.
    - Should be noiseless.
    - Don't play with it.

13. **Watches**

    - Watchstrap should be in good repair.
    - Preferably thin, plain metallic.
    - Avoid calculator or skin diver styles.
    - Avoid wearing a stretch band.

14. **Glasses**

    - Use contacts whenever possible in front of audience.
    - Wide at the temple.
    - Wider than the widest part of your face.
    - Eyebrows should show.
    - Half glasses may make you look older.
    - Match hair color to frame.
    - No sunglasses or glasses that change tint.

15. **Hair**

    - Regardless of length, should be clean, trimmed and neat.
    - Beard and mustache also should be clean, trimmed and neat.
    - No dandruff please - check shoulders.
    - Avoid extreme hair coloring.
    - Do not use excessive spray, gels or creams.

16. **For Large Men**

    - Avoid deep dark suits.
    - Never wear vests.
    - Avoid strong color contrasts.
    - Wear light soled shoes.

17. **For Small Men**

    - Wear pinstripe for authority.
    - Best shirt is solid white.
    - Glasses, if necessary, should be heavy.

Toll Free: 1-800-66-Speak
www.customlearning.com
copyright © 1988

Dress For Speaking Success (Continued)

C. For Women Only

1. The Outfit

- Goal is not to be imitation of a man.
- Black is out, as this is a fun event.
- White is reserved for the bride.
- Avoid competing with the wedding party, goal should be same "tone" of formality.
- Dress with jacket OK.
- Separates should be well coordinated.
- Avoid loud color.
- Skirt length modest but attractive on your leg.
- Medium to straight skirt.
- Never allow skirt or dress to show from underneath.
- Underclothes should never show.
- No hat please. Afternoon - OK.
- Don't wear anything that is too tight, too low, too loud, too clinging or that is see-through.
- Avoid clothing that needs adjusting, eg. long slip, spaghetti straps, etc.

2. Jackets

- Do not remove when speaking.

3. Blouse - Shirt

- Shirt sleeve should peek out a little.
- Necklines should not be too low.

4. Shoes

- Pump with moderate heel.

5. Nylons

- Should be flesh coloured or subdued-coordinated.
- Should be run-free.
- Take a spare pair just in case.

Dress For Speaking Success (Continued)

6. **Jewelry**

   - Less is more.
   - Wear jewelry that does not clank or distract from face or speech.

7. **Purse**

   - Should be compact, in proportion to size.
   - Leave at table.

8. **Glasses**

   - If you need to wear them, don't wear on a string around your neck.

9. **Make-Up**

   - Perfume should not arrive before you do.
   - Avoid excessive amounts.
   - Nail polish should not be chipped. Avoid excessive nail length.
   - No make up lines at chin.

In conclusion, make sure you are well-groomed.

Toll Free: 1-800-66-Speak
www.customlearning.com
copyright © 1988

Customer Service,
Professional Development

Author Profile   446

6 Powerful Reasons to put Brian Lee to work for you   447

Brian Lee CSP - Keynote/Seminar Topics   448

Brian's Clients Say It Best   449

Reader Satisfaction Survey   450

Brian Lee's Book Library   453

World Class Presentation Skills   454

World Class Customer Satisfaciton & Service Empowerment
Leadership   456

World Class Sales & Marketing   458

World Class Professional Development   460

Product Order Form   463

Business Reply Cards   465

Authored by Brian Lee, CSP
"Mr. Customer Satisfaction"
"Canada's "Mr. Enthusiasm"

Brian Lee CSP
Profile of an Author and World Class Professional Speaker

Active as a public speaker from the age of 15 when he completed a Junior Achievement course, Brian Lee CSP has applied his exceptional communications skills in a host of ways.

Becoming successful in business as the Vice-President of a major retail firm by the age of 25, he then entered politics 2 years later and was elected Calgary's youngest-ever Alderman. Nine productive years in public life on City Council and as a Provincial MLA provided Brian with public speaking opportunities on a daily basis.

Brian Lee's Career Highlights

❑ With twenty-one years (and some 60 weddings) M.C.'ing experience behind him, Brian Lee is also a past president of the Canadian Association of Professional Speakers (Alberta Chapter) and past Assistant Area Governor, Toastmasters International as well as past president of the University of Calgary Oxford Debating Society.

❑ Brian Lee, CSP is one of North America's leading experts in the field of World Class Customer Satisfaction and Change Leadership and is author of 4 books including "Satisfaction Guaranteed . . . How to Master the 6 Secrets of Lifetime Customer Loyalty."

❑ For two consecutive years, Brian has been evaluated by the International Customer Service Association Conference as the number one rated Customer Service Speaker in the World.

❑ Mr. "Customer Satisfaction" travels over 200,000 miles a year, delivering over 200 keynotes and seminars, and has spoken in 54 states and provinces and 12 countries worldwide.

❑ As both a speaker and implementation consultant to over 100 Fortune 500 corporations and Health Care Organizations, Brian is sought after as an advisor/coach to senior management, specializing in long term strategic solutions.

❑ He has been awarded the National Speakers Association Professional Designation CSP (Certified Speaking Professional), becoming one of only nine in Canada, and 270 in the world.

❑ Brian and his wife, Valerie Cade Lee, reside in Calgary, Alberta.

Put Brian Lee to work for your next conference or meeting.

1-800-66-SPEAK (667-7325)

*Keynotes * Seminars * Consulting * Coaching*
(for further information, see Pages 453 to 461)

Toll Free: 1-800-66-Speak
www.customlearning.com
copyright © 1988

6 Powerful Reasons to Put Brian Lee to Work for You:

☑ 1. Brian Lee is a World Class Author:
In addition to his busy speaking calendar, Brian brings the credibility of having authored four books:

➤ **Satisfaction Guranteed**
How to Satisfy Every Customer Every Time!

➤ **Leadership Strategies**
A Leadership Anthology with introduction by F. Lee Bailey

➤ **One Minute Name Memory**
How to Remember Every Name . . Every Time . . . Forever!

➤ **The Wedding MC**
How to MC and Speak at Weddings

Brian also has produced two dozen popular audio and video cassette albums, as well as numerous articles.

☑ 2. Brian Lee Gets Immediate Results:
With a track record of personally speaking to over 750,000 people in the past 14 years as a professional speaker, Brian consistently earns an astonishing audience rating of 4.8 (out of a possible 5). Each year Brian receives hundreds of letters testifying to the long-term impact and influence he has in the work place and with people's careers.

✔ 3. Brian Lee's Remarkable Customizing
☐ Skills are his Trademark:
Every speaking engagement is created from scratch for each new audience. This quote from Rick Martinez's unsolicited letter is typical of the feedback received from literally hundreds of meeting planners, who consistently rave about Brian's unique 37 step process of custom-tailoring and personalizing each and every presentation, right down to the detail of remembering the names of everyone in his audience.

☑ 4. Brian Lee Educates, Empowers, Entertains and Recommends:
Brian is not just a motivational speaker. He is a leading edge, high content educator who enhances his crystal clear delivery skills with a unique combination of sincerity, relevant humour and passion, with step-by-step recommendations for implementation. Put Brian on the platform for you, then get ready to see your people take action.

☑ 5. Brian Lee is a CSP . . . Certified Speaking Professional
Certified speaking Professional (CSP) is an earned designation conferred by the National Speakers Association to recognize demonstrated commitment to the speaking profession through proven speaking experience. In 1993, Brian Lee received this prestigious certification. Only 9 speakers in Canada and 263 people in the world have passed the rigorous criteria to attain this conveted designation.

☑ 6. Brian Lee IS Canada's Mr. Enthusiasm
Brian Lee focuses on the joy that is gained from a job well done. The nickname "Mr. Enthusiasm" wasn't created by a public relations firm, but rather "leapt" from the pages of tens of thousands of audience evaluation forms from Brian's diary of over 2500 speaking engagements during the past 14 years.

> Ⓦ **Westinghouse Hanford Company**
> "I am especially impressed with your ability to grasp the issues we're struggling with at Westinghouse in the nuclear industry and to be able to incorporate them into the seminars. In fact, one Human Resource manager commented, 'I'm embarassed because Brian knows more about my company than I do.' Your research and homework obviously paid off."
> Rick Martinez,
> Human Resources Specialist
> Westinghouse Hanford Company

Toll Free: 1-800-66-Speak
www.customlearning.com
copyright © 1988

447

Brian Lee CSP - Keynote/Seminar Topics

 Yes, we may be interested in a Brian Lee CSP presentation on:

A The following topic(s) that are listed in the audio/video/book library listed on pages 453 to 461.

Title(s) _____

_____

B The following topic(s) listed below:

❑ **Feature Conference Keynotes**

- ❑ Thriving on Change
- ❑ Anything You Can Do, You Can Do Better
- ❑ The Six Secrets of People Empowerment
- ❑ The Challenge of Leadership Excellence
- ❑ The Six Secrets of Personal Enthusiasm
- ❑ Reinventing Training
- ❑ Succeed From Adversity
- ❑ Creating Opportunity Through Personal Entrepeneurship

❑ **Customer Satisfaction**

- ❑ The 13 Secrets of Creating World Class Customer Satisfaction
- ❑ Change Your Culture or Be Doomed to Repeat the Past

❑ **Health Care**

- ❑ The Service Excellence Advisor Train the Trainer-Initiative
- ❑ The Challenge of Sustaining & Growing a Medical Practice Through the Year 2000
- ❑ Growing Through Cultural Diversity

❑ **Team Work**

- ❑ Building Self-Empowered Teams
- ❑ Creating High Performance Teamwork with People you Don't Know or Like

❑ **Change Leadership**

- ❑ Take Charge of our Future Change Leadership Summit

❑ **Communication**

- ❑ Communication Dynamics
- ❑ Why People Do What They Do

❑ **Professional Development**

- ❑ The Dynamics of Effective Boards
- ❑ The Power of Professional Development
- ❑ G.O.A.L. Master

❑ **Government**

- ❑ Vision, Values & Empowering Public Sector Leadership
- ❑ S.E.R.V.I.C.E. Your Connstituents and Save Your Sanity
- ❑ The Wit and Humour of Politics

Toll Free: 1-800-66-Speak
www.customlearning.com
copyright © 1988

Brian's Clients Say it Best:

"Brian is the Norman Vincent Peale of Customer Service."

Debbie Wagner,
Systems Professional,
Ford Motor Company

"You now hold the world's record for the greatest number of participants in class for the last session of the conference."

Susan Goewey
Director of Administration
State Government Affairs Council

"The seminar effectively blended values with practical communication skills development. And, in doing so, you re-affirmed and revitalized our staff's commitment to quality service."

Stephen R. Robertson
Director of Human Resources
St. Mary Medical Center

"Energetic, dynamic, informative and interesting. Motivates you about the topic in a manner that makes you want to run out and implement new ideas immediately."

Jim Murphy
City Manager
City of Normandy Park

"In my experience, the memory of most seminars fades within a week or two. The unique thing about your seminar is that six months later, we are still talking about it and still practicing the ideas you implemented."

Yasmin Jackson
Manager, Systems and Administration
Bell Canada International

"Dynamic, challenging and headed toward the 21st century."

Lawrence Derry
Program Supervisor AADAC
Downtown Treatment Edmonton

"I couldn't have hoped for a more dynamic, focused and useful presentation! 'The Challenge of Municipal Excellence' was one of the best sessions on leadership held during the conference and received consistenly high ratings from mayors and council members."

Thomas H. McCloud
Director of Public Affairs
National League of Cities

"Fantastic! Thanks for the superb job . . . people are skill quoting you . . . and the most complementary thing being said about you . . . 'During the whole session my mind never day dreamed to other issues . . . I kept listening to his every word.'"

Hugo Graff
Plan Manager,
Chromalox Inc.

Toll Free: 1-800-66-Speak
www.customlearning.com
copyright © 1988

449

Reader Satisfaction Survey

Brian Lee CSP
Author, The Wedding M.C.

Dear Fellow Wedding M.C.,

This book came about as the result of years of experience combined with suggestions and ideas from hundreds of sources.

Feedback is truly the "breakfast of champions", and your experience, ideas and suggestions will contribute to making this book better for future users.

Accordingly, I would appreciate it if you would share with me your observations by completing the attached Reorder Satisfaction Survey.

With thanks in advance,

Brian C. Lee CSP
Author
The Wedding M.C.

Toll Free: 1-800-66-Speak
www.customlearning.com
copyright © 1988

Reader Satisfaction Survey

(Brian, now that the wedding is complete, I/we would like you to know . . .)

To: **Brian Lee CSP**
The Wedding M.C.
Custom Learning Systems Group Ltd.
#201, 1505 - 17 Avenue SW
Calgary, Alberta Canada T2T 0E2
Fax: 403-228-6776   Emai: brian @customlearning.com
www.customlearning.com

From: Name: _____

Address: _____

City: _____

Province/State: _____ P C./Zip_____

Bus. Phone: (___)_____ Fax: (___)_____

Email: _____

Re: Comments/Observations - The Wedding M.C.

I.   **The best idea/technique gained and used from the book is:**

_____

_____

_____

2.   **Comments, feedback received from Wedding Couple and others in attendance:**

_____

_____

_____

3.   **Suggestion for improving existing ideas, content, format:**

_____

_____

_____

4.   **Suggested "Best Idea" that could be added:**

_____

_____

Toll Free: 1-800-66-Speak
www.customlearning.com
copyright © 1988

451

Reader Satisfaction Survey - continued

5. **I became aware of the book by/through:**

_____

_____

_____

6. **For the Archives:** _____

Wedding Date: _____

City/Location: _____

Bride's Name: _____

Groom's Name: _____

Size of Reception: _____

7. **P.S.**

_____

_____

_____

_____

8. **Please find attached a photo(s)/wedding invitation/of the couple/event:**

9. **On a scale of 1-5, The Wedding M.C. was:** (5 = Valuable, 1 = Poor)

    1. Practical, helpful and relevant   5   4   3   2   1
    2. Well organized   5   4   3   2   1
    3. Easy to use, reader friendly   5   4   3   2   1
    4. Good value for the money   5   4   3   2   1
    5. *__Overall__* I rate The Wedding M.C.   5   4   3   2   1
    6. What could we do to serve you better?

_____

_____

_____

Toll Free: 1-800-66-Speak
www.customlearning.com
copyright © 1988

Brian Lee's Book Library

Satisfaction Guaranteed
by Brian Lee CSP
"Master the Six Secrets of Creating World Class Customer Satisfaction"
(PB 600) **$24.95**

One Minute Name Memory
by Brian Lee CSP
"How to Remember Every Name, . . . Every Time . . . Forever!"
(PB1455C) **$24.95**

Wisdon Worth Quoting
by Brian Lee CSP
"52 Certificates Suitable for Framing"
(PB 200) **$39.95**

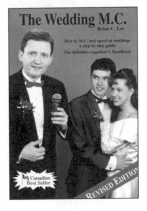

The Wedding M.C.
by Brian Lee CSP

"How to M.C. and speak at Weddings. A step by step guide."
(PB400) **$29.95**

Put Brian Lee's
World Class Presentation Skills
Training Tools to work for You

Advanced Presentation Skills Six Star ™ Train and Trainer Course
by Brian Lee CSP
"How to Design & Deliver the Best Training Program of your Life Every Time"

12 Cassette Audio Album
(PA2501) **$177.77**

Advanced Presentation Skills (A.P.S.) Participant Workbook
by Brian Lee CSP
A 250 Page Manual to accompany the APS 12 hour course (above).
Workbook (W2501) **$95.00**

Special Offer — **10% Off when you buy the whole set!**

The Wedding M.C. Presentation Skills
"MASTER LIBRARY"

WEDDING M.C. LIBRARY

APS.12 Cassette Set	PA2501	$177.77
APS Manual	W2501	$ 95.00
1 Minite Name Memory	PA1455C	$ 24.95
Audience Participation	PV2555	$ 95.00
The Wedding M.C.	PB400	$ 29.95
Total		$422.67

All 5 Products **$379**

Toll Free: 1-800-66-Speak
www.customlearning.com
copyright © 1988

Canada's
"Mr. Customer Satisfaction"
presents

Brian Lee, CSP

The 6 Secrets of
ONE MINUTE
NAME MEMORY

"How to
Remember
Every Name,
. . . Every Time
. . . Forever!"

**The Six Secrets of
One Minute
Name Memory**
by Brian Lee CSP
*"How to Remember
Every Name...
Every Time... Forever!"*

2 Cassette Audio Album
(PA 1455C) **$24.95**

Canada's
"Mr. Customer Satisfaction"
presents

**THE GENIUS OF
GREAT AUDIENCE
PARTICIPATION**

*"How to
Empower and Create
Audience Ownership"*

Brian Lee, CSP

**The Genius of Great
Audience Participation**
by Brian Lee CSP
*"How to Empower and Create
Audience Ownership"*

1 Volume Video
(PV2555) **$95.00**

The Wedding M.C.

The Wedding M.C.
by Brian Lee CSP
*"How to M.C. and speak at
Weddings. A step by step guide."*
(PB400) **$29.95**

Six Star™ Customer Satisfaction Series
by Brian Lee CSP
"Creating World Class Customer Satisfaction"

12 Cassette Audio Album
(PA 544A) **$177.77**

12 Volume video Album
(PV 544A) **$595.00**

Individual Six Star Customer Satisfaction Albums

❏ **Satisfaction Guaranteed**
"How to Create Lifetime Customer Loyalty"
2 Video Set (PV545A) $175.00
2 Audio Set (PA545) $29.95
16 pg. Workbook (W545) $ 3.00
120 pg. Book (PB600) $22.00

❏ **Winning With Difficult Customers**
"How You Can Say to the Most Difficult Customer in the World . . . Come and Get Me!"
2 Video Set (PV550A) $175.00
2 Audio Set (PA550A) $29.95
16 pg. Workbook (W545) $ 3.00

❏ **Stress Free Service Excellence**
"How to Create a Stress-Free Environment for You and Your Customers"
2 Video Set (PV555A) $175.00
2 Audio Set (PA545) $29.95
16 pg. Workbook (W545) $ 3.00

❏ **One Minute Service Selling**
"How to Gain a Competitive Advantage by Helping Others Get What they Want."
2 Video Set (PV560A) $175.00
2 Audio Set (PA560A) $29.95
16 pg. Workbook (W560A) $ 3.00

❏ **Managing Moments of Truth**
"How to Continuously Improve Customer Satisfaction"
2 Video Set (PV656A) $175.00
2 Audio Set (PA656A) $29.95
16 pg. Workbook (W656A) $ 3.00

❏ **Self Esteem & Service Superstars**
"Enhanced Self-Esteem Equals Enhanced Service Excellence."
2 Video Set (PV570A) $175.00
2 Audio Set (PA570A) $29.95
16 pg. Workbook (W570A) $ 3.00

Toll Free: 1-800-66-Speak
www.customlearning.com
copyright © 1988

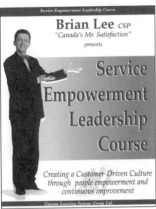

Service Empowerment Leadership Course
by Brian Lee CSP
"Creating a Customer Driven Culture through People Empowerement and Continuous Improvement"

12 Cassette Audio Album
(PA 2320A) **$177.77**

12 Volume Video Album
(PV 2320A) **$595.00**

Individual Service Empowerment Leadership Course Albums

❑ **Vision, Values & Inspired Leadership**
"How to Create a Customer Driven Culture"
2 Video Set (PV2340A) $175.00
2 Audio Set (PA2340A) $29.95
16 pg. Workbook (W2340A) $ 3.00

❑ **Thriving on Change**
"How to Survive and Thrive in the Midst of Change"
2 Video Set (PV2345A) $175.00
2 Audio Set (PA2345A) $29.95
16 pg. Workbook (W2345A) $ 3.00

❑ **The Genius of People Empowerment**
"How to Motivate and Empower for Peak Performance"
2 Video Set (PV2350A) $175.00
2 Audio Set (PA2350A) $29.95
16 pg. Workbook (W2350A) $ 3.00

❑ **The Power of Continuous Improvement**
"How to Measure and Significantly Improve Customer Perception and Satisfaction"
2 Video Set (PV2355A) $175.00
2 Audio Set (PA2355A) $29.95
16 pg. Workbook (W2355A) $ 3.00

❑ **Total Quality Leadership**
"How to Implement the 13 Steps of Total Quality Process Improvement"
2 Video Set (PV2360A) $175.00
2 Audio Set (PA2360A) $29.95
16 pg. Workbook (W2360A) $ 3.00

❑ **The Challenge of Innovative Excellence**
"How to Continuously Improve Service While Creatively Reducing Costs"
2 Video Set (PV2365A) $175.00
2 Audio Set (PA2365A) $29.95
16 pg. Workbook (W2365A) $ 3.00

Put Brian Lee's
World Class Sales & Marketing
Training Tools to work for You

**Advanced Professional
S.E.R.V.I.C.E. Selling**
by Brian Lee CSP
*"How to Double Sales Productivity Through
the 7 Values of Sales Mastery"*
12 Cassette Audio Album
(PA1903) **$197.77**

**Advanced Professional *Auto*
S.E.R.V.I.C.E. Selling**
by Brian Lee. CSP
*"How to Double Auto Sales Productivity
Through the 7 Values of Sales Mastery"*
24 Cassette Audio Album
(PA1903AUTO) **$295.00**

**The Six Secrets of Sales
Empowerment**
by Brian Lee CSP
*"How to Recruit, Hire, Motivate and
Empower Peak Sales Performance"*
1 Volume Video
(PV 472H) **$175.00**

Trade Show Marketing Effectiveness
by Brian Lee. CSP
*"Trade Show Marketing Strategies For Planning,
Selling and Exhibiting Success"*
6 cassette Audio Album
(PA 2480) **$89.95**

Toll Free: 1-800-66-Speak
www.customlearning.com
copyright © 1988

Reinventing Sales & Marketing in a Professional Services Practice
by Brian Lee CSP
"How to Achieve a Long Term Competitive Advantage by Creating a Customer Driven, Sales Focused Culture"
6 Cassette Audio Album
(PA1909) **$89.95**

Telemarketing Sales & Communication Effectiveness
by Brian Lee CSP
"How to Achieve Extraordinary, Cost Effective Results through Sales and Communication Mastery"
6 Cassette Audio Album
(PA1450) **$89.95**

The Six Secrets of Networking & Highly Effective Business Marketing
by Brian Lee CSP
"How to Transform Informal Contacts into Unlimited Business and Social Opportunities."
1 Volume Video
(PV 471G) **$149.95**

Thriving on Multiple Priorities
by Brian Lee CSP
"How to Balance Conflicting Priorities & Get Things Done"

2 Volume Video
(PV1786) **$175.00**

4 Cassette Audio Album
(PA1782) **$69.95**

The 7 Attributes of Meeting Mastery
by Brian Lee CSP
"How to Organize the Best Meeting of Your Life Everytime"

4 Cassette Audio Album
(PA2742A) **$69.95**

Stress Master
by Brian Lee CSP
"How to Survive and Thrive in Spite of Stress & Fatigue"

6 Cassette Audio Album
(PA1776) **$89.95**

Toll Free: 1-800-66-Speak
www.customlearning.com
copyright © 1988

Winning with Difficult People
by Brian Lee CSP
"How You Can Say to the Most Difficult People in the World... Come and Get Me"

3 Volume Video
(PV1793 A1-A3) **$195.00**

6 Cassette Audio Album
(PA1793) **$89.95**

The 13 Secrets of Creating World Class Customer Satisfaction
by Brian Lee CSP
"How to Create a Customer Driven Culture Through People Empowerment & Continuous Improvement"

1 Volume Video
(PV481) **$95.95**

Anything You Can Do... You Can Do Better
by Brian Lee CSP
"How to Put the Power of Excellence to Work in Your Professional Carreer & Personal Life"

2 Volume Videos
(PV408E) **$24.95**

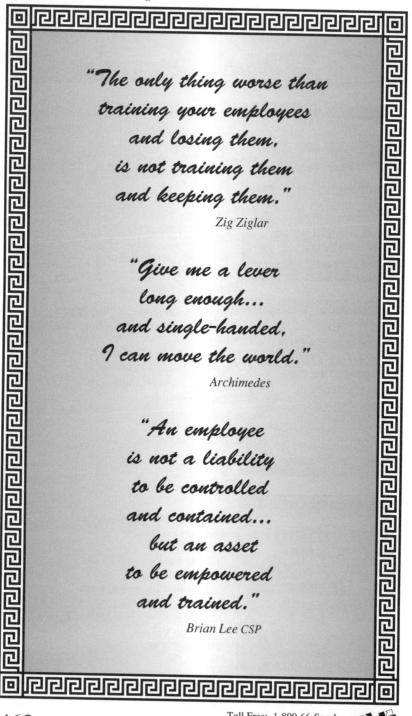

*"The only thing worse than
training your employees
and losing them,
is not training them
and keeping them."*

Zig Ziglar

*"Give me a lever
long enough...
and single-handed,
I can move the world."*

Archimedes

*"An employee
is not a liability
to be controlled
and contained...
but an asset
to be empowered
and trained."*

Brian Lee CSP

Toll Free: 1-800-66-Speak
www.customlearning.com
copyright © 1988

Product Order From

Order by:

Name: _____ Title _____
Organization: _____
Address: _____
City: _____ State/Prov.: _____
Country: _____ Zip/P.C.: _____
Daytime Phone: _____ Fax: _____
E-Mail: _____

Ship to: (if different from above)

Name: _____ Title _____
Organization: _____
Address: _____
City: _____ State/Prov.: _____
Country: _____ Zip/P.C.: _____
Daytime Phone: _____ Fax: _____

Order:

Quantity	Title	Order Number	Audio	Video	Other	Unit Price	Total
						Merchandise Total	
						Shipping & Handling	
						Sub-Total	
						G.S.T.	
						GRAND TOTAL	

Shipping & Handling

$ 0 – $ 50	$ 8.95	$151 – $200	$11.95
$ 51 – $100	$ 9.95	$201 – $250	$12.95
$101 – $150	$10.95	$251 – $300	$13.95

For orders totalling over $300, add $1 for each additional $50 of purchasees.

Method of Payment

☐ Cheque #

Made payable to:

Custom Learning Systems Group Ltd.
#201, 1505 - 17 Avenue S.W.
Calgary, Alberta T2T 0E2
Fax (403) 228-6776
Toll Free: 1-800-667-7325

☐ Charge to:

  ☐ MasterCard

  ☐ Visa

Card #: _____

Expiry: _____

Cardholder
Signature: _____

Toll Free: 1-800-66-Speak
www.customlearning.com
copyright © 1988

Toll Free: 1-800-66-Speak
www.customlearning.com
copyright © 1988

Business
Reply Mail

Affix
Postage
Here

Custom Learning Systems Group Ltd.
#201, 1505 - 17 Avenue S.W.,
Calgary, Alberta, Canada T2T 0E2

Business
Reply Mail

Affix
Postage
Here

Custom Learning Systems Group Ltd.
#201, 1505 - 17 Avenue S.W.,
Calgary, Alberta, Canada T2T 0E2

Gift Order Form

I Do want you to rush me:
The Wedding M.C. best seller

❑ Complete Book _____ copies @ $29.95 = $ _____

    Postage & Handling _____ items @ $ 7.50 = $ _____

                                 G.S.T. $ _____

                                 Total $ _____

Ship To:
Name: _____ Title _____

Organization: _____

Address: _____

City: _____ State/Prov.: _____

Country: _____ Zip/P.C.: _____

Daytime Phone: _____ Fax: _____

E-Mail: _____

Method of Payment

❑   Cheque # _____

    Made payable to:

        Custom Learning Systems Group Ltd.

        #201, 1505 - 17 Avenue S.W.

        Calgary, Alberta T2T 0E2

        Fax (403) 228-6776

        Toll Free: 1-800-667-7325

❑   Charge to: Credit Card orders
   ❑ MasterCard   can be Faxed or
   ❑ Visa   Phoned in.

Card #: _____

Expiry: _____

Cardholder
Signature: _____

Wedding M.C. Order Form

I Do want you to rush me:
The Wedding M.C. best seller

❑ Complete Book _____ copies @ $29.95 = $ _____

    Postage & Handling _____ items @ $ 7.50 = $ _____

                                   G.S.T. $ _____

                                 Total $ _____

Ship To:
Name: _____ Title _____

Organization: _____

Address: _____

City: _____ State/Prov.: _____

Country: _____ Zip/P.C.: _____

Daytime Phone: _____ Fax: _____

E-Mail: _____

Method of Payment

❑   Cheque # _____

    Made payable to:

        Custom Learning Systems Group Ltd.

        #201, 1505 - 17 Avenue S.W.

        Calgary, Alberta T2T 0E2

        Fax (403) 228-6776

        Toll Free: 1-800-667-7325

❑   Charge to: Credit Card orders
   ❑ MasterCard   can be Faxed or
   ❑ Visa   Phoned in.

Card #: _____

Expiry: _____

Cardholder
Signature: _____